Mrs. George Sumner

Our Holiday in the East

Mrs. George Sumner

Our Holiday in the East

ISBN/EAN: 9783337288587

Printed in Europe, USA, Canada, Australia, Japan

Cover: Foto ©Andreas Hilbeck / pixelio.de

More available books at **www.hansebooks.com**

OUR HOLIDAY
IN THE EAST.

BY

MRS. GEORGE SUMNER.

EDITED BY

THE REV. GEORGE HENRY SUMNER,
HON. CANON OF WINCHESTER, AND RECTOR OF OLD ALRESFORD, HANTS.

LONDON:
HURST AND BLACKETT, PUBLISHERS,
13 GREAT MARLBOROUGH STREET.
1881.

All Rights reserved.

PREFACE.

A VISIT to the East—and especially to those Oriental lands consecrated by their connection with Biblical history—has for long been a dream which both my wife and I earnestly desired should one day become a reality. During the spring of this year we were able to carry out these long cherished wishes, and, with our daughter and a few friends, to visit localities familiar to us all by name from our earliest childhood, and rendered dear by their association with the Sacred Story of our Lord's Life on earth.

My wife has endeavoured in the following pages, by enlarging her journal written at the time, to convey to others an idea of the scenes which gave us such intense pleasure. She has had much diffidence in publishing this sketch of our travels, and I do not know that she would have ventured to do so at all if, on our return home, our friends had not inundated us with questions which showed that, to many persons at any rate, a few details of our tour would not be without interest. No attempt has been made to solve any of the knotty questions connected with disputed holy sites in Palestine, for our stay in the East was not sufficiently prolonged to enable us to enter upon such controverted topics.

If some degree of the pleasure which she has experienced in writing, and which I have also felt in editing, the records of that happy time be shared by her readers, her object will be fully accomplished.

GEORGE HENRY SUMNER.

Old Alresford Rectory, Hants.
Christmas, 1880.

CONTENTS.

CHAPTER I.—EASTWARD BOUND.

Start for the East—Life on Board the *Pera*—Landing at Alexandria—Novel Experiences—Introduction to our Dragoman, Michel-el-Hani—Varied Nationalities at Alexandria—Historical Reminiscences—Removal of Pompey's Pillar—Railway to Cairo—Aspect of the Country—The Natives—The Villages—Donkey-riding in Cairo—Fascination of the Place—The Syces, Bazaars, and Mode of Bargaining—The Pyramids—The Sphinx 3

CHAPTER II.—CAIRO TO JAFFA.

Sunday at Cairo—Mosque of Mehemet Ali—Old Cairo—Heliopolis—Ancient Obelisk—The Virgin's Well—Miss Whateley's Mission School—Difficulties Gradually Surmounted—Gross Superstition of the Dervishes—Introduction to the Wife of the Khedive—Court Customs—Mahmoud Pasha's Hareem—The Condition of the Labouring Classes—Bridal Processions—Customs with Regard to Prayer—The Scavengers of Cairo—The Nile—The Way in which it Irrigates and Fertilizes the Country—Railway to Ismailia—Aspect of the Desert—Suez Canal—The Mirage—Arrival at Port Said—Violent Storm—Arrival at Jaffa . . . 37

CHAPTER III.—THE HOLY LAND.

Difficult Landing at Jaffa—First Introduction to Tent Life—Unexpected Comforts—House of Simon the Tanner—*En Route* for Lydda—Road to Jerusalem—Orange and Lemon

Groves—The Plain of Sharon—Beauty of the Flowers—Our First Mid-day Halt—Ramleh—Lydda—Night Experiences—General Order of Marching—Filth of Lydda—St George's Church—Beth-horon—View from the Sheikh's House—Gibeon—Neby Samwil—First View of Jerusalem—Desolate Appearance of the Country—Suicidal Policy of the Government 69

CHAPTER IV.—JERUSALEM.

First Thoughts on Reaching Jerusalem—Encampment Outside the Damascus Gate, near the Supposed Site of the Crucifixion—The Church of the Holy Sepulchre, Common to Roman Catholics, Greeks, Copts, and Armenians—Holy Places in the Church—Reverence of the Pilgrims—Regiment of Turkish Soldiers to Keep Order in the Church—Sale of Curiosities Outside the Church—The Citadel—The Haram—Kubbet-es-Sakhra—Mosque-el-Aksa—Subterranean Vaults—The Golden Gate—Pool of Bethesda—Palm Sunday—Walk to and from Bethany—View of Jerusalem—Joab's Well—Flow of Water—Group of Lepers—Jewish Funeral Procession—Plans for our Expedition to the Dead Sea . 93

CHAPTER V.—JERICHO AND THE DEAD SEA.

Arrangements for the Journey to the Jordan—Sheikh of Abudis takes the Party in Charge—Road from Jerusalem to Jericho—Flora of Judæa—Native Mode of Sport—Jericho—Elisha's Fountain—Native Dance—Modern Jericho—Bedoueen Salutation—The Dead Sea—Fords of the Jordan—An Alarm—Adventure in Crossing the Cherith—Return to Jerusalem—Mohammedan at Prayer—Camp in the Karama Sheikh . 117

CHAPTER VI.—JERUSALEM.

Good Friday at Jerusalem—The Cœnaculum—The Jews' Wailing-place—Affecting Scene—Celebration of the Passover—Arch of the Ecce Homo—The Church of the Holy Sepulchre—Easter Services—Visit to the Convent of Marsaba—Bethlehem—Church of the Nativity—Site of Our Lord's

Birth—St. Jerome's Grotto—Domestic Troubles—Visit to a Sheikh—Garden of Gethsemane—Preparations for Leaving Jerusalem 143

CHAPTER VII.—JERUSALEM TO NAZARETH.

Departure from Jerusalem—Ramah—Beeroth—Bethel—Encampment at Sinjil—Threatening Aspect of a Bedoueen—Jacob's Well—Nablous—Mounts Ebal and Gerizim—Mission Work at Nablous—The Samaritan Pentateuch—Samaria—Wonderful Ruins—Fulfilment of Prophecy—Dothan—Joseph's Well—Camp at Jenin—Plain of Esdraelon—Gideon's Well —Jezreel—Shunem—Nain . . . 175

CHAPTER VIII.—NAZARETH TO SYRIA.

Situation of Nazareth—Why left so Inaccessible—The Virgin's Fountain—Beauty of the Women—Sunday at Nazareth— View from the Hill above the Town—Concourse of Russian Pilgrims—The Holy Sites at Nazareth—Cana of Galilee— Tiberias—Camp by the Lake—Contrast of the Present with the Past—Disputed Sites of Capernaum, Bethsaida, and Chorazin—We Camp at Kahn-Minyeh—Storm on the Lake —A Quiet Morning—Safed, "The City set on an Hill"— Bedoueen Encampment—A Metawileh Sheikh—Algerine Colony at Deshun—Distribution of Meat—Kadesh Naphtali —Vandalism—Dan—Source of the Jordan—Scene of Rob Roy's Capture—Banias—We Leave the Holy Land . 203

CHAPTER IX.—DAMASCUS.

Farewell to Palestine—Bitumen Works—Maronite and Druse Women—The Rival Sects—The Massacre of 1860—Sunday at Hasbeya—Source of the Jordan—Rasheya—Welcome by School-children—Ruins of Rukleh and Deir-el-Ashayir— Hurricane at Dimas—Night in the Khan—Beauty of the Abana—First View of Damascus—Dimitri's Hotel—The Great Mosque—Bazaars—Visit to Abd-el-Kadir and the Grand Mufti—Houses of Damascus—Ali Bey's Hareem— Summary Justice—Burial-grounds—The "Street called

Straight"—Mission Work in Damascus—Dancing Dervishes . 241

CHAPTER X.—DAMASCUS TO BEYROUT.

Departure from Damascus—Halt at Ain-Fijeh—Beauty of the Barada—Camp at Suk-Wady-Barada and Yahfufeh—Wonderful Colouring of the Buka'a Plain—We Reach Baalbek—Magnificent Ruins—Massive Stones—Interior of a Native House at Baalbek—Zachleh—Lovely Camp—Regret at its being our Last—Backsheesh Distributed—The Lebanon Pass—First Sight of Beyrout—Our Dragoman's Family—Mrs. Mott's Schools, Mothers' Meetings, etc.—Persecution of Christians—Interesting Service on Sunday—Native Hareem—Bridal Customs—General Dislike of the Turkish Government—Farewell to Syria . . . 281

CHAPTER XI.—WESTWARD HO!

Cyprus: Improved by English Occupation—Third-class Passengers on the *Hungaria*—Beauty of Rhodes—A Day at Smyrna—Sunday at Syra—Greek Easter—Arrival at Athens—Mars' Hill—The Parthenon—Restoration of the Elgin Marbles—Funeral Procession—Through the Dardanelles to Constantinople—Lovely View of the City—The Sultan at His Devotions—Assemblage of Fashionables at "The Sweet Waters"—The Mosque of St. Sophia—Cemetery at Scutari Well Kept—Magnificence of the Dolma-Batchi Palace—We Leave Constantinople for Varna—Aspect of the Bulgarians—From Rustchuk to Bucharest—We Reach Vienna *viâ* Buda-Pesth—Arrival in England . 315

ILLUSTRATIONS.

FRONTISPIECE—"Mount Tabor."
VIGNETTE—"Arab and Dromedary."

From Photographs published by F. FRITH & Co.

CHAPTER I.

EASTWARD BOUND.

START FOR THE EAST—LIFE ON BOARD "THE PERA"—LANDING AT ALEXANDRIA—NOVEL EXPERIENCES—INTRODUCTION TO OUR DRAGOMAN, MICHEL-EL-HANI—VARIED NATIONALITIES AT ALEXANDRIA—HISTORICAL REMINISCENCES—REMOVAL OF POMPEY'S PILLAR—RAILWAY TO CAIRO—ASPECT OF THE COUNTRY—THE NATIVES—THE VILLAGES—DONKEY-RIDING IN CAIRO—FASCINATION OF THE PLACE—THE SYCES, BAZAARS, AND MODE OF BARGAINING—THE PYRAMIDS—THE SPHINX.

CHAPTER I.

ON Monday, February 23rd, 1880, our party, consisting of my cousin and niece Mr. and Miss Heywood, two friends Mr. and Miss Scudamore Stanhope, my husband, my daughter, and myself, started for the East. We glided out of the Charing Cross Station into the thick, foggy, evening gloom, followed by hearty good wishes for the success of our pilgrimage to the Holy Land on the part of kind friends who had come to see us off.

A week's run across Europe brought us to Brindisi, and we found ourselves on board the Peninsular and Oriental steamer, *Pera*, a well-appointed vessel, clean and comfortable. The discipline on board was almost of a man-of-war character. Captain Hyde, who commanded the steamer, had at one time been in the Queen's service, and had evidently not forgotten the lessons learned there. He was always followed at a distance of a few yards by a little sailor-boy in spotless white trousers, ready at a moment's notice to carry his commands to the other end of the vessel. The boy's orders were never to stand in front of the captain, and his manœuvres to keep in the rear were very droll, and an endless source of amusement. He revolved round him like a satellite. As the captain turned, the boy turned; when the captain stopped, the boy stopped; and the only time when we saw him relax from this rigid conformity to duty was on one occasion when the captain was enjoying an afternoon siesta, and the little fellow, taking advantage of the situation, indulged in a furtive run on his own account.

Our boat carried the mail-bags, and the accumulation of letters and newspapers was marvellous. There were no fewer than six hundred and thirty large sackfuls for India, China, and Australia. It took two hours to get this literary cargo on board at Brindisi; for, with an inconceivable want of energy on the part of the Italians, the train from Bologna disgorges its contents about a quarter of a mile from the quay, so that all the mail-bags have first to be packed in mule-carts, and then once more unloaded to be brought on board ship. Representations on the subject have been made over and over again to the proper authorities, but hitherto without effect. Brindisi is a dreary place, and we were glad to steam away into the blue Adriatic, past the Castle of Otranto, with the Italian coast full in view.

Next morning we were within eight or ten miles of the Morea; the Bay of Navarino was before us, and the beautiful outline of the Greek coast stretched far away towards the South.

The mountains of the Morea looked very lovely, piled up one behind the other, with the snow glittering on their summits; but the land seemed bare and desolate, and the only signs of life were small villages at rare intervals nestling under the great hills. Late in the afternoon we passed Cape Matapan and the Island of Cerigo (the ancient Cythera), and bade farewell to Greece. The next morning, when we came on deck, Crete was nearly out of sight.

We glided along over the placid, lake-like, still, and waveless sea in a sort of dreamy way which was very delicious, and a party of us sat from time to time on the poop, singing, reciting, reading, talking, and rejoicing over our good fortune in having such a passage. We saw very little shipping, not more than three or four sail in the course of twelve hours. Sea-gulls were our only companions, for ever hovering over us, gleaming like silver in the sunshine as they whirled round and round in graceful sweeps, enjoying life to the utmost.

It was at two o'clock on the afternoon of the 4th of March that we anchored off Alexandria, and our eyes first opened upon Eastern colouring. Alexandria looked like a golden city, lying on a golden shore between two great bands of blue— the sky and the sea. It stood out sharp and clear, with its palm-trees and minarets, against the sky-line, like a picture of Goodall's—hot, dry, and arid, but very wonderful and beautiful to northern eyes accustomed for so long to clouds and sunlessness. As soon as we anchored, crowds of gay little boats and boatmen buzzed round our vessel, and a rabble of Arabs came on board dressed in full white trousers and tunics of green, blue, or scarlet, with turbans or tarbouches on their heads, and at once changed the quiet and decorum of our stately vessel into a Babel-like confusion. The men hustled, bustled, chattered, shouted, and gesticulated. They fought one with another over the luggage, struggling, pushing, and screaming like lunatics.

Before leaving England we had engaged the services of a dragoman for the Holy Land, who had been privately recommended to us—Michel-El-Hani. He had written to say that he would meet us at Alexandria, and he soon came on board from one of the boats, and we felt our hands grasped by a stranger, a tall, dark Syrian, in European dress, with a fine eager face. From that moment we belonged to him, and he to us, and most carefully and successfully did he pioneer us through all our journeys. At this particular moment he extricated us triumphantly from the pandemonium, and we were soon, under his protection, safely landed.*

* Michel-El-Hani, of whom it is impossible to speak too highly, was dragoman to "Rob Roy," when canoeing on the Jordan. Mr. Macgregor thus speaks of him—"At Ismailia there met me the brave and faithful companion of my future journey, Michael Hani, well known to me as my dragoman in 1849, frequently trusted since by large parties sent to his charge; most welcome now as the man without whose aid I could scarcely have ventured to take the *Rob Roy* through the journey we are about to relate."—"*Rob Roy*" *on the Jordan, p.* 16.

A crowd of Alexandrians, dirty, and sparsely clad, received us as we landed on the shore of Egypt. Their one shout was "Backsheesh!"—"Give us something!" This, indeed, is the first and the last word you hear in the East; it is the first cry of the Oriental infant, and the last whine of the aged; it is hurled with a loud voice at you from the fields, even as you whirl by in a railway train, and pervades all classes, from the Pasha down to the poor leper. The sound of it is never ceasing. It meets you everywhere. On this particular occasion backsheesh stood us in good stead, for the administration of a few francs by Hani enabled us to pass without question through the shabby, dirty out-houses on the wharf, which served as the custom-house.

It is quite impossible to convey even a faint idea of the wonders of Eastern life and colouring. We felt very much as if we had waked up in another planet. The aspect of everything was so absolutely different from more conventional Europe, with its darker skies, its duller colouring, and its unpicturesque style of dress; and, merely from an artistic point of view, this first introduction to the land of Egypt was full of interest and delight.

We walked through the streets of Alexandria in a sort of dream, gazing at jet black Nubians, gaily-dressed Turks, yellow-slippered Persians, veiled women, and picturesque figures of all ages and varied nationalities, attired in dresses of bright, beautiful colours, and with drapery hanging in graceful folds over their lithesome figures. The very beggars throw their rags about them in artistic fashion.

Over all this scene the sun reigned supreme, lighting up land and sea with a brilliancy so intense and vivid that it is quite indescribable. The heat was overwhelming. We had left England in a cold, dark fog, and now we suddenly found ourselves in blazing heat under a fierce sun and cloudless sky. The change was magical. The cry on board the *Pera* had been, " Oh for the sun ! we have not seen it for weeks !" or, " I am flying to the sunny south in search of warmth. I can bear the chill darkness of our climate no longer." And here we were basking in tropical heat and glare, with dust and flat roofs, palm-trees, darkened houses, and mosquito curtains, and with an exquisite feeling of being in a new world, which opened out like a revelation to us.

After four days at sea, the sense of terra firma, the memory of a successful voyage, letters of good news from home, and the novelty of Eastern life made us all very happy. From the windows of our hotel we looked out on to gardens filled with tropical plants, palms, and tamarisk-trees, intermingled with flat-roofed houses, veiled women and picturesque men, while camels, and donkeys in smart trappings crowded the streets, and, as we passed through the corridors of the hotel, black youths, clad in loose white garments,—the housemaids of the establishment,—salaamed respectfully whenever we came near them.

There is little in modern Alexandria of special interest, but it is rich in historic memories, and dear to the Church of Christ in connection with the noble stand made by St. Athanasius against the Arian heresies, and as the birth-place of Apollos, that "certain Jew," so eloquent and mighty in the Scriptures, so fervent in spirit, who must have been such an infinite joy and comfort to the great apostle of the Gentiles, with his burning enthusiasm and his craving for human sympathy.

We drove about the town, and went to see

Pompey's pillar: a monolith, with a Corinthian capital, of exquisitely beautiful proportions. A background of graceful palm-trees made it look quite lovely.

The Egyptian government have recently presented to the city of New York an obelisk very similar to Cleopatra's Needle: which was being packed for transmission to America when we were at Alexandria. It certainly does seem a great pity that these national monuments should be removed from their native soil; but, in talking to the very courteous American who was superintending the removal of the column, we felt that, when we called to mind the Thames Embankment and Cleopatra's Needle, our lips, at any rate, were closed on the subject.

The next day saw us en route for Cairo, one hundred and thirty miles by rail.

The whole line through the Delta of the Nile—
—the green region of Egypt—is deeply interesting to a stranger, although the country is flat and ugly, and the palm and tamarisk-trees are few and far between, and there is nothing to shade from the heat, or to relieve from the glare of the sun's rays. The crops are very green, and

the land seems rich and fertile. The effect of the water of the Nile upon the desert is simply magical. Irrigate the land, and it at once brings forth abundant crops. The owners of the soil are well aware of this, and from the train we saw on all sides the peasants actively engaged in directing the streams of water aright. They were wonderfully busy ploughing the ground with a yoke of oxen, harnessed to straight wooden ploughs such as you see in Scriptural pictures.

A beaten track, which serves as a road, runs along by the side of the railway from Alexandria to Cairo. It happened to be Friday, the Moslem sabbath, when we passed in the train. The road was crowded with people; some walking, some riding donkeys, some on camels. The stations, too, were filled with fellaheen of the poorest class. It seemed to be the sabbath lounge. Many were in rags and tatters; many were trying to sell their wares, oranges, lettuces, or water. The Arab villages which we passed are deplorable. They look as if a number of boxes were piled up one behind another. Each adobe, or mud-baked cabin, has one door, but no window, and a flat roof covered with reeds or roughly tempered mud. Large heaps of dusty refuse are banked up around them on every side; children of all ages and degrees of nudeness roll about on the dust heaps; scavenger dogs prowl in and out, or lie sleeping in the sun. Groups of camels and donkeys, picturesque-looking men wearing the abba (a coarse, woollen outer garment, with broad white and brown stripes), and gracefully draped women carrying large water-jars, like the pictures of Rebekah at the well, move about amidst filth and squalor, and under feathery palm-trees. There is generally a group of these trees near each village.

We were told that the "fellaheen," or Egyptian peasants, are really well off, in spite of appearances to the contrary, and that they accumulate money, which they hide in the ground.

They pay a tax of ten shillings a year on every donkey, sixteen shillings for a camel, and a pound for every horse. Their wants seem very few, and they have no luxuries. They live on coarse bread, eggs, cheese, rice, lentils, vegetables, fruit, and raw sugar-cane; they drink cold water and milk, and seem to thrive on the simple fare.

The contrast of grace and beauty in dress and form, combined with degradation of habits, is most extraordinary. The people are handsome and well made. They have very commonly a lofty bearing and noble countenances, not unlike those which are found on old Egyptian bas-reliefs of the ancient worshippers of Osiris, and they drape themselves so artistically that it is a pleasure to look at them. Then, on the other hand, how they can live in such degrading dirt, and with habits so uncivilised, is almost inconceivable to a European.

Both the cotton and the corn crops of 1879 were most abundant, and the natives seem quiet and contented under the rule of the present Khedive. They appear to have confidence in the quasi-European protection which they enjoy. The country is certainly advancing rapidly in prosperity. The imports of 1879 at £5,130,000 show an advance of £200,000, and the exports in the same year have leaped from £8,304,000 to £13,783,000. Of this sum cotton supplies £9,676,000, the remainder consisting of wheat, rice, barley, lentils, ostrich feathers, elephant teeth, &c.

Almost the first object which met our view on entering Cairo was the figure of a very tall English fellow-traveller, riding on an exceedingly small donkey—so small, indeed, that it was difficult to be quite sure whether he was walking with the donkey under him, or whether the donkey was in any way supporting him. A very lightly clothed, mahogany-coloured boy, with a long stick, was urging on the animal, till it broke into a gallop, and the appearance of our tall friend was very comical. He had already prepared us for this kind of locomotion, and had pointed out the peculiar advantage of it—that, if at any moment you prefer walking, you have only to put your feet down to the ground, let the donkey go on from under you, and quietly pursue your own way. In point of fact, the donkeys of Cairo play the part of hansom cabs in London. It may be said broadly that no gentleman, if unaccompanied by ladies, uses any other means of locomotion. A donkey-boy always runs behind, making the most extraordinary noises in order to urge his donkey on, and also to warn foot-passengers of the dangers they incur if they obstruct his onward progress. Occasionally, too, when the rider is inwardly congratulating himself upon the successful way in which he is balancing himself upon his quadruped, a violent blow from behind on the legs of his unfortunate animal disturbs his tranquillity, and oftentimes his equilibrium also. The movement of the donkey under these trying circumstances is not unlike that of a cab suddenly swerving to one side when caught in the groove of a tram-car.

One word about the donkey-boys. They are quite an institution of Cairo, and as full of fun as an Irish car-driver. The way in which they puff off the qualities of their donkeys is irresistible. "Mine vary good donkey, saar." "Take mine, saar." "Mine Dr. Kenealy—mine best, saar," and so on.

Cairo is a town which fairly takes the traveller by storm. Whether he will or not, he surrenders sooner or later to its captivating influences. You are in the midst of Oriental magnificence united with European luxuries. You go out into the bazaars, and revel in all the glories of colouring for which the Eastern nations are so conspicuous. You fancy yourself living in the days of the Arabian Nights, and you return to your hotel to enjoy all the comforts of modern civilization. Nowhere are the two so closely united. Damascus, which is sometimes compared with Cairo, falls far short of it in this respect. Damascus is a city whose prime is passed. Fanaticism, and the baneful influences of an infamous government, have shorn her of her splendour. But Cairo is a rising city. The late Khedive has been much abused, but he certainly did a great deal to advance the national prosperity and civilization of Egypt. Cairo responds to good treatment, and trade and commerce flourish.

The New Grand Hotel, at which we stayed in Cairo, was built by the late Khedive to take in some of the many notabilities who came to Egypt for the opening of the Suez Canal. It is a fine European hotel, clean and well appointed, situated in one of the principal thoroughfares of Cairo. The gardens in front are filled with lovely flowers and shrubs—brugmantias, and bananas twenty feet high, bright purple bougainvilleas streaming in a profusion of festoons, salvias, tree mallows, fan-shaped palms, roses, and geraniums. It is all very lovely, and the view from the balcony is most charming—the public gardens, the town and citadel, mosques and minarets, the for-ever-passing crowd of walkers, and riders, and drivers, the carriages with running syces, and an endless succession of picturesque figures, like slides in a magic lantern.

A word must be said about these running syces of Cairo, for they are a great element of beauty in the streets, clad in fine white garments, bound round the waist with a sash, long loose sleeves, which, as they run, are caught by the wind, and have the effect of wings, gold-embroidered waistcoat of scarlet or blue, white full trousers reaching to the knee, with bare legs and feet. They carry a long cane in their hands, and run in front of the carriages, shouting, "Ouah! ouah!"—"Make way! make way!" They are lithesome and agile young fellows, and the streets are so crowded from morning to night (for every-one lives in the open air) that these runners are not so much a luxury as a necessity. They generally get up on the box of the carriage, or behind it, if you go outside the town.

It was not long after our arrival before we sallied forth to reconnoitre the bazaars. Who has not heard and read of the bazaars of the East!

And yet there are few scenes more difficult to realize. The whole thing is so absolutely different from anything you ever see in Europe. It upsets so entirely all your pre-conceived ideas as to sale and purchase. Everything is done by contraries. The seller, instead of displaying his wares, very frequently—always, if of value—conceals them in the recesses of an iron safe, which is opened with difficulty and reluctance. The shopman sits, the buyer stands. The waresman puts on the most nonchalant air, as if the conclusion of any transaction in the way of trade was the very last thing which would occupy his thoughts.

The principal street in which the bazaars are is called the Mouski. It is long and narrow, unpaved, and on wet days, therefore, ankle-deep in mud. But "it never rains at Cairo," as the saying is, and so the dust is a more tangible evil than the mud. All the various shopkeepers belonging to one trade congregate in the same quarter, so that if you want to make various purchases of different articles, you have to pass, not merely from shop to shop, but from quarter to quarter. At one moment you are bewildered by gay horse-trappings and magnificent saddles, which are displayed prominently to tempt the native riders,—they delight in colour,—and the saddles really are most gorgeous. Then a turn brings you to the shoe quarter, full of red and yellow slippers, with the toes turned up in a peak. After that you pass on to the Manchester cotton goods, filling a small street of stalls. Then comes the narrow, dull, silversmiths' quarter, where necklaces of the most beautiful workmanship are hidden away in remote corners, and then the Oriental stuffs and embroideries, rich and rare, with the well-known stall of "Far Away Moses."

The shops, however, are of the most insignificant character, generally speaking little more than an open front of seven, eight, or ten feet square, on the boards of which the vendor sits cross-legged among his goods, smoking a narghileh. If you want to make a purchase he invites you to come and sit down by him, sometimes pressing upon you small glasses of hot sweet tea. The narrow footways between the shops are generally covered over with open wood-work, and mats thrown upon it, or with festoons of creepers or close trellis—anything, in short, which may serve as shelter from the rays of the sun. The streets are thus darkened, which is refreshing in the glare of the East.

Such were the bazaars to which we went, and there is a charm about them which it is impossible for those who have not seen them to understand. There is a perpetually moving throng of variously-dressed people of every shade of complexion, from the jet-black Ethiopian to the fair European. There are Egyptians, Arabs and Nubians, Bedouins and Greeks, Syrians and English, and representatives of every sort of nationality. There are closely-veiled women with yashmaks, children with scarcely a rag on, dogs, donkeys, mules, Pashas in grand carriages, with gaily-dressed syces running before them, Cook's tourists on donkeys, camels carrying great loads of grass, or long trunks of trees. Every instant you are in jeopardy. The cry of "Ouah! Ouah!" is heard almost ceaselessly, warning you to take care of your limbs, and you leap aside just in time to avoid being knocked down by an advancing string of camels. Then perhaps a native lady, riding straddle-wise on a donkey, muffled up in a black silk garment, which gives the appearance of an inflated balloon, bears down upon you, and you have to exercise all your skill to give her free passage. The probability is that in avoiding Charybdis you fall into Scylla, and knock over either a money-changer with his table, or some vendor of sweetmeats, who ensconce themselves at the corners of the streets. The novelty of the whole scene was so bewildering that we were quite glad to return to the calm and quiet of our hotel.

We were all anxious that our first expedition should be to the Pyramids. We lost no time, therefore, in making the necessary arrangements. There is now a fairly good road all the way from Cairo to the Pyramids of Ghizeh—about an hour and a half's drive. As we crossed the Nile the spot where Moses is said to have been found was pointed out to us. This was the first Scriptural ground we had trodden, and although the exact place must be mere supposition, yet the very fact of standing by a river so often mentioned in the Bible was a matter of the greatest interest. The Nile stretched out before us, with the Pyramids in the distance, and we pictured the figures of the Egyptian Princess and her maidens walking down for their evening bath, the little ark of bulrushes, the wailing child, the faithful sister, the poor, anxious mother, and the brilliant future in store for the helpless infant. It is supposed that the ark of bulrushes was made of the papyrus, and not of the reeds which grow abundantly in every little watercourse in Egypt. The Nile, where we first saw it, is about the size of the Thames at London, and the water looked somewhat thick and dark-coloured. But the Egyptians love it as a sort of divinity, for their very life hangs on its rise and fall, and every blade of green in the land depends on its waters for existence.

The road along which we drove has been recently made and planted with an avenue of trees by the late Khedive, in honour of their European Majesties who came to Egypt for the opening of the Suez Canal. Rows of camels were continually passing us with their plaintive, patient faces, led by tall, swarthy fellaheen. It is about nine miles from Cairo to the Pyramids; and unfortunately, when we had gone about half way, the springs of one of our carriages broke, and there was nothing to be done but to send the ladies on in the carriage which was still sound, and for the gentlemen to walk, while one of the syces was sent back to Cairo to get another conveyance.

Happily for those who walked, there were banks of clouds which shielded them somewhat from the piercing rays of the sun. The Pyramids were full in sight all the way, and you never get wearied of gazing at them. The Pyramids! Strange indeed it seemed really to see what had been from childhood one of the unknown wonders of the world. And yet, is it not true that, even to those who visit them, they are still unknown wonders? Who shall disclose their secret history? Who shall read aright the teachings of those vast erections? The object of those ancient fabrics, and the names of their builders, will probably always remain more or less of a mystery. There are three large pyramids of Ghizeh, and several smaller ones. The great pyramid of Cheops is four hundred and fifty-one feet high, or rather more than a hundred feet higher than the dome of St. Paul's, and covers an area of very nearly thirteen acres. It is difficult to realise its height, owing to the ponderous shape of the structure, and it is only after climbing up some distance, and seeing how diminutive are the figures left below, that you begin to realise how high it really is.

The Pyramids lie at the very entrance of the desert, one side turning towards Cairo instinct with life and modern activity, the other looking on the bare sandy plain which speaks of ages of sterility and desolation. Nowhere, perhaps, are the two brought into closer juxtaposition. At the base of the largest of the three, the late Khedive built reception-rooms for the Prince of Wales, when, at the time of the opening of the Suez Canal, he paid a visit to the Pyramids. It is a monstrous erection, very unsuitable in so venerable a precinct, and, by its common-place style, suggests a comparison between the sublime and the ridiculous.

Majestic and grand as these Pyramids are now, they must have been far more splendid in their original state, when they were cased with smooth white or yellow limestone, or red granite from the first cataract. Sculptures, too, in all probability ornamented the outside, and, with the surrounding monuments now fallen into decay or hidden by the sand, the sight must have been a very glorious one.

As soon as we drew near the sandy platform on which the Pyramids are built, our troubles began. We found ourselves beset, surrounded, and completely enclosed by an army of picturesque Arabs, of various degrees of dirt and griminess, who, with wild gesticulations, implored us to engage them for the ascent, or for any other office required. We were deafened with the squabbling and altercation which ensued, but one man stood out as pre-eminently attractive. "Ibrahim Tahoul." He had already been riding by our carriage, talking to us in doggerel English, and we had been struck by his handsome face and graceful garments. So he was elected to be the chief leader of the Pyramid-party, and under him were several other strong Arabs, with a large contingent of supernumeraries.

The ascent of the Great Pyramid is no easy task, but four of our party determined to climb up it, and after watching them for a short time, unknown to my husband, who was afraid it would be too tiring for me, I started to follow them. The steps up which we had to scramble are about four or five feet high. The Arabs, however, leave very little necessity for personal exertion in the matter. One man seizes one arm, another seizes the other, and, whilst you are thus being hoisted up, there comes a most surprising series of pushes from behind, and your feet are planted in the exact place you are aiming at, on an eminence about the height of your chest. Each traveller has a contingent of four Arabs to propel him up, and there is a flying squadron of unattached helpers who catch hold of your foot or your arm, or any other portion of your person which is not already in the possession of the lucky four, and give it a hoist or a push, for which volunteer assistance they clamorously demand "backsheesh," when the time of settlement comes. All this is very ignominious, but without this aid it really would be impossible for anyone but Mr. Whymper himself to reach the top.

Many travellers have recounted their sad experience as regards the almost compulsory backsheesh extorted from them while scaling the Pyramids. We obviated this by openly placing all our valuables, including our purses, in the hands of one of our party who remained below. When, therefore, as is the custom of the Arabs, backsheesh was demanded about half way up, we gave them to understand that it was absolutely useless for them to say one word about it, for everything connected with backsheesh had been left behind, but that at the end they should be well satisfied. It is only fair to say that when we left the place, and had settled with the men, they were very grateful and profuse in Eastern compliments. Funny fellows they were, and their tongues were never silent for a moment. When they were not squabbling amongst themselves in strong-sounding Arabic, they exhorted me in this wise,

"Look up dere—dere—look up dere," pointing to a ledge of the Pyramid far overhead. "Dere you see your husband. No you fear me—me strong man;" and then followed a hoist and a push, and I was up another ledge, panting and astonished. I paused for reflection, and my chief guide must have thought I was afraid; for, by this time, the rest of the party were high above my head, and looked like flies on the mountain of stone steps above me. "No you fear me, lady. Your eye same colour my eye." This is considered to be a very re-assuring observation in the East. By the time I had gone a quarter of the way up I felt too giddy to go any higher. I could not look down the depth below without such discomfort that I reluctantly decided to give up the attempt, and I was lifted down, ledge after ledge, by my Arab attendants with very little effort on my own part. They are as strong as lions, and as agile as gazelles.

Meanwhile, my husband and daughter were nearly at the top of the Pyramid. Ibrahim, who was in charge of them, suddenly turned round to my husband, and said,

" Yankee Doodle ?"

" No," was the response. " English."

" Jack and Jill," said the Arab.

"I hope we shall not break our crowns," replied my husband. And then, to his surprise, the guide repeated the whole of that classic poem.

There is an area of something like one hundred and twenty square yards at the top of the Pyramid, and the view thence is most striking. My husband gives the following account of it :—

" To the south, the desert stretches as far as the eye can reach. It is not one monotonous level of sand, but rather ridges like waves of the sea, every now and then broken by a sand mountain. There was not a single oasis to be seen, but in the far distance we descried a caravan, winding along with an interminable string of camels. Immediately underneath us lay the Sphinx; and to the north the verdure and fertility of the banks of the Nile were backed by the minarets and domes of Cairo glittering in the sun."

Our party remained some time at the top. The Arabs wanted them to cut their names on the stone. It is hardly necessary to say that they indignantly declined to do so. Some one has been wicked enough to commit a forgery, and to inscribe there, " A. P. of Wales!"

The descent was, if possible, more ignominious than the ascent. Two Arabs in front receive the traveller on landing on each successive step, whilst a rope placed round his waist, and held firmly by another Arab behind, lets the unfortunate sufferer down gently. Truth to tell, it was rather giddy work; something like climbing down the outside of the dome of St. Paul's by a ladder, each step being three or four feet deep.

"L'appetit vient en mangeant," and though, a short time before, great doubts had been expressed by all our party as to whether they should go inside the Pyramid or not, yet no sooner had the external difficulties been successfully grappled with than my husband and daughter determined to penetrate into the inmost recesses of the vast structure.

The entrance to the interior of the Great Pyramid is about fifty feet from the ground. Seven Arabs went in with them, two of them carrying lighted candles. The passage is extremely low at first, only about three or four feet high, and descends rapidly. Then you ascend, in some places quite precipitously, and, of course, all in the dark. The marble is very slippery and difficult to walk on. At last a great hall is reached, out of which a passage leads to the King's Chamber, in which is the sarcophagus, supposed by some to have been the receptacle of the bones of King Cheops.

When they got into the King's Chamber, the Arabs set up a loud "hurrah," and brandished their arms about with wild gesticulations. It must have been a strange, weird scene—the intense heat, the swarthy Arabs in their flowing dresses, the absolute darkness of the whole place, save where the two dim candles threw their flickering light. The outer world was for a time absolutely shut out, and they were alone with their wild, excited guides. There is something overawing in the whole aspect of the Pyramids, whether viewed from without, or whether contemplated from their own internal recesses.

The Sphinx, which was our next object of interest, is only a few hundred yards from the Great Pyramid. We were followed on our way thither by a screaming crowd of Arabs, as before, buzzing round like hornets, and teasing for backsheesh, till we were driven into a state bordering on distraction. The Sphinx is a wonderful ruin, and appeared to me even more striking than the Pyramids themselves. It rears its great mutilated head above the surging sand, smiling blandly, without a nose, and with ruined eyes, but with the wreck of much beauty and nobleness. There it has stood for countless ages. Men have come and men have gone, but it remains for ever. Through the mighty past it has been calmly gazing, with the same fixed smile, at the long procession of generations that have lived and died since the days of Cheops, the builder of the Pyramid,—since the time of the Pharaohs, —the Israelites,—Joseph,—and Moses,—down to the great day when the Lord Jesus was brought, an infant, into the land of Egypt by the

Virgin Mary; still on and on, to the present time of enlightenment and civilization, when English and American tourists eat sandwiches in its august presence, and say scornfully, as we overheard one of them remark, "Oh, this is the Sphinx, is it? I don't think much of it!"

There were originally, it is said, two Sphinxes, guarding the entrance to a temple. The body and paws of the one which alone remains are hidden under the sand, though to a certain extent you can make out the length of the body. From the crown of the head to the pavement on which the fore-legs of the Sphinx rest is said to be sixty-six feet. The ear is four and a half feet long, the nose five feet seven inches, and the mouth seven feet in length.

We stood for a long time meditating over this marvellous old monument. Five hundred yards further through the desert brought us to an excavated temple, the gigantic stones of which must have been transported (like the outer coating of the Pyramids) some hundred and eighty miles, a fact which shows that at any rate the engineers of those days were no tyros in their art. It was discovered by Monsieur Mariette in 1853, and, when we were there, a troupe of little Arab children were trying to keep the building clear by filling baskets full of sand and carrying them on their heads some short distance off, where they disgorged their contents. Thirty of the smallest navvies we had ever seen were occupied in this manner, singing in unison a monotonous sort of minor chant, and laughing merrily, as though at play. They get a trifling payment from government for this jovial labour, but, truth to tell, the amount of work done was very infinitesimal.

The ruins of this ancient temple are exceedingly fine, chiefly composed of blocks of granite and alabaster. It is said by some that a great city once occupied this site, and that the Nile flowed past it. Our Arab guide insisted upon the correctness of this theory. It may have been so, but in that case the river must have shifted its course about six miles. This is not at all unlikely to have happened, for, owing to the nature of the soil, the Nile even now continually changes its bed. Our drive back from the Pyramids was a pleasant rest after the toils of the day, and the incessant clamouring for backsheesh. It was sunset before we reached our hotel, and the evening lights were beautiful.

CHAPTER II.

CAIRO TO JAFFA.

SUNDAY AT CAIRO—MOSQUE OF MEHEMET ALI—OLD CAIRO—HELIOPOLIS—ANCIENT OBELISK—THE VIRGIN'S WELL—MISS WHATELEY'S MISSION SCHOOL—DIFFICULTIES GRADUALLY SURMOUNTED—GROSS SUPERSTITION OF THE DERVISHES—INTRODUCTION TO THE WIFE OF THE KHEDIVE—COURT CUSTOMS—MAHMOUD PASHA'S HAREEM—THE CONDITION OF THE LABOURING CLASSES—BRIDAL PROCESSIONS—CUSTOMS WITH REGARD TO PRAYER—THE SCAVENGERS OF CAIRO—THE NILE—THE WAY IN WHICH IT IRRIGATES AND FERTILIZES THE COUNTRY—RAILWAY TO ISMAILIA—ASPECT OF THE DESERT—SUEZ CANAL—THE MIRAGE—ARRIVAL AT PORT SAÏD—VIOLENT STORM—ARRIVAL AT JAFFA.

CHAPTER II.

WE spent a delightful Sunday at Cairo. It was so pleasant to find a well-built English church close to our hotel, with early, morning and afternoon services; and, as it was the fourth Sunday in Lent, one of the lessons for the day was Gen. xlii., and I cannot describe the interest we felt in listening to the story of Joseph in the very country in which he had made for himself so great a name.

The next few days were fully occupied in sight-seeing. This is no guide-book, and therefore I will not enumerate the various bazaars, streets, mosques, and ancient ruins we saw; but a few words must be said concerning the mosque of Mehemet Ali. It is a comparatively modern building, magnificently placed on the brow of a hill on which stands the citadel overlooking the town. Unluckily, when we were there, a gale was blowing which almost blinded us with sand, for Cairo is built just on the edge of the desert. But, notwithstanding this, the view was very grand—the beautiful grey old city, with its countless minarets, domes, and gardens, the green plain, through which flows the life-giving Nile, and the desert, with the Pyramids rising majestically out of a sea of sand.

On entering the mosque, we had to put on our slippers. We had prudently brought our own with us, and thus avoided the necessity of wearing some of the many dirty, ragged pairs placed in rows at the entrance-door, and hired out to those who need them.

The slippers are put on over the shoes, the theory being that the floor of the sacred building is not to be desecrated by any outer dust being shaken off upon it. In order further to show your respect for the place, and in accordance with the entire bouleversement of European ideas which characterises the East, gentlemen have to keep their hats on, instead of, as with us, taking them off. The outer court, in the centre of which is a well (Hanefiyeh) for the necessary ablutions, is entirely of alabaster—both floor, walls, and pillars.

As we entered, a Moslem was in the act of performing his ablutions, for all faithful sons of the Prophet invariably wash before they worship. In the building itself we found groups of Mohammedans squatted on the floor, which is covered over with Turkey carpets, repeating their prayers, and swaying their bodies gently to and fro as they muttered passages from the Koran in a low, crooning chant. They looked up as we entered, and watched us attentively, but did not interrupt their service.

The mosque is richly decorated inside. Hundreds of lamps hang from the ceiling. No woman is allowed to visit the mosque on Friday (the Mohammedan Sunday), but on other days they are permitted to enter for their devotions.

It is hardly necessary to say that we were shown the Mameluke jump, the Khedive's reception palace, the tombs of the Mamelukes, and the royal mortuary mosque, where Khedives and their wives are interred in gaudy mausoleums. Sometimes portions of food are placed on their tombs, so that the departed spirits, when perambulating the mosque, as they are said to do at night, may find something wherewith to refresh themselves. The out-door tombs of the Moslems are usually painted a glaring white, with an upright stone at the head and another at the feet, representing, as we were told, the good and the bad angel of the person interred underneath.

We returned through "old Cairo" while a gale was raging, and the dust was almost blinding. On the way we passed some fine, ancient, decayed old mosques in the most picturesque narrow streets; the houses having projecting balconies, and windows closely latticed to prevent the women inside from being seen.

It was interesting to go through the bazaars of native productions, well filled with the usual artistic-looking crowds, dirty camels, and donkeys, lovely bits of Moorish architecture, dogs in countless numbers sleeping or prowling about, mingled with ragged children, and beggars of every degree of deformity; and all lit up with a blazing sun. The smells were occasionally overpowering, and in one of the ruined mosques, still used for worship by poorer Moslems, the evil odours were so horrible that we were forced to retire speedily. But, notwithstanding all this, crowds of poor, maimed, blind, diseased creatures were lying about in the entrance, eating, sleeping, and living in it as if it was their home.

One day of our stay at Cairo was devoted to a visit to Heliopolis, the ancient On. Here lived, in old times, the priest of On, and Asenath, his daughter, Joseph's wife.

The drive to Heliopolis was very interesting. As a matter of course, we passed a palace of the Khedive's, surrounded by luxuriant gardens. I say as a matter of course, for it is a notable fact that if you see any very large building in Egypt, and inquire what it is, the answer you receive is almost invariably the same: "A palace belonging to the Khedive." The late Khedive had an extraordinary mania for building. Skirting the desert, and passing through avenues of lebbek-trees (like acacias), we reached the land of Goshen, where we at once exchanged barrenness for fertility. The land of Goshen is well irrigated, and teeming with bright green vegetation; palm-trees, groves of orange and lemon-trees, hedges of prickly pears (cactus), fields in which Indian corn, leeks, onions, garlic, cucumbers, and all manner of cereals are grown amid sparkling streams of water, rippling and flowing in all directions, with a delicious and refreshing sound. It was indeed "a watered garden," "a garden of herbs." We went back in thought to the pastoral days of old Jacob, when he lived in this good land with his children, and his children's children, his flocks and his herds, and saw once more, in the great and mighty Joseph, the long lost son of his beloved Rachel. Goshen must have seemed very lovely to him after the wild and rocky uplands of Canaan.

The great point of interest at Heliopolis is the obelisk, which is supposed to be the oldest in the world standing on its original site. It rises from the midst of a green field of wheat, with a teeming population of ragged beggar children hovering about in hopes of backsheesh.

No doubt the eyes of Joseph had often rested on this very monolith under which we stood. Was it irreverent to suppose that this venerable old obelisk had probably looked down upon the love-making between Joseph and Asenath, as well as on the heathen rites of the old Egyptian worship? Was it unnatural to long that it could speak to us of the days when Egypt was the centre of learning and civilization, and when the light of true religion dawned upon it in Joseph's teaching and example? Our Blessed Lord, too, Himself was probably brought under its shadow by the Virgin Mary and Joseph, for at a well close by, under the wide-spreading branches of an old sycamore-tree, tradition says that they rested in their flight into Egypt.

It was a most delicious and refreshing place. The great wheel of the sakiyeh, moved by a buffalo, turned and creaked, filling the little earthen pitchers with which it was furnished, and emptying them into channels which watered the neighbouring flower-garden through numberless tiny rills. We sat down in the grateful shade by the trickling, splashing water, to meditate on the great historic past. This sweet haven of rest may well have tempted the Holy Family to pause awhile, after their painful journey through the scorching desert.

This, then, was a place most memorable in the history of our tour, because, for the first time, we were brought into close connection with our Lord's life upon earth. We were treading in His footsteps.

During our stay at Cairo we went to see Miss

Whateley's Mission School. Her educational labours amongst the Arabs are well known, and we were surprised and astonished at the immense success she has achieved, in spite of difficulties which would have completely disheartened a less heroic spirit. About five hundred Arabian and Coptic children are now being educated in her schools. They are all taught to read the Bible, though only a few of them are baptised Christians. If any attempt were made to proselytise, the whole thing would be stopped at once, but it is hoped and believed that the Scriptural teaching will have a Christianising effect upon them. Such, indeed, is found to be the case, for many of them, we were told, become Christians after they leave the school. My husband examined two or three of the boys' classes in English (which all learn), and he was perfectly amazed at the sharpness and thoughtfulness of their answers. The reading-book placed in his hands was rather difficult, but the first-class explained clearly and intelligently the following words which occurred in the lesson : "computation," "divine dispensation," "external symbols," "the Messiah," "fulfilment of prophecy."

Nor was it the mere meaning of the words which they had taken in; for my husband asked them a variety of questions, and their answering throughout was sharp, accurate, and thoughtful, showing that they had been well-grounded in the general truths of the Christian faith. It was a pleasure to see their eager, bright faces gleaming with delight at being questioned by a stranger. The girls sang for us, and showed their needle-work, which was excellent.

Miss Whateley spoke to us of her first years at Cairo, when she was abused, insulted, and cursed in the streets by the fanatical Moslems, when dust was thrown at her as she passed, and every sort of opposition placed in her way. It was up-hill work then, and nothing but God's blessing on her brave, indomitable energy, and the motive power of love in her heart, could have enabled her to grapple with such overwhelming difficulties. She has now added to her educational work a most interesting and successful medical mission among the sick and suffering, and her name is a household word in Cairo.

Every year she takes a Dahabeeah, and pursues

her work of love among the villages bordering on the Nile. Her knowledge of Arabic is perfect, and she gathers the natives around her, talks to them, instructs and doctors them with intense zeal and philanthropy. Before long, it is to be hoped that Mohammedan prejudice will break down before the influence of Christianity. At any rate, Miss Whately is now carrying on her noble work without being absolutely stopped, and we left her school with an earnest prayer that such unselfish labours may be abundantly blessed.

Christianising influences are sorely needed at Cairo, as will be seen from the following account of one of the Mohammedan customs which I heard from an eye-witness.

The rite described to me is called "Tizreh." Seven hundred dervishes drugged with haki entered into a courtyard where the ceremony was to be enacted, yelling, raving, piercing themselves with needles and pointed instruments, till they bled profusely. They then placed themselves on the ground in order, lying close together, foaming at the mouth. A hundred and fifty yards of human beings were thus arranged, so as to make a roadway of bodies, along which a Sheikh mounted on horseback was to ride. He had great difficulty in making the horse tread on this living pavement, and the animal stumbled and plunged, and tried its utmost to escape, but he was urged on by his rider, and the shouts of the bystanders and the clang of instruments of music drowned the groans of the wretched fanatics. After the ceremony, the poor sufferers were removed by their friends, wailing piteously. Not unfrequently death ensues. The present Khedive is said to be most anxious to put a stop to this barbarous and disgusting rite. The religious theory of it seems to be that evil spirits are exorcised and sin driven out by the horse's tread.

During our stay at Cairo, I was fortunate enough to be introduced, together with the ladies of our party, to the wife of the Khedive by Madame Turabe-Bey, who was connected with the Court, and to whom we had been introduced. The following extract from my journal gives the particulars of the visit:—

"*March* 10*th*.—To-day we went to the Ismailia Palace, and were most courteously and kindly received by the Princess. Tall black Nubians handed us out of the carriage, and led us up the marble steps to the door of the harcem, where a group of the Princess's attendants, gaily dressed in bright-coloured satin robes, were in waiting to take us into the palace. We passed through a large dark hall, luxuriously furnished with divans and sofas and heavy hangings, to an inner *salon*, decorated in blue and gold, with European furniture. On an ottoman at one end sat the Princess, looking very bright and pleasant. She is only twenty-one years old. We went forward and made the Eastern salutation. She was very gracious, and gave us a courteous welcome, speaking in French.

"The attendant maidens brought chairs and placed us in a semi-circle round her. Cigarettes were handed to us, and coffee in exceedingly small cups with gold filigree stands like egg-cups. The tray was hidden, according to custom, by a gorgeous velvet screen embroidered heavily in gold, held at each end by one of the attendants. Ten of these young girls were gliding about the room very noiselessly. Ere long two princesses came in, leaving their yashmaks in the antechamber, and saluted the Khedive's wife in Oriental fashion, bowing towards the ground, and then, with a graceful circular sweep of the hand, touching chin, forehead, and heart. Fortunately for us, they all spoke a little French, so we could carry on a conversation. The Princess good-naturedly sent one of her ladies to put on an Oriental Court dress, so that we might see the Eastern state costume. By-and-by she returned, wearing a train of pink silk many yards in length richly embroidered, and a bodice of yellow silk and gold brocade. Her face was concealed by a white yashmak.

"Shortly after this, we rose to take our leave, but the Princess asked us to remain, as she had sent for her musicians to entertain us. In a short time, six young girls appeared in red and blue dresses, with embroidered slippers, and sat in a row at the further end of the room. One played on a violin, another on a lute; two had huge zithers, and the two others tambourines. With this accompaniment, they sang Arabian ballads. The music was strange and wild, in excellent time, but absolutely devoid of melody. They went on and on from one song to another, singing with high shrill voices an interminable number of verses without any appearance of hesitation or fatigue. It really seemed as if nothing would ever stop them, so I hazarded a complimentary remark as to their extraordinary memory, upon which the Princess eagerly assured me they could sing more than a thousand such songs by heart. This was somewhat startling, as they had already sung for an hour with scarcely a moment's breathing space, and it was time for us to rejoin the gentlemen of our party at the hotel; so we rose to take our leave. The Princess very graciously sent for her two little sons of five and six years old to see us before we left. Dear little fellows they were —so pretty and well-mannered; they spoke English nicely, and shook hands with us in European fashion. She then gave me a cabinet photograph of the Khedive, which one of the slave-girls wrapped up in a large square of pink silk. We thanked her for her kindness and courtesy, and requested her, according to the usual custom, to convey our compliments to the Khedive."

Thus ended our interview in the hareem of the Khedive. It is said that he is anxious to have his sons well-educated, and he certainly has lost no time in doing so, for an English tutor has been appointed to superintend their education. He moreover had the good sense to apply to one of our great public schools in England, and the post is at present held by an ex-master of Winchester College, who is attached to the Khedive's court, and, in straight-cut coat and red fez, looks altogether Oriental.*

We drove to another harcem, that of Mahmoud Pasha, a younger brother of the Khedive. Here we waited for some time in a large hall, furnished with divans, and the floor covered with soft Persian carpets like velvet. The hall looked out into a very pretty garden filled with tropical plants, and with a fountain in the centre. By-and-by Prince Mahmoud entered with his wife. He had lived for some years in Paris, so we talked with him in French. Cigarettes and coffee were again handed, and slave-girls flitted about. There was much less state and formality in this visit, but we did not remain long, as it was getting so late.

Having said thus much about the Court, it may be well to add a few particulars respecting the labouring classes in Cairo. An acquaintance of ours, who employs a good many of the fellaheen

---

* The fez is never taken off, either indoors or out-of-doors.

in his works, told us that the rate of wages is four pence a day. They make huts for themselves on waste ground outside the town, and even if they have to hire a lodging, it only costs them one shilling and four pence a month. They eat sugar-cane and baked bread, so that their maintenance is not expensive.

We chanced one day to see a funeral procession in one of the crowded streets. The body was on a bier, covered with a piece of carpet. A few men walked in front, repeating prayers out of the Koran, while four veiled women, riding astride on donkeys, brought up the rear, uttering wails in a high shrill voice. Great, indeed, was the contrast between this scene and our reverent English funerals. The wailing, too, had an artificial ring about it, which did not denote true sorrow.

There is the same sort of unreal character about their wedding processions. We saw two matrimonial parties. In one case a band of noisy musicians led the way through the crowded Mouski. The bride followed, under a pink canopy, and enveloped in a large thick white veil, which entirely covered and concealed her figure and face. Veiled women supported her on the right and on the left, while little bridesmaids clad in red garments ran in front, and the whole company moved along very rapidly.

The other marriage procession that we saw was that of a bridegroom. It passed our hotel late at night, a band playing, torches gleaming, and large crowds accompanying it. It was a sight that made us realise more strongly almost than anything else that we were in the land of the Bible, and vividly illustrated the words, "Behold the Bridegroom cometh."

The Mohammedan customs with regard to prayer are very peculiar. A faithful Moslem performs his devotions five times a day, and the hours of prayer are proclaimed from the minarets by the Muezzins. The first call is Subh, at daybreak; the second Duhr, at midday; then follows Asr, about an hour and a half before sunset; Maghrib, shortly after sunset; and, lastly, Ashâ, at nightfall. The call varies, but it is often times the following:

"Allah is great. There is no God but Allah, and Mohammed is the prophet of Allah. Come to prayer. Come to worship. Allah is great. There is no God but Allah."

These words are often repeated. Whenever

it is the hour of prayer the Moslem turns towards Mecca, kneels upon his prayer-mat, bit of carpet, or upon the bare ground, and prostrates himself with his forehead touching the earth. He rises up again and stretches out his hands towards heaven in an attitude of entreaty, repeating words out of the Koran. This is continued for about five minutes. On one occasion, as we were returning through the public gardens, we saw two men at work throw down their tools, when the cry of the Muezzin was heard, turn towards Mecca, and begin a series of prostrations. It was impossible not to be struck with their fearlessness of profession, or to help wishing that members of our pure Church would be equally bold in their Christian ritual!

In a land where all is new and strange, one of the most surprising arrangements is the work allotted to dogs as quadrupedal scavengers. Thousands of them prowl about the city. They are ownerless and undomesticated. No one cares for them, and they in their turn care for nobody. They never bite, but in whatever direction you may look, you are sure to see a dozen or two of them lying about in the streets. They never get out of your way, and sometimes occupy the whole pavement. They are a privileged class. Their organization at night, when they consider the town to be their own property, is supposed to be very perfect; for there is a tacit arrangement amongst them that certain districts should be assigned to certain herds of dogs. An interloper from one part of the town to another finds himself in a very unpleasant position, for he is at once set upon by the dogs of the district into which he has intruded. The refuse and offal is devoured by them, and certainly Cairo is freer from odours than many a town with a theoretical system of sewerage. But they make night hideous by their noise, and it requires some practice to get accustomed to the howling and fighting, which never cease.

One night we were roused by a greater tumult of noises than usual. In the midst of the ordinary barking and howling there came a loud cackling, as if a score of indignant hens, rolled into one, were expostulating with some tormentor. Louder and louder it grew, till, at last, the dogs were so exasperated that there was a sound as of a violent and desperate pitched battle; then a stampede, with a confused chorus of yells, howls, barks, and unearthly cries. We heard afterwards that the noise arose from some vultures and dogs fighting over carrion, till they were dispersed by one of the native watchmen.

One word about the river. Some of our party went to the Nilometer, and learnt many things concerning the Nile—the bounteous fertilising Nile; the one river of Egypt, which is loved and reverenced, and almost worshipped by the people; for it is the mainspring of their physical life. Rain, though of more frequent occurrence of late years than formerly, falls but very rarely in Egypt, perhaps some half dozen times in the course of the year. And the crops, therefore, of that very small portion of the land which can be cultivated, are wholly dependent upon the annual overflow of the river. The inundation, which usually commences in June, is caused by the melting of the snow in the mountains of the Upper Nile. The water rises gradually for about a couple of months, and then, after receding, for a considerable time rises and falls alternately. Its progress is anxiously watched, and duly recorded by the Nilometer.

We were reminded of the great recumbent figure of the river-god in the Vatican, surrounded by those sixteen joyous, merry little children playing pranks around the solemn old Nile, and representing the sixteen cubits, or Egyptian ells, which it is necessary for the river to rise before it irrigates the land. When it reaches this height, the various embankments by which the water is dammed back are cut, and the life-giving stream is allowed to irrigate the country far and near. Its course is directed into various channels cut for the purpose, and carefully spread over the flat surface of the ground.

The effect of the Nile water is simply marvellous. Sandy desert, when irrigated, soon becomes alluvial soil, and the influence of the great river extends far and wide. Of course, the rise in the upper part of the Nile is much more than at Cairo and at its mouth. At Thebes it is considered satisfactory if the water rises about thirty-six feet, while at Cairo from twenty-four to twenty-seven feet is sufficient. The rise at the Rosetta and the Damietta mouths would then be about three or four feet.

We passed along the Delta in March, before the Nile had begun to rise, and the natives were then irrigating the fields by the most primitive artificial methods. Sometimes two Arabs, nearly nude, were swinging leathern buckets, filled from a lower and emptied on to a higher level, with an uninterrupted motion, regular as clockwork. More effective is the sakiyeh, a wheel with a succession of buckets attached to it, which are filled on passing through the water, and empty themselves when inverted by the turning of the wheel. Evidently the natives appreciate the value of the water, and grudge no labour or pains to utilize it.

Friday, March 12th, was our last day at Cairo, and we were heartily sorry to leave it. We had been lodged in comfort and luxury at the New Grand Hotel, and we fully realised the fact that we should find no such palatial hostelries in the land to which our steps were now turned. But this was only one element in our regret. The fascination of Cairo seems to arise from its intense and vivid Oriental character, its cloudless sky, dazzling sunshine, pure, transparent air, and its cosmopolitan assortment of nationalities. Nowhere else can you see European civilization side by side with people and habits and customs that carry you back to the days of the Pharaohs.

We were accompanied to the station by our good friends at Cairo, and started regretfully for Ismailia. The Egyptian railway-carriages are on a par with those of the Italian lines. The third-class are extremely dirty, and are said to be peopled with live animals who pay no fare. Those carriages which are made for the ladies of the hareem of the Khedive are constructed in such a way that no one can possibly see into them, nor can the ladies look out.

The train lunched in the middle of the journey at Zak-â-zik. If the first-class carriages had an English appearance, there were certainly not wanting reminders that we were in Egypt, for in watching the luggage being shifted from one train to another, we observed that the head-porter brandished about a stick, with which he not only kept off intrusive boys, but also occasionally belaboured the porters. In one corner of the station, a party of travelling Bedoueens were squatting in a circle, with their long guns over their shoulders, looking sensational and formidable. In another corner a native juggler was exhibiting his tricks, with a crowd around him in rapt attention. These jugglers, descendants of

Jannes and Jambres, are a regular institution in Egypt, and their incantations to the evil one are most extraordinary.

The journey to Ismailia occupied about six hours. The country throughout is perfectly flat, with a few mud villages and palm-trees, and numberless water-dykes. After Zak-â-zîk, the line runs through the Arabian desert, and nothing meets the eye but long waves of sand and pebbles. It is melancholy in the extreme; there is no living thing to relieve the depressing monotony but a few stunted ash-coloured thorn-bushes. The sun beats down on these vast deserted wastes as in flames of fire, and both here and in the desert near Cairo we learned the full meaning of those words, "The people thirsted there for water," "Our soul is dried away," "The great and terrible wilderness." The fierce heat, the loneliness, the silence, the hopeless barrenness, and the vastness of a desert, are terrible to look upon.

We reached Ismailia at five o'clock. This town, midway between Suez and Port Saîd, is situated on an oasis in the desert formed by the overflow from the fresh water canal, as it is called, which brings the water of the Nile from the neighbourhood of Zak-â-zîk. It really is marvellous to see, as you do at Ismailia, a town made in the desert, with excellent roads, shops, and cafés, and avenues of the lebbek-tree. Its mushroom growth is due to the energy of Monsieur De Lesseps.

There are two hotels in the town, several now deserted villas, a small Roman Catholic church, some shops, and a palace, built by the late Khedive for the Emperor and Empress of the French, when the Suez Canal was opened. The festivities connected with the opening are said to have cost the Khedive four millions of money.

We found the Hôtel de Paris, which was our abode for the night, fairly comfortable. It was a comical sort of building, with a series of very small rooms, all giving on to a kitchen garden, and presided over by a neat French landlady, and was perfectly clean, but absolutely primeval in all its arrangements.

The next morning, at early dawn, we took our seats on the little steamer which plies between Ismailia and Port Saîd. We had been told that we should soon grow weary of the Suez Canal, that the one word "monotonous" described the whole passage, and that we should be thankful when it was only an experience of the past. But it was not so at all. Whether we were more easily interested than other travellers it is impossible for us to decide, but certainly we none of us found the day long or wearisome.

Ismailia itself is on the borders of Lake Timsâh, or the Crocodile Lake. Monsieur De Lesseps, in forming his canal, utilised several large lakes *en route*, one of a thousand square miles.

We heard a melancholy account of the sufferings of the poor Arabs who worked at the canal. Thousands of them were forced by the Khedive to work for nothing but their food, and this was so insufficient, owing to the difficulty of carriage across the desert, that vast numbers of them died of starvation and thirst. Lord Palmerston was reported to have done his best, though unsuccessfully, to prevent this cruelty.

The canal itself is about one hundred miles long, and a hundred yards or so wide. On each side the eye travels over sand-hills and dales as far as it can reach. But you feel within the range of civilization, for four or five telegraph wires run alongside of the canal, as well as a water-pipe, which brings Nile water, which is excellent for drinking purposes, from Ismailia to Port Saîd.

Every now and then we came to a station, where a boat put off sometimes with a native passenger, sometimes with merchandise; and occasionally we passed large steamers, on their way to the Red Sea. But the great interest was at midday, when we were fortunate enough to have an admirable sight of the mirage of the desert, for several hours, on the Asiatic side of the canal. A calm, glistening sea was distinctly visible in the distance, with islands dotted over it; bays with rocky shores, and mountains towering up into the air. We could hardly believe that what we saw was only a phantasmagoria lying on the arid, dreary desert, till we came abreast of these illusions, when they vanished from our sight.

At El Kantarah, a small hostelry on the canal, where we lunched at midday, there was an excellent view from a sand-hill close by of the Lake Menzaleh, a large shallow piece of water on the African side. From here, too, we saw the distant horizon absolutely white with thousands of flamingoes. Suddenly, as we were looking at them, they flew up simultaneously into the air, and the effect of their beautiful red under-wings was like a shower of rose-leaves floating in the sky.

There was an unfortunate English telegraph officer at Kantarah, who seemed delighted to see us and to exchange a few words with a fellow-countryman. He is quite alone in this dreary place, looking after the telegraph, and has lived here for years, far away from friends, and home, and country. We were glad to be able to cheer him by a few words of good news from Old England.

It was between two and three o'clock when we landed at the Hotel des Pays Bas at Port Saîd. We found excellent quarters here, but the town of Port Saîd itself is singularly uninteresting. It is very new, very French, very ugly, and, we were told, very wicked. Gaming and drinking-houses abound, and the population seem to include some of the naval scum of every nation. There is some difficulty in keeping the harbour, which is five hundred and seventy acres in area, free from the mud deposited by Mediterranean currents. The whole place is instinct with the usual bustle and confusion of a seaport town.

We spent Sunday there, and were glad to have our English services in the Mission room, and again in our hotel in the evening, which were cheering and refreshing.

But the elements were determined to prolong our stay at Port Saîd. A storm such as they had not experienced for fifteen years raged with great violence, and the captain of the *Mendoza* would not leave the shelter of the harbour till Tuesday night. The disembarkation at Jaffa, for which port we were bound, is a matter of considerable difficulty, and, in stormy weather, absolutely impossible. Fortunately for us there was a very large number of French pilgrims on board, whom the captain had guaranteed to land at Jaffa, and his policy therefore was not to leave Port Saîd till there was a reasonable probability of his being able to effect a landing there. Had it not been for this fortunate circumstance, we probably should have left Port Saîd much sooner, and been carried on to Haifa or Beyrout!

From the thirteen or fourteen hours' experience that we had of the *Mendoza*, we certainly had no wish that our passage in her should be unnecessarily prolonged. Our voyage from Port Saîd to

Jaffa, which lasted from four o'clock on Tuesday afternoon to five o'clock the next morning, was the only thoroughly miserable passage we had in all our Eastern tour. The sea had scarcely recovered from a gale which had swept over it for three days. The vessel itself was full of pilgrims going to Jerusalem, whose manners and customs were not altogether appetising, and the whole organization of the steamer was unpleasant. But,

> "Be the day weary, or be the day long,
> At length it ringeth to evensong,"

and we soon forgot the miseries of the night when we found ourselves anchoring a short mile or so from the Holy Land, with Jaffa full in sight.

CHAPTER III.

THE HOLY LAND.

DIFFICULT LANDING AT JAFFA—FIRST INTRODUCTION TO TENT LIFE—UNEXPECTED COMFORTS—HOUSE OF SIMON THE TANNER—EN ROUTE FOR LYDDA—ROAD TO JERUSALEM—ORANGE AND LEMON GROVES—THE PLAIN OF SHARON—BEAUTY OF THE FLOWERS—OUR FIRST MID-DAY HALT—RAMLEH—LYDDA—NIGHT EXPERIENCES—GENERAL ORDER OF MARCHING—FILTH OF LYDDA—ST. GEORGE'S CHURCH—BETH-HORON—VIEW FROM THE SHEIKH'S HOUSE—GIBEON—NEBY SAMWIL—FIRST VIEW OF JERUSALEM—DESOLATE APPEARANCE OF THE COUNTRY—SUICIDAL POLICY OF THE GOVERNMENT.

CHAPTER III.

BUILT up in tiers on the hill-side, surrounded by rich orange groves, and bathed in golden sunshine, Jaffa looked true to her name—"Beautiful."

Soon a whole fleet of little boats—we counted seventeen—buzzed round our steamer, with the usual clatter and chatter of Eastern boatmen, screaming, arguing, and gesticulating for passengers to the shore. As each boat had some fifteen or twenty Arabs in it, the confusion and hubbub when they were all disgorged on to the *Mendoza* may be more easily imagined than described. Fortunately for us our dragoman Hani, who had left us at Cairo, and here met us again, brought a boat out specially for us, and we soon found ourselves and our luggage, under his protection, nearing the Holy Land.

No wonder there is difficulty in landing at Jaffa,

for the whole place is rock-girt, and the passage through the reefs so narrow that the boatmen had to ship their oars in order to pass through.

The moment when we first set foot on the Holy Land was an era in our lives, and our thoughts were of too sacred a character to be expressed in words. There was not one of us who did not feel it very solemnizing.

We walked up an exceedingly steep and precipitous stairway to the town, and continued mounting through narrow streets till we reached a grassy platform overlooking Jaffa, with its white, flat-roofed buildings, surrounded by acres of orange and lemon-trees, and the blue sea beyond. Here we found our encampment—five stately tents, adorned within most brilliantly with appliqué work, in red, white, crimson, and blue patterns. There were three sleeping bell-tents for our party, comfortably fitted up with Persian rugs, iron bedsteads, the whitest of bedding, camp-stools, and tables, with washing apparatus. The two other tents were devoted, the one to cooking purposes, the other to serve as our general sitting and dining-room. Outside the tents, about eight and twenty horses and mules were picketed, with the Arab muleteers grooming them. A bell soon informed us that breakfast was ready, and never was any meal more appreciated by hungry travellers. We had expected to fare somewhat roughly, and after a gipsy fashion, but, to our surprise, found a most inviting breakfast spread on a long table, which was covered with a spotless cloth—eggs, omelettes, cutlets, coffee, and white bread, with excellent butter and jam—and there was a general air of comfort and luxury pervading the whole arrangements. George and Tannous, our two Arab servants, and Giovanni, a Greek, were standing within the tent, ready to anticipate our every wish, and Hani himself was in the gangway, enjoying our delight and astonishment. It was camping out made easy.

The Union Jack floated over the central tent, and gave *éclat* to our encampment, and we began to feel the grandeur and freedom of nomad life. Here we were in this wonderful sacred and historic old country, with a ready-made and portable home, free to go or to remain, according to the dictates of our own will and fancy, and our first realization of gipsy life was highly exhilarating.

There was not, however, much time for contemplating our new and strange position, for immediately after breakfast we walked down through quaint narrow arched ways and streets to the house of Simon the tanner. It stands close to the sea shore, and, though not the identical building, yet the site is probably the same as that on which St. Peter saw the heavenly vision. The present house is stone vaulted inside, and we climbed up to the flat roof, which commands a charming view of the Mediterranean and picturesque-looking town, and read the passages of Scripture which describe this and other incidents connected with the place.

In the course of our wanderings through Jaffa, we fell in with many bands of our fellow-passengers, the French pilgrims occupied, like ourselves, in visiting places of Scriptural interest.

By the time we got back to the camp our horses were ready for us to start—seven strong little Arabs, well groomed, and apparently eager to be off. We had sent out our own saddles from England, which for ladies, at any rate, is a great and almost necessary luxury.

We were soon *en route*, the horses curvetting

and prancing about a good deal. The day was splendid—sunny, and yet not oppressively hot. Our course for the greater part of the way lay along the only carriage road in Palestine, that from Jaffa to Jerusalem, and this hardly deserves to be dignified with such a name. It is heavily furrowed with ruts, bored deep with holes, and seamed with ridges in every imaginable position. A carriage must bump, and roll, and pitch from side to side in a cruel way, and the poor sufferers within must surely arrive at Jerusalem with bruised and tortured bodies, probably rueing the day when they started on such a journey. The omnibus from Jaffa to Jerusalem, which we saw afterwards at the Holy City, is as barbarous as the road itself. It is merely an open van with rows of seats across it, of antediluvian formation. To look at it, you would say that it would fall to pieces before it got to Ramleh, but its organization seems to suit the road on which it has to travel, and it jogs and jerks along, and pulls through the mud, and out of the chasms, and over the ridges, and somehow or other reaches Jerusalem in safety. We were thankful that we had arranged for our horses to meet us at Jaffa, and were thus spared so painful an experience.

The first mile out of the town took us through beautiful groves of orange and lemon-trees, as large as apple-trees in England. The size of the fruit is gigantic. Numbers of oranges are grown here for the Eastern markets, and at the time of the blossoming of the trees their sweet perfume fills the air so strongly that not only is the town of Jaffa redolent with it, but sailors some miles out at sea can tell that they are approaching the coast from the orange scent which is wafted to them from the luxuriant shore.

We emerged from these fragrant groves into the plain of Sharon, with the snow-capped range of Hebron in the distance. Scarlet anemones and Vanthol tulips carpeted the ground. The hedges were of prickly pears some ten or twelve feet high.

At mid-day we stopped for luncheon at a little well and mosque by the roadside. Our Arabs spread a white cloth on the ground, and on it plates, knives, forks, and glasses, together with cold chicken, hard eggs, bread, butter, jam, oranges, and biscuits. There was evidently no fear of our starving. As the majority of our party were total abstainers (and it may be well to say in passing that we never felt the least inconvenience or inability to endure fatigue from it), a kettle was soon boiled, and excellent tea, with milk, provided. This midday tea was a never-failing refreshment to us in our long tiring days. Everything around us was very strange, and it felt rather as if we were living in a dream. Our horses were picketed near us; numbers of native men and women in flowing garments, with camels and donkeys, were grouped by the well, as interested in watching us as we were in watching them; and, while we were resting, a French traveller, with his dragoman, both well armed, stopped to water their horses and exchange salutations with us.

We reached Ramleh shortly before sundown. The long olive groves here form a dark oasis in the bare, treeless plain, above which rises the tower of Ramleh, belonging to the old ruined "white mosque." Just outside the town, three lepers sat by the wayside, stretching out their arms to us with piteous cries for backsheesh, and showing their poor leprous limbs. They did not attempt to get up and come near us.

We had determined not to go by the usual route to Jerusalem, but to pass through more interesting country by way of Beth-horon. Accordingly, at Ramleh we left the high road, and rode along a green track between cactus-hedges twelve feet high and perfectly impenetrable, till we reached Ludd, the ancient Lydda. Our horses and mules, with luggage and servants, had passed us while we were halting at midday, and by the time we reached Ludd, everything was ready for our reception—tents pitched, and hot coffee prepared to refresh us after our ride.

Dinner was at seven o'clock, and it may be said once for all that our meals were most excellent. Hani was the mainspring of this, as well as of everything else which concerned our comfort; but he had a merry-looking Arab cook under him, who made wonderful sweets and *entrées*, with a kitchen range of simple design, in the form of an iron trough, about four feet long, supported on iron legs, and filled with a charcoal fire, which was fanned by a bundle of feathers. How the dinners which we enjoyed were produced out of this exceedingly archaic cooking apparatus was a perpetual source of marvel to us.

And now, how shall I describe our first night in camp? It was exciting, to say the least of it.

The sensations experienced by those who play at being Bedouoens are certainly peculiar and unique. My husband and I shut our tent door tight; we buttoned it over inside, made ourselves as secure as we could, and lay down, hoping to rest in peace; but anything like the succession of noises which then began it is difficult to conceive. In the first place, the Arabs slept in the open air, according to the custom of the country, all round our camp. We thought they never would cease their talking. What could they have to say?

"Now surely they have done, and we shall have quiet."

Vain hope! A moment's lull only led to louder talk than ever. They settled themselves round the camp fire, and never ceased their endless stories. Then, in a circle outside the muleteers, the horses and mules were picketed. They, too, seemed to be making a night of it, endlessly fidgeting, fighting one with another, every now and then getting loose, and rushing through the tent-ropes, whilst occasionally we heard a donkey's bray by way of variety. Then the dogs of Lydda began to bark. One dog had attached himself to our camp—Beyrout, we called him—and we hoped he would be with us throughout our travels. He was our watch-dog, and his business was to keep off all intruders, human or canine, and this he did effectually. Over and over again during the night troops of dogs, apparently thirty or more in number, came to our camp, but they recognized his authority, asserted by his own peculiarly sharp, snappish bark, and retired, probably vowing vengeance on a future day. This was not conducive to sleep.

Twice, by way of change, a number of jackals, which we recognized by their shrill cry, came near us. They seemed close to the prickly pears by which our camp was surrounded, and this, of course, made the dogs bark more furiously than ever. But the night wore on, and a faint grey dawn crept over the landscape. The muleteers ceased their jabber, but some peasants with musical talent droned out in the neighbouring fields a dreary Gregorian sort of chants. We were not sorry when our first experience of night life in camp came to an end.

The next morning we had to be up at cockcrow, and on horseback before eight o'clock.

The sun shone brilliantly upon our little camp, already fast melting away. It was quite a study to watch the process of decamping—there was such method and rapidity in it. We left our sleeping-tents before seven o'clock, to find breakfast ready in the *salon*, and, when we looked out again half an hour later, there was but little vestige left of our night abodes. The tents were folded and packed, the luggage was strapped on to the mules, the kitchen and dining paraphernalia were disposed of in long narrow boxes—there was a place for everything, and everything was in its place before the signal was given to start.

The order of the day was as follows: When everything was in readiness, we mounted our horses and started, leaving the mules and baggage to follow on a little later. We always halted at mid-day, when the luggage train passed on without stopping, and so, on our arrival at our camping-ground at four or five in the afternoon, we always found our tents pitched, and everything ready for our reception. Hani usually led the way, and we were accompanied by two syces (grooms on foot), Abdullah and Alraschid, with bare legs, their feet being protected by yellow slippers against the sharp rocks. It was marvellous to see how these Arabs walked gaily along the whole day, always ready to do whatever was wanted to the horse-gear, or to run here and there to pick wild flowers, and then merrily to groom the horses and take them to water on our arrival at our destination at the close of each day. They never seemed to be weary, or cross, or footsore.

And so we rode, on the morning of the 18th of March, into Ludd—Lod of the Old Testament, Lydda of the New. We read the story of St. Peter curing Æneas, and of the messengers coming from Joppa to tell him of the death of Dorcas; and as we waded through the narrow, muddy, dirty, and miserable streets of Lydda, it seemed almost a desecration to suppose that St. Peter could have spent even an hour in so unpleasant and dismal a place.

This difficulty of realizing the exquisite Scriptural stories in modern degraded Palestine was a constant source of disappointment, meeting us continually as we journeyed on through the Holy Land. Mud was literally flowing in a dull stream through Lydda; the slush was at least a foot deep. Between the walls of the houses a few lean dogs were sadly struggling through the mire; men and women ankle-deep in mud were passing along, but the filth baffles description, and we were thankful, after dismounting for a short time at the church of St. George, to find ourselves in the open mountain track.

As the legend runs, St. George was born at Ludd, fought the dragon in the neighbourhood of Beyrout, was martyred at the end of the third century, and was buried in this church. His knuckle and finger-bone, set in a silver casket, are shown to the passing traveller, and the church is ornamented with a picture of his conflict with the dragon. Strange to say, in this Greek church there was a gallery at the back, very high up, where the women can worship unseen. Even the Christian women here follow the Moslem custom, and entirely veil their faces.

Our route, on leaving Lydda, lay in the open plain, among cornfields and olive-trees, through a rich, fertile land, till we reached the rocky region in the neighbourhood of Beth-horon.

Crossing a valley by a stony path, we soon began a rugged ascent, and the track by which we wound round a succession of bleak mountainsides was more like the precipitous bed of a torrent than a road. We were never once during the whole day able to go beyond a foot's pace, but our little Arabs picked their way amongst the huge stones, and clambered up great boulders of rocks in a marvellous manner. We found by experience that it was best to leave them entirely to themselves, and they proved worthy of our confidence.

We had lunch at mid-day under "the shadow of a great rock." My niece picked a nosegay of twenty-seven different sorts of flowers from out of the floral profusion around us. The ground was perfectly enamelled with scarlet anemones, purple and white cyclamens, abundant as English primroses, and as large as in a well-kept greenhouse, pink linum, ranunculuses, camomile, planta genista, and many others.

We passed Lower, and, about four o'clock in the afternoon, reached Upper Beth-horon—"Bet-ur-el-Foka"—which was to be our camping-place for the night. Upper Beth-horon stands between two and three thousand feet above the sea; and on a grassy slope, near the old mud village which was perched upon a hill overlooking the camp, we found our tents pitched, the English flag flying, and hot coffee ready, to refresh us after our weary ride.

A party of Arabs from Beth-horon ranged themselves in a semi-circle around us to watch our proceedings with a solemn and rapt attention, after the manner of Easterns.

The village Sheikh was presented to us by Hani. He was about eighty years old, and very dirty, but his tattered garments hung about him with a strange dignity, and he at once advanced to lionize us over the village, and up to the citadel on the top of the hill. The latter turned out ultimately to be the roof of the Sheikh's mud house. His abode only differed from the other ordinary houses by being a little larger, and occupying the most elevated spot in Beth-horon. On to this vantage-ground we scrambled, surrounded, apparently, by the majority of the population of the place. Such a crowd of very insufficiently-clothed and dirty human beings could hardly be imagined. But they came round us, and rushed hither and thither, and executed war-dances in front of us, shouting out for backsheesh. It was with difficulty that the Sheikh could keep anything like order.

I was very anxious to enter one of the mud houses, but Hani described the interior of the native dwellings in such a graphic manner, and so earnestly deprecated our doing anything of the kind, for fear of ulterior consequences, that we refrained from indulging our curiosity. There is no furniture in these wretched adobe hovels, and often hardly room for all the family to squeeze into them. They generally sleep on the roof or outside the houses, and make as little use as they can of their unattractive homes.

The view from the Sheikh's house was very interesting, overlooking the western side of the territory of Ephraim and Benjamin, and part of Judah, the plain of Sharon, over which we had passed the previous day, Philistia, and the broad blue line of the sea beyond. The valley of Ajalon stretched out towards the south, and, as we gazed upon the scene, we tried to picture to ourselves Joshua pursuing the Amorites "along the way that goeth up to Beth-horon," smiting them to Azekah and Makeddah, where the Lord interposed in his servants' behalf by casting great hail-stones upon them from heaven that they died, and where that wondrous miracle was enacted of the sun standing still upon Gibeon, and the moon in the valley of Ajalon.

The night was bitterly cold. Snow, which very rarely falls in Palestine, had blocked the road some days before, and still lay in patches on the ground. We had some difficulty in keeping ourselves warm in our narrow beds, and had to make use of all our fur cloaks, ulsters, and shawls. The moon shone out gloriously, and as the Sheikh, in answer to Hani's request, had refused to make himself responsible for the honesty of the villagers, two of our Arab muleteers were told off to keep watch. Our night, however, was not so disturbed as the previous one had been, but it undoubtedly requires some breaking in to sleep comfortably in tents in Palestine.

The next day was one of the deepest excitement to us all, for we expected in the course of it to reach the Holy City, Jerusalem. The road at first was terribly steep and rocky, but, viewed scripturally, most interesting. We left our wild, lonely camp at eight o'clock, and soon wound round the base of the hill on which Gibeon once stood.

This must have been a wonderful natural fortress when it was one of the four cities of the Hivites; now it is only a miserable mud village, all the inhabitants of which turned out to stare at us as we passed along. In the valley below Gibeon Asahel the swift of foot was slain. It looked very lone and desolate, and solemn cranes stalked about, fearless of molestation. Through swamp and bog our horses floundered across this valley, and thence mounted to Neby Samwil, upwards of three thousand feet above the sea level, the ancient Mizpeh, the city of Benjamin, and the seat of the national assemblies when the judges ruled.

We climbed up to the top of the now ruined mosque of Neby Samwil, and, with a strange, overwhelming emotion, for the first time gazed on the distant city of Jerusalem—the Royal City, "the joy of the whole earth." It is situated on the ridge of a hill two thousand three hundred feet high, its domes sharply marked out against the clear sky, surrounded on all sides by mountain ranges, and with no particular beauty of outline. In the far distance we could see the high lands of Moab, and, just beyond Jerusalem, Bethlehem, and the Hebron range still tinged with snow.

Bare, stony hills stretched out between us and

Jerusalem, and the country was dreary and desolate in the extreme. But earthly beauty seemed to be as nothing—it was not needed. The city which we were at this moment privileged to see had a beauty and an interest quite distinct and apart from earthly associations or material loveliness. No Christian can gaze for the first time, even though it be from a distance, on the city of the Great King without a mingled feeling of intense awe, reverence, and devotion.

Our mid-day halting-place was about a mile below Neby Samwil, on a stony hillside, where a few olive-trees afforded feeble shade, full in sight of the mosque-crowned mountain. Here we sat whilst one of our party read the many scriptural histories connected with Mizpeh, contrasting the present with the past—the days when "all the children of Israel went out, and the congregation was gathered together as one man from Dan even to Beersheba, with the land of Gilead, unto the Lord in Mizpeh;" when, on this very spot, Samuel judged the children of Israel; and when, later on, they shouted in honour of their newly-elected leader, "God save the King!"

The tide of the nation's life was then at its flood, and as we cast our eyes over the stony, trackless wastes and solitudes around us, we realised, as, in truth, we did during the whole time of our sojourn in Palestine, that it is a land of ruins, paralysed and forsaken, trodden down of the Gentiles, lying in dust and ashes. Certainly no one can cross the mountainous region of Bethhoron without having this thought indelibly stamped on his memory. Hills and valleys, stony, rugged, desolate, neglected, silent, and lifeless, succeed one another, as though the anger of God rested on this land, once flowing with milk and honey. Judea is not beautiful. A shroud of sadness hangs over it like a pall, and forces even an unbeliever to observe that it is different from any other land in the world. Bad government may account for much, a false religion may account for more; but, after all, there is a sort of death which broods over the greater part of Palestine that cannot be attributed to either one or the other.

When you see on all sides the brilliant flowers of every colour growing amidst the stones—flowers rich and rare, which would be a credit to any well-kept English garden—and when you see, as you occasionally do, the valleys standing thick with corn, it is impossible to resist the conviction that Palestine is capable of the most luxuriant produce. Vines, figs, and olives might cover the hills and mountain-sides, as once they did. Palms and pomegranates, peaches and bananas, might flourish in the valleys. Tamarisk and other trees might be cultivated to attract the rainfall, and cereals of every kind might be made to yield abundantly in the rich soil of the lowlands. Under the Turkish government this is impossible. The present aspect of the greater part of Palestine is as though the heavens had rained stones upon it for centuries. Every tree is cut down, a few stunted, ashy-grey thorns only being left, which the Bedouin uses for fuel with which to bake his daily bread. There is no encouragement on the part of the government to improvement. They checkmate every effort at private enterprise by laying a double tax on land which is cultivated. The taxes are arbitrarily levied. It depends on the fancy of the Pasha and his agent, and whether he is greedy of gain or not. The government expects him to hand over a certain sum into the Imperial exchequer, and does not inquire too curiously how he gets it. The Pasha sometimes farms out the district to underlings, who with cruelty and injustice extract money from the poor land-tillers.

And so this noble, grand, sacred old country, with the highest genealogy and the most magnificent history in the world, is overrun, desecrated, and down-trodden by an alien nation. The "joy of the land is ceased; she is cast down from heaven unto the earth; her beauty is departed; she spreadeth forth her hands, and there is none to comfort her." How is the mighty fallen! May the day soon arise when Christian nations shall unite together to wrest the Holy Land from its despoilers, and restore it, under God's good providence, to beauty and prosperity!

The latter part of our ride from Neby Samwil was coloured by such lamentations, and longings for the future. We crossed a rocky river-bed, near which David is supposed to have slain Goliath, and mounted to the brow of a steep, precipitous hill. Just before us was a deep ravine, with a mountain rising high above it, planted with olive-trees, and crowned with a church at the summit; nearer to us a great city, walled in with domes and mosques. My heart burned within me; tears of emotion rushed to my eyes; and Hani quietly said,

"The Mount of Olives—Jerusalem."

CHAPTER IV.

JERUSALEM.

FIRST THOUGHTS ON REACHING JERUSALEM—ENCAMPMENT OUTSIDE THE DAMASCUS GATE, NEAR THE SUPPOSED SITE OF THE CRUCIFIXION—THE CHURCH OF THE HOLY SEPULCHRE, COMMON TO ROMAN CATHOLICS, GREEKS, COPTS, AND ARMENIANS—HOLY PLACES IN THE CHURCH—REVERENCE OF THE PILGRIMS—REGIMENT OF TURKISH SOLDIERS TO KEEP ORDER IN THE CHURCH—SALE OF CURIOSITIES OUTSIDE THE CHURCH—THE CITADEL—THE HARAM — KUBBET-ES-SAKHRA — MOSQUE-EL-AKSA—SUBTERRANEAN VAULTS—THE GOLDEN GATE—POOL OF BETHESDA—PALM SUNDAY—WALK TO AND FROM BETHANY—VIEW OF JERUSALEM—JOAB'S WELL—FLOW OF WATER—GROUP OF LEPERS—JEWISH FUNERAL PROCESSION—PLANS FOR OUR EXPEDITION TO THE DEAD SEA.

CHAPTER IV.

OUR first thought was that of thankfulness to God for being permitted in safety to reach the goal of our hopes. Then came an inrush of sacred memories, like an overwhelming torrent. It would have seemed irreverent to have spoken. There, lying straight before us, was the sacred mount where our Blessed Lord's Feet had trod—where, in the garden, His sweat was, as it were, great drops of blood. There was the city wherein He had preached, and done all manner of wonderful works, and where He had laid down His life for us men, and for our salvation. It was like a wonderful vision, but we longed to take it into our hearts as a solemn reality, so that our love and gratitude towards Him might be quickened and deepened by treading on earth in His very footsteps.

Our tents were pitched not far from the Damascus Gate, some little distance from the usual camping-ground, which is close to the Jaffa Gate. We purposely avoided this, thinking it better not to encamp upon ground which had been used for that purpose over and over again.

There was a great advantage in our site, for it was almost immediately at the base of the hillock which Lieutenant Conder, of the Palestine Exploration, believes to have been the actual place to which our Blessed Lord was led out for crucifixion. A green grass rounded knoll, bare of trees, rises not far from the Damascus Gate, near the main track to Nablous, which the Jews still call "Beth-hac-Sekilah," the place of stoning. The greater part of it is even now used as a Mohammedan cemetery.

As we gazed at it evening after evening from the doors of our tents, we could more clearly realise the greatest event that ever took place in this sin-stricken world—the grandest and most amazing act of Divine love, which gathers to itself in endless adoration the heart of all Christendom. We could imagine the three crosses raised high upon that grassy knoll, the mysterious and awful darkness, the insulting crowd, the broken-hearted Mother, the sorrowing disciples, and that one God-like patient Sufferer, hanging in all the majesty of grief, and uniting heaven and earth by His bitter cross and passion.

It was easier to picture the wonderful scene in the silence and quiet of that "green hill far away" than in the Church of the Holy Sepulchre, amid teeming crowds and artificial surroundings. And yet there is something very solemnizing about the Church of the Holy Sepulchre. It was one of the first objects of interest which we visited under the guidance of our local *cicerone*, "Elias Salem." The custody of the church is shared by Roman Catholics, Greeks, Copts, and Armenians. Each church has a chapel and altar of its own under the same roof, and the holy places within the building are common to all. The Stone of Unction on which the Body of our Lord is said to have been placed when anointed by Nicodemus, and the slab of marble over the supposed sepulchre, are enclosed in a shrine in the centre of the church, which you enter by a low door, and in which many lamps are always kept burning by the faithful. Only a few can enter this chapel at the same time, and the constant succession of pilgrims anxious to kneel, kiss the marble, and pray, is uninterrupted.

The Greek chapel is by far the most gorgeous in all its surroundings, and, by way of contrast, the chapel of the Copts is small, poor, and mean.

At every turn you come upon a chapel in memory of some of the scenes of our Lord's life —the parting of the raiment, the crowning with thorns, the scourging. Pre-eminent above all in interest is the Golgotha, or Mount Calvary. You reach it by a long flight of steps, and in a dim religious light mark the place assigned by tradition to the sacred Tragedy.

Whether these sites be the real ones or not, it is impossible to be in the Church of the Holy Sepulchre without a deep sense of the solemn memories with which it is interwoven. When you see, day after day, the tearful faces and kneeling figures bending low before the Stone of Unction, or the site of the raising of the Cross— when you see them kissing humbly and lovingly the sacred spots of which they themselves entertain no doubt, we felt the sympathy of that great love which unites all who believe in our

Lord Jesus Christ. We mourned over the divisions which have rent the seamless robe of Christ, and longed that faith throughout the Christian world might be one, true, and pure.

Services are perpetually going on in the different chapels. Franciscans march from station to station chaunting; Armenians break in with a monotonous drone; pilgrims kneel about in every corner, curl themselves up to sleep, or eat their meagre fare within the sacred precincts.* Copts in large loose robes and heavy turbans (the Coptic women being closely veiled and draped in gracefully-flowing garments), Russians, Greeks, Syrians, Egyptians, English, French, and Americans, in every variety of costume and colour, wander about the church in never-ceasing crowds, worshipping, idling about, or gazing on the holy places.

It was sad to see, as we did at the early service on Palm Sunday morning, the whole church occupied by Turkish soldiers drawn up in line to keep order. So great has been at times the animus between the four Christian Churches that the

* The Church of the Holy Sepulchre is treated like home by the many pilgrims who flock there, and it is counted no desecration if they eat, drink, and sleep, as well as worship, in it.

Turkish Government has found it necessary to interpose for the safety of the worshippers. It is painful and humiliating to think of Christian Churches thus exposed to the taunts and sneers of the Mohammedan.

On the Greek Easter day, when the imposture of the Holy Fire is enacted, the scenes are occasionally most sad and revolting. But by that time we were far away in the Archipelago, and so did not witness it ourselves.

Outside the church of the Holy Sepulchre is an open space, which is the most prolific field of enterprise for numberless hawkers. Immediately on emerging from the church you are surrounded on all sides by vendors of rosaries, pictures, glass bracelets, olive-wood ornaments, Bethlehem shells, and other works of local art. Their goods are cleverly disposed around them on the pavement, and they ply the traveller with ceaseless entreaties to buy.

According to Eastern custom, the price first asked for every article is more than double its value, and a perpetual huxtering and bargaining goes on. Four francs perhaps are offered when ten are asked, and this is the signal for a dramatic scene of virtuous indignation on one side and British determination on the other. The Arab salesman takes back his article as though deeply affronted at your offer, gives you to understand that he would rather throw up his business altogether than allow you to cheat him so grossly. He returns it to its place, and assumes an air of injured innocence, until he sees you are preparing to pass on to another salesman. He then cries piteously, "Hawaji! Hawaji!" and, making gesticulations indicating the ruin which this transaction would bring upon him, he hands to you the desired article at your own assessment. After all, probably, you feel that he has got the best of the bargain! We were told that it would not be safe for any Jew to pass in front of the Holy Sepulchre along this open space. It would be as much as his life was worth.

On leaving the church, we picked our way through narrow, dirty, dark streets, shut in for the most part by high walls, and arched over in many places. The streets of Jerusalem are not cheerful thoroughfares, although the shops are all open after the manner of the East.

We followed along the Via Dolorosa, a steep,

narrow, arched street, gloomy and picturesque, leading up from St. Stephen's Gate towards the Holy Sepulchre, and marked by many traditional sites of interest: the houses of Dives and Lazarus, the arch from which Pilate is said to have watched Our Lord coming up the Via Dolorosa to Calvary, and others; but as the whole of modern Jerusalem is some twenty or thirty feet above the level of the ancient city, imagination must be brought in to fill up the outlines of localities the truth of which you are reluctantly compelled to doubt. Ever since the first great siege of Titus, when not one stone was left upon another, down through all subsequent ages, the accumulation of *débris* has obliterated historic landmarks. A few architectural relics have been exhumed and built into the walls of the mosques of Omar and Aksa, but such memorials are few and far between.

From the top of the citadel we had a good view of the whole city, and tried to learn the geography of its principal features. Members of a Turkish military band, unfortunately for us, were practising on their instruments. Each performer was learning his respective part simultaneously with the others, and, as it seemed to us, in a different key. The effect may be imagined, and the chaos of frightful sounds could hardly, we thought, be of use in cultivating the national taste for music. But Orientals seem to have no musical gifts; their songs consist of a droning chaunt, sung through the nose on seven or eight notes, on which they wander up and down, according to fancy, with now and then a high note introduced apparently at hap-hazard. The very birds of Palestine are unmusical, and, if not silent, utter grating and discordant sounds. The bulbul, the nightingale of the country, is the exception which proves the rule, but this bird is rarely found except in the neighbourhood of Nablous and Damascus. It is, however, only fair to say that excellent voices are heard in some of the Christian Syrian schools.

From the flat roof on which we stood we looked right over the Haram, or Temple area, a walled enclosure occupying nearly a quarter of the modern city. It is now sacredly guarded by the Moslems from the intrusion of Christians. Since the Crimean war travellers from a distance can, on payment of a certain sum, obtain admission from their Consul, but no local Christian is ever allowed to enter the sacred precincts.

The grassy enclosure was just below us, planted with olives and cypresses, and furnished with numerous fountains for the ablutions of the Mohammedans. The great Mosque of Omar, Kubbet-es-Sakhrah, or the Dome of the Rock, was the principal object within the Haram, with its richly enamelled dome covering the sacred rock, the summit of Mount Moriah. This dome, glittering in the sun, is the most striking object in the distant view of Jerusalem. As we looked down into the Haram, we could see white figures of Mohammedan women wandering about, and Moslems entering the mosques, or preparing to worship as soon as the Muezzin had ended his drawling chaunt from the minaret hard by.

Above us was Mount Zion, "the stronghold of Zion," "My holy hill of Zion," the nucleus of the city, "Beautiful for situation, the joy of the whole earth." It is difficult to conceive the glory of these former days in the decay, ruin, and degradation of the present, but is it not written in the prophecies concerning the Jews that thus it should be? The seven hills were all before us: Mount Zion, Ophel, Moriah, Bezetha, Scopus, Mount of Olives, and Akra. The valley of Jehoshaphat lay deep down beneath Mount Moriah, at the bottom of which is the channel of the Kedron, with the Mount of Olives rising high above it.

We sat for a full hour gazing at this wondrous view, surpassed in interest by no other on the face of the earth, and we felt a new power and beauty in those glorious words, "As the mountains are round about Jerusalem, so the Lord is round about His people from henceforth, even for ever."—Ps. cxxv. 2.

We could not linger too long outside the walls of the Haram, for the Consul's Cavass, or servant, adorned in a gaily embroidered blue jacket, full trousers, and with an imposing scimitar in his sash, was waiting for us, bearing in his hand our authority for entering into the jealously guarded sanctum. A soldier also accompanied us throughout our circuit of the place.

At the door of the mosque, Kubbet-es-Sakhra, we were met by a tall custodian, the Sheikh of the mosque, who shook hands with us in a stately and condescending manner. A pretty child was by his side, clinging to his flowing robe, and seeing, by our looks, that we admired her, he said, with a gratified smile, "C'est ma fille!" and drew her closer to him, as if he dreaded the Giaour's evil eye.

We put on our slippers and entered the building. The little damsel came round with us as well as her father, but she did not invite any blandishments from Christians, and evidently shrank from notice. The custodian told us a variety of surprising Moslem stories and legends concerning the Haram-es-Sherîf, which did not, to say the least, consort well with the facts of Scripture.

One Mohammedan prophecy, however, struck us as being very curious. They show a horizontal column projecting from the Eastern wall of the Haram, and they tell you that at the last day, when Mohammed stands to judge the world in the valley of Jehoshaphat, all who can walk, with the help of good angels, along a hair stretched from the column to the top of Olivet will go to heaven.

The mosque itself is unique, for it is an octagonal building, covering the summit of Mount Moriah, but with the original rock, fifty-seven feet long by forty-three wide, and rising some six feet above the pavement, left bare and rugged in the centre of the building. The dome over the rock is resplendent with mosaics, and stained glass windows of marvellous beauty shed a subdued, solemn light on the marble pavement and the rich decorations, while the rock itself stands out dark and grim from the gorgeous surroundings. Here was the site of the threshing-place of Araunah the Jebusite, and (unless Dean Stanley's theory as to Gerizim having been the site be correct) the spot where Abraham prepared to offer up his son.

Within the precincts of the Haram stands also the mosque El Aksa, near the south-west corner. The history of this mosque is curious. Built originally by the Emperor Justinian in the sixth century, in honour of the Virgin, it was found in ruins two centuries and a half later, and then rebuilt, and subsequently became once more a Christian temple on the taking of the city by the Crusaders. It was called the Palace Porch, or Temple of Solomon, and a part of it was assigned by Baldwin to a new military order, the members of which thence took the name of Knight-Templars. Afterwards it was once more transformed into a mosque. It is full of interest. In many places pillars of twisted marble with graceful capitals are built into the walls, taken in all probability from the old Jewish temple.

Of scarcely less interest are the subterranean vaults in the south-eastern quarter of the Haram, sometimes called Solomon's Stables. Massive square pillars, with connecting arches, meet the eye on all sides, and doubtless further excavations would bring to light much which is now hidden by *débris*. It is an ascertained fact that the Crusaders used the place for a stable, and even now the holes in which were iron rings for the purpose of fastening their horses may be seen in the pillars.

But the part of the Haram which most deeply impressed me was "The Golden Gate," now built into the wall, and with comparatively modern surroundings; yet the gate itself is undoubtedly ancient, and through this Our Lord entered the temple on Palm Sunday, when the children cried "Hosanna to the Son of David!" and the jealous, bitter Scribes and Pharisees stood looking on with war in their hearts and meditating fierce designs for the destruction of the Holy One.

As we left the Haram, we passed the site traditionally known as the Pool of Bethesda, now little more than a mass of *débris* and rubbish filling up the fosse. On the western side are two arches, supposed to be the remains of the porches. It is said that a wealthy foreigner, fired by religious zeal, offered to the Turkish government to restore the pool, clear out the accumulation of rubbish and refuse by which it is now defiled, and put it into such a state as would be more befitting a place where the Lord had wrought one of His mighty works. The Turkish government, in reply, gave the required permission, but with this proviso, that, when he had finished his excavations, he should replace everything exactly as he had found it!

When we returned to our camping-ground, we found our dog, Beyrout, just in the act of pinning a man by his cloak, who on inquiry turned out to be the owner of the ground. He had come, not perhaps altogether unreasonably, to make inquiries of the intruders into his fields. This was the second *soi-disant* owner who had put in an appearance. Of course Hani was prepared to pay whatever was right, but he arranged to do it through the Consul, who would know the real owner. We felt sorry for the poor man, thus gripped and held fast by the dog, for it certainly was adding insult to injury to attack the proprietor of the soil on his own ground. Naturally enough, the man was furious, and threw himself into a perfect hurricane of indignation; but it was of short duration. Easterns are subject to paroxysms of wrath which are allayed as quickly as they are roused.

March the twenty-first was to us a memorable day. It was Palm Sunday, and after morning service in the English church, which was crowded, we determined to walk to Bethany, and so return back to Jerusalem along the very same road which Our Lord had trodden on the first Palm Sunday.

Bethany lies on the other side of the Mount of Olives, between two and three miles from Jerusalem. The road, which wound along the mountainside, was wild and rocky. The blue iris and bright crimson anemones (called "drops of blood" by the pilgrims) studded the hill-sides. Occasionally we passed fig-trees, bearing, as is usual at that season, small early figs.

The interest of our walk culminated as we returned towards Jerusalem, and rounded one of the shoulders of Mount Olivet, when the view of

Jerusalem suddenly burst upon us, and we felt that we must be standing at the very point where Our Lord halted as He rode from Bethany. The valley of Jehoshaphat was immediately beneath us; the Holy City crowned the mountain beyond. It was spread out before us like an ideal city, surrounded by battlemented walls, adorned with domes and minarets gleaming in the sun, almost like the pictorial descriptions of the heavenly Jerusalem.

This, then, was the very spot whence Our Lord beheld the city and wept over it. He saw the coming sorrow, the crowning sin, the rejected blessing, the doomed city, the ruined nation. As God, He saw it all, and wept as none other could weep. He would have gathered them even as a hen gathereth her chickens under her wing, but they would not. He yearned over them, but they knew not the time of their visitation. They spurned the mightiest gift that was ever offered to this weary, heavy-laden world, and from thenceforth the darkness of ruin and despair slowly gathered over the Promised Land—the land flowing with milk and honey—the Holy Land. We see the curse now. Palestine is like a forlorn, forsaken widow, lying in dust and ashes till the dawn of a good day heralds in the return and restoration of God's chosen people.

From the high ground whereon we stood, it was easy to trace the whole of the road along which Our Lord must have passed, crossing the brook Kedron amidst the enthusiastic shouts of the fickle multitude—"Hosanna to the Son of David!" up the steep ascent to the Golden Gate, through which He entered into the Temple.

We stopped by the roadside and read all the details of His great triumphal entry, gathering up such treasures of thought concerning His last days on earth as will make Palm Sunday at Jerusalem a memory for our lives.

It is impossible to describe the numberless places of interest, in and around Jerusalem, which we saw daily. Suffice it to say that our time was fully occupied from morning to night. The tombs of the kings; the Anglican Mission Church for the Arabs (outside the Jaffa Gate); Absalom's tomb, against which the passing Jews throw stones to express their abhorrence at a rebellious son; the pool of Siloam in the valley of Jehoshaphat; the Aceldama, or field of blood, a place still used to bury strangers in, and a visit to Joab's well, occupied us the next day.

The road to Joab's well is steep and precipitous. It is in the valley of Jehoshaphat, not far from "the king's garden," and only overflows at certain seasons. It so happened that at the time of our visit much water was flowing, and a sort of fête was being held on the banks of the stream, which rushed like a mountain torrent into the valley beneath. We rode down to the olive orchard, through which the brook bubbled and danced, and the sun shone over a pretty and gay scene. Groups of white-robed women sat by the stream gazing at it, rejoicing over it, putting their hands into it, while the children dabbled and paddled in it. They seemed content to sit patiently for hours and hours listening to its murmurs, and revelling in the unwonted sound.

It is difficult for us to form a conception of the refreshment of a clear rushing stream to Easterns, accustomed as they are to dry, arid rocks and a scorching sun. "Living water," "Streams in the desert," "The pure river of water of life," are to them not merely beautiful illustrations, but vital realities. Those only who have witnessed such a scene as we saw at the pool of Siloam can fully understand the deep force and significance of such words as:

"The glorious Lord will be unto us a place of broad rivers and streams."

" As rivers of water in a dry place."

" I will pour water upon him that is thirsty, and floods upon the dry ground."

" My soul is athirst for God."

"If any man thirst, let him come unto Me, and drink."

On our way back we passed some twenty poor lepers, many of them quite blind, stretching out their hands imploringly for backsheesh, and calling out to us in a husky, sepulchral voice. We gave some money for distribution amongst them. Piteous objects they were, with their limbs in many cases half eaten off, and their faces swollen and distorted by the fearful disease. They are not allowed to live in the city, but there is a building erected near the Kedron for them. A Moravian clergyman devotes himself to the work of ministering to them, and he has a house in which about twenty of these poor creatures live with him. These lepers are supported by Government.

And so we passed on through the Dung Gate, which was repaired by " Malchiah the Son of Rechab . . . he built it and set up the doors thereof" (Nehem. iii. 14). Here a Jewish funeral procession met us, and a saddening sight it was. We were shocked by the utter lack of reverence and decorum. Ten Jews came running down the steep side of the hill, carrying a body placed on a rough wooden bier, barely covered with a white cloth. They were laughing and talking loudly, and it was not until they paused at the gate that we realized what was taking place. Then they muttered a few prayers, and, shouldering the bier once more, ran off with it down the mountain side, across the Kedron to the Jews' burial-place, facing the walls of the Temple.

Our guide, Elias, told us that the Jews bury their dead very hurriedly. Immediately after the person is supposed to have died they break his legs, wrap the corpse in a sheet, and carry it out at once for burial. A dead body is an object of horror and pollution, and must be got rid of as quickly as possible.

We had found it so bitterly cold at night that we had determined to make the expedition to the Dead Sea at once, hoping that we should find the weather more genial on our return. All the necessary preparations accordingly were made, and that evening Hani opened the tent-curtain and stood in the doorway to discuss arrangements for the morrow.

"Well, Hani, and what time must we start in the morning?"

"Lady,* at seven o'clock."

Deep groans followed this announcement.

"We are so tired, Hani."

"Well, well, we will say half-past seven; but then we have so many hours to ride."

"We will do exactly as you think best. It is only the young ladies who can't get up."

"Ha! ha! They are very good. I have nothing to say. It will be all right, all right. Seven o'clock, ladies and gentlemen, and I call you at five."

He rubbed his hands with an action like playing on cymbals, which was his usual mode of showing satisfaction.

"Good night, sirs! Good night, ladies!" and the tall figure disappeared. A minute after, he was heard shouting for George, or Huddah, or Tannous, and passing round orders for the next day's march to Jericho.

* Lady is the invariable form of address. So St. John, Ep. ii. 5. "Now, I beseech thee, lady."

CHAPTER V.

JERICHO AND THE DEAD SEA.

ARRANGEMENTS FOR THE JOURNEY TO THE JORDAN—SHEIKH OF ABU-DÎS TAKES THE PARTY IN CHARGE—ROAD FROM JERUSALEM TO JERICHO—FLORA OF JUDÆA—NATIVE MODE OF SPORT—JERICHO—ELISHA'S FOUNTAIN—NATIVE DANCE—MODERN JERICHO—BEDOUEEN SALUTATION—THE DEAD SEA—FORDS OF THE JORDAN—AN ALARM—ADVENTURE IN CROSSING THE CHERITH—RETURN TO JERUSALEM—MOHAMMEDAN AT PRAYER—CAMP IN THE KARAMA SHEIKH.

CHAPTER V.

THE next morning dawned bright and beautiful. The sun seemed to reproach us for seeking the warmer climate of the Jordan. But, had we wished it, we could not then have changed our plans, for all the arrangements were made for our visit to Jericho and the Dead Sea. In order to ensure the safety of the expedition, a sort of blackmail has to be paid to the Arabs. It appears to be a recognized privilege of the Sheikh of Abu-Dîs to send one of their family with travellers as a guarantee, which is recognized by the tribe to which they belong, that the proper payment has been made. The Sheikh's ægis is then extended over you.

This Sheikh rode early into our camp on a little grey Arab horse, most picturesquely attired in a white shirt with long sleeves, a garment of olive-green thrown over his shoulders, black embroidered waistcoat, loose white trousers, stuffed into high boots, and a dead-gold kafiyeh on his head, bound round with a cord of camel's hair. A couple of pistols in his sash, and a scimitar by his side, showed that he was ready for any emergency. "Sheikh Mohammed, of the tribe of Areeat," was the title which he gave himself in writing in my journal-book.

We started from Jerusalem a cavalcade of eleven on horseback. The baggage-mules were to follow. The road between Jerusalem and Jericho—about twenty miles—is as dreary and lonely as can be imagined. "A certain man," it is said in the Gospels, "went *down* to Jericho." And no doubt he did, for Jerusalem is 2,300 feet above, while Jericho is about 1,000 feet below, the level of the sea. The consequence is that the climate of the plains of the Jordan is almost tropical, and the inhabitants well-nigh the colour of Africans.

Our route lay along the Bethany road, round the Mount of Olives, and down a rugged, deep descent to a desolate ravine, where, we were told, the traveller of the Scriptures " fell among thieves, which stripped him of his raiment, and wounded him, and departed, leaving him half dead." The surrounding district still bears a very bad name, and even the little shepherd boys are armed. A gun slung over the shoulder, a couple of pistols in the belt, and a dirk or scimitar at the side, is what every Syrian seems to wear as naturally as a European does his clothes.

In the course of the morning some half dozen Bedoueens on horseback passed us; splendid fellows they were, armed to the teeth, with spears twelve or fourteen feet long, on their way from the country of Moab to Jerusalem. Hani told us they were Christians from Ramoth Gilead, and we heard from Mr. Zeller, the missionary at Jerusalem, that there were a good many Christians in that district.

There was little to redeem the barren rocks and stony, desolate hill-sides from hopeless gloom, except the beautiful flowers, and they were quite wonderful. The large yellow pyrethrum, scarlet and purple anemones, poppies of various hues, ranunculuses, pink linums, marigolds, fumitory, burrage, scabious, desert spike, camomile, tulips, pheasant's eye, cyclamens, convolvulus, rock stock, and many others, covered the ground in brilliant profusion. It is impossible to convey an idea of the wealth and splendour of the wild flowers of Palestine, but they give a picturesque force to those sacred words, "Solomon, in all his glory, was not arrayed like one of these." Our syces were sent hither and thither to pick flowers, and our hands were soon filled with nosegays of all the colours of the rainbow.

We halted for our midday rest at Khan-el-Ahmah, a rocky cavern by the road-side, which afforded some refreshing shade. Twelve Arabs, armed with long guns, sat round and watched us during our meal. One of them was father to Sheikh Mohammed. He was the patriarch of the tribe, a thin, haggard, leathery-looking old man, miserably clothed. When Hani saw him he rushed forward with an exclamation of delight, and kissed him with effusion. Then, taking him by the hand, he presented him to us with the words,

"This is a capital fellow. He has been my friend in these parts for many years. Ah! we know each other, don't we?" And he patted him fondly on the back.

When we had finished our luncheon, Hani invited him, with his son and another Sheikh, to a select meal apart from the others. It was "high life below stairs" in the desert. They sat cross-legged, eating up the remains of our chickens with the utmost dignity. There is a strange sort of majesty and loftiness about these Arabs, which sometimes consorts oddly enough with their faded costumes and poor surroundings. One of them showed us the way in which they shot birds. He had a skin stretched over canes, painted like an animal, with projecting ears, and two holes pierced for his eyes, and, with this in front of him, he stalked after his game. In the course of the evening he came into our camp with a partridge, hoopoo, and pigeon, to prove to us the success of his stratagem, but the absence of any life in these regions, as far, at any rate, as the ordinary traveller can see, is very remarkable.

Not long after leaving the Khan-el-Ahmah we rode along a magnificent gorge of wild, abrupt rocks, which is identified with the valley of Achor, in which Achan was stoned, and at the bottom of which the brook Cherith flows. From the summit of this gorge we had a splendid view of the plains of Jericho, the Jordan, and the Dead Sea, with the purple-tinged mountains of Moab in the distance.

We descended into the valley by a rocky, precipitous pass, and, after fording the Cherith, entered the plains of Jordan near Jericho. These are rich and fertile, and full of capabilities, but no one seems to take much interest in their cultivation. The shadow of the trans-Jordanic tribes lies deep upon the land, and paralyses industry.

About three o'clock in the afternoon we reached our camping-ground, close to the ruins of old Jericho, "the city of palm-trees." It is now little more than a piled-up heap of rubbish, and not a single palm-tree remains. A good many nebk-trees, or spina Christi, grow in the neighbourhood, and the ground was carpeted with thousands of rainbow-coloured flowers, like the most gorgeous embroidery. The climate was soft and enervating, a great contrast to the brisk fresh air of Jerusalem.

The site of our camp was charming, about half a mile from the regular camping-ground, which a few hours later on was occupied by a party of "Gaze's" tourists. Behind us rose the mountains of Quarantania, some thousand feet high, bleak, desolate, and grim, the supposed scene of Our Blessed Lord's temptation. Close to us was the Ain-es-Sultân, the spring which Elisha sweetened. It bursts out from the midst of rank, rich vegetation, amid tall reeds and wild fig-trees, and forms at once an eddying stream, which even now is accounted the sweetest water in Palestine. On the brink of this clear sparkling pool we stationed ourselves, and read the various passages in the Bible concerning ancient Jericho and Gilgal.

In the evening, just as dinner was over, Hani told us that a troupe of natives had come from the modern Jericho to perform their national dance before us.

"The people of Riha want to give you an entertainment," said he.

"What is it like?"

Hani shrugged his shoulders.

"Ah! it is not beautiful, but then they have their customs."

"And demand backsheesh for the performance?"

"Certainly, certainly."

"Well, well: tell them to begin at once, and you had better settle with them."

It was night, and the moon shone brightly. About thirty natives, of whom half a dozen were women, formed a semi-circle in front of us, in the space round which our tents were pitched. Our whole party, including the two Sheikhs (for a second had joined us as we passed Abu-Dis), sat opposite to the performers. I had been cautioned beforehand not to show any signs of fear, and certainly the caution was not unnecessary.

It is impossible to imagine more hideous, wild, uncanny performers than these inhabitants of Jericho. They looked like savages with their tattooed faces, glaring eyes, dark complexions, and dishevelled hair. At first the men and women formed a close living wall in front of us, swinging to and fro, singing with a low, discordant rhythm, and clapping their hands together to mark the time. Soon two of the women advanced to the centre of the circle, clad in dark drapery which swept the ground. They waved their arms aloft, swaying them in graceful movements and regular cadence to the wild music, themselves singing the same weird, monotonous tune. Suddenly the dancing-women uttered with startling effect a high, shrill noise like a bird-whistle, and then the men handed to them scimitars, which they brandished over our heads, waving them in fantastic circles, keeping time to the music, and every now and again passing them dangerously near our faces. It was evident that they wished to frighten us, but we had learned our lesson, and sat looking on at the strange scene with stolid, impassive faces. We almost fancied ourselves in Central Africa.

When the women had done their worst, the men began making a succession of simultaneous barks and groans, forming themselves into a very close rank and bowing to and fro, while one of their number tried in vain to break through the line.

When we thought it not uncourteous to stop them, we asked Hani to thank the natives for the entertainment they had given us, secretly rejoicing that it had come to an end, and then we offered in return to sing to them. They were delighted at our proposal, and we performed a selection of glees and songs, which seemed to please them, for they clapped us most vigorously at the conclusion. It was a barbaric audience, and there was a sort of dreamy wildness about the whole scene which it is impossible to describe. The desolate plain of Jericho, the lonely little camp, the wild-looking Arabs, the cold moon lighting up the whole company, each and all combined to produce a very strange experience.

They seemed well-satisfied with our backsheesh, and for long we heard the shrill bird-whistle and confused hum of voices gradually fading away in the far distance.

Our Sheikh's sister joined him from Jericho that night. She was a gaunt young woman, the colour of old parchment, with her hair hanging about her face in wild disorder. She and her two brothers sat round the watch-fire, near our tents, all night through, and safely guarded us from any midnight marauders.

The next morning we were astir soon after five o'clock, anxious to be *en route* as early as we could, so as to avoid the mid-day heat. As we left old Jericho, the great mountain of the temptation stood out grandly in the early sunlight. The morning air was sweet with the fragrant scent of flowers; hoopoos, with their smart, jaunty tufts, were flying about in all directions, and we caught an infectious exhilaration. The beautiful plain of Jericho stretched out before us invitingly, and we rode through luxuriant corn-fields, cultivated in a wild, careless manner, and brilliant with gay flowers and weeds. Nebk-trees, zizyphus and balsam-trees, grew here and there. After less than a mile we reached Riha or Eriha, the modern Jericho.

If the truth must be told, my ideas about this place had been somewhat hazy. Just before leaving Jerusalem, I had said to Hani that I hoped to be able to buy some trifling article at Jericho, which I had neglected to do at Jerusalem. Hani looked at me in blank astonishment.

"Lady," he said, "I do not think you will get much there."

As a matter of fact, you might as well expect to find bazaars in the centre of the Sahara desert as at Riha, which consists of a few straggling mud hovels, with ruined walls, and dried brushwood serving the purpose of a roof. Riha has been supposed to be the site of the ancient Gilgal, though Lieutenant Conder places it about a mile off.

Miserable and degraded indeed the place looked; the inhabitants were like dried mummies, sharing their hovels in common with cocks and hens, and dogs and filth. There is one fairly decent house in the place, which belongs to some Russian monks. Some of the fair danseuses of the previous evening recognized us in the distance, and greeted us with their shrill, guttural cry, and the Sheikh stood watching us from the top of a dust-heap, from whence he exchanged salutations with us.

Altogether, we formed a goodly cavalcade, for, in addition to our own party of seven, we had the two Sheikhs, Mohammed and Mustapha, riding in front with Hani. Then came on horseback with the provisions Tannous and Georgé, and our two syces, Alraschid and Abdullah, riding double on a donkey—as a special favour allowed to them for the day—brought up the rear. Woe betide the Bedoueens who would venture to attack so gallant a party!

After a long stretch over rich corn-land, atrociously farmed, we came to a sandy plain, with low brushwood, excellent cantering ground, which formed a most delightful contrast to the cruel rocks and stones of the mountain tracks. Our Sheikh, Mohammed, bounded away like a gazelle, and went through a series of the most extraordinary manœuvres, galloping right and left, brandishing his sword aloft, and feigning most tremendous and infuriated excitement, now spearing an imaginary enemy, now cutting him down with his scimitar, and then galloping through our ranks at full speed with drawn sword. It was a pretty exhibition of horsemanship. How his little Arab hack, which did not at all answer to the imaginary beautiful steed of the desert, was able to perform all the evolutions required of him was a marvel to us all.

Miss Stanhope gave a rival exhibition of first-rate riding, and Mohammed watched her with surprise and delight, exclaiming,

"Ah! she rides well."

As we drew nearer to the Dead Sea, the sand was covered in places with bitumen and salt, and the whole surrounding was arid and dreary.

Suddenly we observed in the distance a group of horsemen coming towards us. They seemed to be Bedoueens, and, somewhat to our dismay, one of them left his fellows and galloped up to our party with wild and threatening gesticulations, holding a pistol in his hand, which he fired in the air, when about ten yards from us. He then recognized Hani, and shook hands with him. After this strange mode of salutation, we wanted to know who he was, and what he meant. It turned out that he was in attendance upon the Greek Patriarch, who was returning from the Jordan, whither he had gone to make arrangements for the Greek pilgrims, who come annually during Eastertide by hundreds to bathe in the sacred river. His threatening advance had been merely intended to frighten us, but it was a species of practical joke in the great solitudes of the Dead Sea shores which I hardly relished, and it brought vividly to my mind the Eastern proverb, "In the desert no man meets a friend," and that scene in the "Talisman," when Sheerkof, the Lion of the Mountain, encounters Kenneth, Knight of the Couchant Leopard.

It was rather more than two hours and a half after leaving our camp before we reached the Dead Sea. For the last two miles or more the track lay over a region of absolute desolation. The sand-hills rise to a considerable height, and are of strange shapes. The Dead Sea itself looked very beautiful, still and motionless, shut in on the one side by the mountains of Moab, on the other by the hill-region of Judæa. The Jordan runs into it just at the very spot where we approached it, and there is no exit at the southern extremity.

> "That death-full lake,
> No turning hath or issue thence is found." *

The Dead Sea varies from five to eight miles in breadth, and is about forty miles long, nearly the same length as the lake of Geneva. We all dismounted and sat on some bare trunks of trees which lie blanched on the shores like giant bones. A lifeless little island of stones was just in front of us, and the heavy, blue, clear water settled quietly round it, beautiful and still as death. The great silence of the Dead Sea has a strange and solemnising effect, but we did not find the scenery gloomy, as we expected. The sunshine was so brilliant, and the mountains which encircled the blue sea so richly shaded with exquisite, soft tints of purple, that our prevailing sensation was one of delight; but we were told that the southern

* FLETCHER.

end is far more dreary and repelling than the northern. The smell of the water is very disagreeable, and its taste nauseous in the extreme, salt, bitter, and burning. There were several little dead fish on the shore, which had come down the Jordan and had been killed by the sulphurous water. My husband bathed in the Dead Sea, and so great is the buoyancy of the water that he was able to lie down at full length, without moving a finger, as comfortably and with as great a feeling of security as if he had been lying on a mattress.

Hani told us of an adventure which had happened on one occasion when he was in charge of a party at this place. Two ladies were bathing; and one, having lost her balance, could not recover it again, and swallowed such a quantity of the Dead Sea water that she became unconscious. Hani, fortunately, was on the watch, sprang into the water and drew her to the shore. From the effects of the poisonous water she suffered the greatest agony, and for many hours her life was despaired of, but the remedies used were happily effectual, and she finally recovered.

About an hour and a half's ride from the Dead

Sea brought us to the fords of the Jordan. As we drew near, we saw some Bedoueens on horseback on a hill in front of us. One of our Sheikhs galloped off at once to reconnoitre, and by-and-by returned, having discovered that they belonged to a friendly tribe.

It was mid-day when we reached the Jordan, with which we were all rather disappointed. It is brown as the Tiber at Rome, muddy and narrow. The banks are bordered with tamarisk-trees, reeds, and rushes, and the sides of the river are composed of thick, muddy red clay which cakes and cracks into brick-like hardness. Our halt was at Kasr-el-Yehudi, the chief resort for pilgrims. Here there is an opening in the thicket which fringes the banks of the Jordan, and under a beautiful tree with a great stem and large overhanging branches we had our carpets spread out and luncheon prepared, while we gazed on the most historically important and the most sacred river in the world. How many events had happened in connection with this little commonplace-looking stream! Through it the Israelites came by a miracle. David had crossed it. Elijah had divided its waters; and Elisha, too, waving over it the mantle which he inherited from his master, made for himself a dry path through its bed. Above all, Our Blessed Lord had stood in its waters when, at the hands of John the Baptist, he had received the rite of Holy Baptism, and the Father's voice proclaimed from Heaven, " This is my Beloved Son, in whom I am well pleased."

Hani advised us not to stray about, for the Jordan ford is a notorious place for Bedoueen robbers, whose aim is to plunder isolated travellers, and we found three additional armed retainers of Mohammed waiting our arrival here to keep guard over us.

Whilst my husband was bathing in the river, two men from the other side swam across, somewhat startling the rest, for, on reaching the bank, they bounded away *in puris naturalibus*. Several horses, as it turned out, had been stolen by some of the trans-Jordanic tribes, and these men had crossed the river, hoping to recover the missing animals. Their search had been ineffectual.

It was two o'clock before we left Kasr-el-Yehudi, and the shade of that great tree by the water side, to ride into a blaze of sunshine and overpowering heat along the plains between us and our Jericho camp, but in spite of sun and glare the ride back to camp was most splendid and delightful. It so happened that we had to ford the brook Cherith, and here the horses were allowed to pause for a draught of water. One of the Arabs persuaded me in an evil moment to let go the reins, so that my horse "Hassan" might drink more freely. A minute afterwards he had got the reins entangled in his legs, and was plunging about with the other horses in a hopeless manner. Thinking that discretion was the better part of valour, I slipped off into the stream (which was only up to my waist) for I could do nothing in managing the horse. Hani and George rushed into the water and had caught me up out of my difficulties before I had time to contemplate the situation, and the whole *fiasco* ended happily.

A ride of four miles in a wet riding-habit is really pleasant in tropical heat.

It was with the most sincere regret that, on the next day, March 25th, we said good-bye to our camp at Jericho. The early sun coloured the hills of Moab with a purple glow, and the foreground was like a jewelled carpet, gleaming with every colour of the rainbow. The mountains of Palestine looked grim, bare, and dark, making a wonderfully effective contrast. It was an effort to turn our faces westward again, for we enjoyed the soft, tropical air, the richer vegetation, and the luxury of riding on the smooth plains, free from the everlasting rocks and stones of the hill country. Henceforth we shall not feel disposed to pity a man who is "sent to Jericho," provided he has Hani as his guide, good tents and horses, as we had, and lovely weather. He will find himself, under such circumstances, very happy and comfortable, and he will taste to perfection the romance and fascination of nomadic life.

We were six hours toiling up the weary road from Jericho to Jerusalem. Large companies of Bedoueens from the other side of the Jordan were continually passing us with camels and mules, returning from Jerusalem to their own country. They were a wild-looking lot, always armed, and I felt glad to be under the protection of Sheikh Mohammed. We passed no human habitations save here and there, at rare intervals, the black camel-hair tents of the Bedoueens. Except when travellers pass, there is not much life to be seen, and the silence is oppressive.

We halted to rest at "The Apostles' Spring," Enshemesh, or spring of the sun, Joshua xv. 7, which rises just at the base of the rocky declivity leading up to Bethany. We sat on the stony bank overlooking the road, and were interested in watching the habits and proceedings of Mohammed. First of all, he washed his hands and feet at the well, and then spread out a mat on the ground, and turning towards Mecca began his devotions; kneeling down, prostrating himself with his forehead touching the ground, rising up and again going through the same genuflections. He looked up now and then to see if we were observing him, and then continued his devotional exercises until they were completed.

Mohammed was very anxious to possess my husband's gay silk Cairo scarf, which he usually wore coiled round his person, and one day he touched the coveted decoration, saying,

"Give me?"

No answer.

With vigorous gesticulations, he first pointed to himself. "Me—take you—safe Jericho—Dead Sea—Jordan—Jerusalem." Then, placing his finger on the silk scarf, "You—give me?"

However, by a little clever management, Mohammed was pacified, and he had money given him instead of the scarf; but I think he felt disappointed, for these Easterns are fond of dress, and the scarf had many colours. It was evident that he was a man much respected by the people of his tribe. Several times, as we were riding along, the Arab shepherds, on seeing him in the distance, left their flocks, ran towards him, and kissed his hand. He seemed to take it very quietly, and as a matter of course.

En route from the Apostles' Spring to Jerusalem, we paused for a while at Bethany. The tomb of Lazarus is excavated out of the rock, and is approached by a series of stone steps. The cave now shown is precisely like what one would fancy the tomb of Lazarus to have been, and we had little difficulty in realizing on the spot that wondrous resurrection scene—the Saviour's command, "Lazarus, come forth!" the white figure, bound in grave-clothes, emerging from the gloomy cave, welcomed to the loving arms of his sisters. Few of the ancient sites of the Holy Land struck us more forcibly than this.

The reputed house of Lazarus is still shown, as well as that of Simon, but both are very doubtful. The modern village of Bethany, although lying picturesquely on the mountain slope, is miserable and unattractive, except in connection with its Biblical associations.

When we reached Jerusalem, skirting the walls from St. Stephen's Gate, we found that during our absence some newly-arrived travellers had appropriated our camping-ground. Fortunately, Hani was acquainted with the owner of a field available for our purpose, not far distant from the Damascus Gate, called Karama-Sheikh. This was the very spot occupied by the Prince of Wales during his visit to Jerusalem in 1862, and the proprietor, out of friendship for Hani, allowed us to pitch our tents on the same place. His own house was close to our encampment—a stone building with a tower, from which there was a fine view of Jerusalem. The wind blew a hurricane by way of welcome, and our men had considerable difficulty in getting up the tents. Half an hour, however, saw us comfortably settled, and the canvas sides firmly secured with heavy stones placed all round to keep them steady.

We found it so cold that we were obliged to get charcoal braziers to warm our saloon tent, and the wind raged and howled furiously around us, but our good tents stood firmly. We felt ourselves in the Arctic regions, and it was a distressful contrast to the soft tropical air and brilliant sunshine of the beautiful plains of Jericho.

CHAPTER VI.

JERUSALEM.

GOOD FRIDAY AT JERUSALEM—THE CŒNACULUM—THE JEWS' WAILING-PLACE—AFFECTING SCENE—CELEBRATION OF THE PASSOVER—ARCH OF THE ECCE HOMO—THE CHURCH OF THE HOLY SEPULCHRE—EASTER SERVICES—VISIT TO THE CONVENT OF MARSABA—BETHLEHEM—CHURCH OF THE NATIVITY—SITE OF OUR LORD'S BIRTH—ST. JEROME'S GROTTO—DOMESTIC TROUBLES—VISIT TO A SHEIKH—GARDEN OF GETHSEMANE—PREPARATIONS FOR LEAVING JERUSALEM.

CHAPTER VI.

GOOD FRIDAY at Jerusalem was a day never to be forgotten. The English services were well attended, and the Bishop of Jerusalem preached an earnest sermon on the great subject of the Crucifixion. It seemed wonderful and solemn to be commemorating the great central fact of our holy faith in the very place where Our Blessed Lord laid down His Life.

After service we went to the Cœnaculum. It is a building outside the Gate of David, immediately over the tomb of the Shepherd King, and many assert that the hall we entered by a flight of steps, a chapel-like room, about fifty feet long by thirty wide, with groined roof supported by arches, was the very same "upper chamber" where the Lord Jesus gathered His disciples around Him for the Last Supper, where those wonderful parting words were spoken which are so precious an inheritance to His Church for evermore, and where the apostate Judas left the little band of faithful followers, and crept out into the dark night to carry out his own darker plot. Here, too, the disciples assembled to wait for the Pentecostal blessing. The whole aspect of this upper chamber was suggestive, and it would be very satisfactory if it could be certified as the veritable place whereon such sacred memories rested secure from dispute; but this is a vain hope, and we learnt to be content with uncertainty, and to fall back on the conviction that it was Our Lord's intention that the most important sites of His earthly sojourn should be shrouded in a veil of mystery and doubt. The Cœnaculum is now in the hands of Mohammedans, and no Christian is allowed to visit the reputed tomb of David.

After spending some time in the afternoon on the Mount of Olives, and in the Garden of Gethsemane, we passed through the miserable streets of the Jews' quarter to their "wailing place." Every Friday the Jews are permitted to assemble under the huge stone walls which shut in the Haram on its northern side, and there weep over the ruin of their city and temple, and pray for its restoration. The massive stones of which the wall is composed are, in all probability, the very same as those which formed part of the old wall of the Temple. Whether that be so or not, these stones represent to the Jews their past history, with all its glory and greatness, and their "dumb mouths," like Cæsar's wounds, are more eloquent than burning words to Jewish hearts.

We stood under the walls at this wailing-place, and watched the crowds assembling. There were Jews gathered together from Germany, Spain, Poland, Russia, and all parts of the world, clad in the quaintest costumes. The Polish Jews wore velvet caps, edged with a trimming of fur, and flowing gabardines of various colours. A long lock of hair is allowed to curl down each side of the face. Old patriarchs and a younger generation of differing physiognomies were there; many with almost Saxon features and fair hair; others with the more usual type of Jewish face, strong features and dark complexions, but all having the subtle Jewish look, which is unmistakable.

The many groups of differing ages, arrayed in garments of varied hues, some with flowing grey

L

locks and long beards, in velvet or satin robes, all standing in solemn sadness under the great wall in its towering height, would inspire an artist with enthusiasm. There must have been about three hundred thus gathered together, with a few women, who kept in the background. The Rabbis began a Litany in a minor key, which was responded to by the whole body of Jews in the same sort of monotone. As many as could get close to the wall pressed their foreheads against its stones, passing their hands fondly over them. Their cry was:

"O God, the heathen are come into Thine inheritance. Thy holy Temple have they defiled. They have laid Jerusalem on heaps."

Then arose a wailing response.

"How long, O Lord—how long? Wilt Thou be angry for ever? They have devoured Jacob, and laid waste his dwelling-place. How long, O Lord? Wilt Thou be angry for ever?"

As the prayer and the cry of entreaty and expostulation increased in fervour, we saw some of the older Jews weeping bitterly, pressing their withered cheeks against the stones again and again, and sobbing out the piteous wail,

"How long, O Lord—how long?"

It was difficult to stand by unmoved. Their forefathers had crucified the Lord of Glory, and they know it not: the true Light is shining, and they see it not: the Messiah for whom they sigh has come, but they believe it not; but the days must be drawing near when they will return to Jerusalem, and have it in possession. In the end the veil will be taken from their hearts, God will build up Zion, and appear in His glory, and "the Jews' wailing-place" shall be no more!

In the evening we were allowed to witness a very interesting ceremony. Mr. Zeller, the missionary, had kindly arranged for us to accompany him to the house of an upper-class Jew, in order that we might be present at the celebration of the Passover. The family consisted of a party of five—grandfather, father and mother, son and daughter. They greeted us very cordially, arrayed in their best clothes and jewelry, representing the raiment and jewels borrowed from the Egyptians. We expressed to Mr. Zeller a little delicacy as to whether we might not be obtruding upon their devotions, but he assured us that they liked to have strangers, properly introduced, to watch their proceedings.

A divan had been prepared for us, and the master of the house seated us on it. In the centre of the room was a table, covered with a white cloth, on which unleavened bread, " the dough before it was leavened," Exod. xii. 36, was placed, together with some lettuce (to represent bitter herbs), wine and wine-glasses. The children were seated one on each side of the father, and next to them the grandfather. The mother sat somewhat apart from the rest, and hardly seemed to join in the service at all, but she turned round to us occasionally with a gratified smile when her little son muttered the responses in an unusually loud tone.

"Ah! qu'il le dit bien, le petit!"

The father took the Talmud, and from it read passages concerning the Passover; both he and his children half closed their eyes, and droned out the words in a sort of chaunt, swaying their bodies to and fro all the time.*

---

* This is their universal habit in prayer. Mr. Zeller told us that, whenever the name of God is mentioned, they are taught to bow the head, and that, as the name of God occurs in their prayers so constantly, lest they might perchance omit to do so at the proper time, they bow the head unceasingly.

Occasionally the father folded up small portions of the bread in lettuce, and gave it to all present. By-and-by a little slip-shod servant maid brought from a cupboard some red compote. This is supposed to represent the bricks made by the Israelites during their bondage in Egypt. They then bared their feet in token of haste, and finally a portion of cold lamb was brought in, "roast with fire," and a dish of chops, every morsel of which was eaten according to the command, "Ye shall let nothing of it remain until the morning."

We thought the service very much lacking in devotion, for the Jews hardly seem to know what reverence is. The father was the only one who appeared in any degree to enter into the real meaning of it, and the maid-servant slipping in and out of the room with loose, white stockings hanging about her feet, while the mother either smiled or paid no attention at all to what was going on, did not impress us with the solemnity of the whole proceedings.

As we rode back, at ten o'clock at night, all the houses of the Jews were lit up, for the same Passover service was being duly celebrated in them.

On Easter Eve we went to the convent of the "Sisters of Zion" in Jerusalem. This is said to have been the site of Pilate's house, and in the chapel beneath the convent is an arch, recently excavated, supposed to be the identical arch under which Our Lord was brought forth and presented to the cruel multitude with the words, "Behold the man!"

Excavations have been made under this chapel to the level of old Jerusalem, and here you are able to walk on what is, without doubt, the very pavement of the ancient city, with the ruts of wheels still visible on it! We could say to ourselves, "the sacred Feet of Jesus trod these very stones. He walked upon this pavement."

Some twenty feet lower still is an arched, subterraneous passage, which we traversed with lights. A spring rises up in the middle of it. It is said to be connected with the mosque of Omar, but the passage is blocked up.

In the afternoon the Bishop of Jerusalem came to our camp. It is thought well that he should keep up a certain amount of state, and his visit was carried out in accordance with this theory, for the Bishop and Mrs. Barclay were preceded by two gorgeous cavasses clad in blue, with a silver mitre on their breasts, and staff of office in their hands. He was very kind and courteous, and gave us much interesting information respecting Jerusalem.

Late in the afternoon we went once more to the Church of the Holy Sepulchre. It was then lighted up with thousands of small, variegated lamps. Crowds were pressing forward to kiss the marble slab over the Sepulchre. The site of the crucifixion was also brilliantly lighted up. A young peasant mother had laid her little baby down on the ground, close to the altar which is erected on the spot. She herself was kneeling and absorbed in her prayers, and the little infant lay rolling and crowing happily, quite unconscious, apparently, of the danger of being trodden under foot by the surging crowd. It was a pretty sight to watch the loving smiles which the passers-by cast upon that little fat child behaving so innocently and irreverently in the sacred place—the place which for ages has been approached with bended knee, bated breath, and streaming eyes.

On Easter Day, March 28th, our own services

at eight o'clock and ten o'clock, and in the evening, were fully attended.

The English church is just inside the Jaffa Gate, near to "David's tower;" and the market-place close by, through which we had to pass, presented a motley scene on Easter morning. Long trains of camels and donkeys bringing vegetables into the town were threading their way through the gate. Soldiers and Bedoueens, market-girls from Bethlehem, priests, Russian pilgrims, dismal and dirty, rabbis, Europeans, Armenians, and fierce Kurds, horsemen with their long spears, women enveloped in long, white "izars," mingled together in inextricable confusion. The French Consul was seen returning from early Mass, with a full-dressed escort, preceded by Janissaries tapping the ground with their long staves to warn the crowd to make way for their master. It would be difficult to find a more heterogeneous multitude in any other part of the world, and the confusion, jostling, haggling, dirt, and Babel-like mixture of tongues, baffle description.

The contrast was very suggestive when, in the quiet of our little English church, we joined in spirit with our loved ones, three thousand miles away, in the blessed service of Easter Day.

It is jarring at all times to see the Holy City trodden down by unbelievers in the Christian Faith, but more than ever at this special season did we long for the time to come when Jerusalem shall be "a rejoicing" and her people "a joy" (Is. lxv.), when the words shall be fulfilled, "The Lord is in the midst of thee; thou shalt not see evil any more. He will save; He will rejoice over thee with joy; He will rest in His love; He will joy over thee with singing," (Zephaniah iii. 14), because "Thou shalt know that I the Lord am thy Saviour and thy Redeemer" (Isaiah vi.).

On Easter Sunday afternoon we spent a long time high up on the Mount of Olives looking over Jerusalem. It was a brilliant day, glorious with sunshine and blue sky, and the view was splendid. In this very place Our Lord Jesus Christ might have sat with His disciples when they came to Him "for to show Him the buildings of the Temple," and when He said, "Verily I say unto you, there shall not be left here one stone upon another that shall not be thrown down." Again the description in the Book of the Revelation of the heavenly Jerusalem forced itself upon our minds as we gazed on the city before us, all radiant and resplendent in the glorious sunlight. "He carried me away in the spirit to a great and high mountain, and showed me that great city, the holy Jerusalem, descending out of Heaven .... and her light was like unto a stone most precious, even like a jasper-stone, clear as crystal; and had a wall great and high, and had twelve gates .... and the city lieth four square .... and the city was pure gold like unto clear glass."

We descended to the Garden of Gethsemane and the Virgin's tomb, and mounted up the steep, precipitous path to St. Stephen's Gate, pausing for awhile at the place assigned by tradition to the stoning of St. Stephen. It is a circular spot half-way up the ascent, shut in on three sides by rock, and with large stones lying around in all directions.

Passing on through St. Stephen's Gate, we went once more to the Church of the Holy Sepulchre, where vespers were being said by the Roman Catholics before the brilliantly-lighted sepulchre. When the Roman ritual was ended, the Armenians began, the priest wearing a high mitre and brocaded silk mantle. A long procession of very poor people followed in a casual sort of way, droning the responses in a melancholy monotone. When this service had reached its climax, another began in the Greek chapel close by. The two processions nearly clashed. Monks, priests, men, women, and children, babies, soldiers, and specimens of various nationalities, were streaming to and fro in every direction, praying, bowing, kissing the holy places, gazing, whispering, and prostrating themselves over and over again. Many, fatigued with their exertions, were lying about asleep, and a few were eating provisions, brought in with them, in out-of-the-way corners. Our own quiet evening service in our tent (for the church was too far off to allow our going there at night) was a grateful contrast to the crowd and bustle of the Holy Sepulchre.

It was arranged that on Easter Monday we should go to the Convent of Marsaba, returning to Jerusalem by Bethlehem, but at the last moment a difficulty arose. Travellers to Marsaba require a tribal escort, and on inquiring from the Sheikh of Abu-Dìs we found that there was no one available for our party. Hani, however, was not to be thus thwarted in his plans, and announced his intention of playing the part of Sheikh for the day.

We were up, therefore, betimes, and next morning at early dawn Hani made his appearance in Eastern costume, with a turban on his head.

"Lady," he said, "I know the paths over the mountains as well as the shepherds. There is not an Arab in the land can guide you better than I can. Come on with Sheikh Hani!"

We were told afterwards that the inhabitants of the district watch travellers from the recesses of their hills, and are apt to waylay them, if they are wandering about without proper protection, but we had the greatest confidence in our guide, and placed ourselves, without a moment's hesitation, under the charge of El-Hani.

The ride to Marsaba—from two and a half to three hours—is dreary in the extreme, across rocky mountains, and through lone, desolate defiles. High up on one of these is perched the extraordinary convent of Marsaba. The rocks in the ravine in which it has been built are strangely worn into long ridges by rain and storm, and are of a dark, dull yellow colour. The gorge is fitly named the Valley of Fire, for in summer the heat is fierce and unbearable.

It has been supposed by some that this glaring, burning wilderness is the one into which the scape-goat was sent, bearing upon him the iniquities of the children of Israel. It certainly answers to the description in Leviticus of a land not inhabited. As we approached Marsaba a tall figure was seen on the top of one of the hills near, keeping watch. The convent is said to be a wealthy one, and guard is kept up continually, for fear of a raid by the Bedoueens.

The convent belongs to the Greek Church, and is a sort of penal settlement for recalcitrant monks. Hanging over a precipice of some four hundred feet, it seems to cling for dear life to the bare cliff on which it is built. Flying buttresses uphold the walls, and every natural resting-place in the rocks is taken advantage of for the support of the building. Ladies are never admitted under any circumstances, but we had obtained the necessary order from the Consul for the gentlemen of our party. They rapped loudly for ten minutes on the iron door, and, after the monks had inspected them through the grating, the door slowly turned on its hinges, and they were admitted into the gloomy building. The monks live a very ascetic life, and were pale and dirty. The countenances of many of them seemed to bear out the theory of its being a place of forced retirement.

The library of the convent is said to be rich in ancient manuscripts, but is jealously guarded from the eyes of the profane. We were not altogether sorry to quit the neighbourhood of the dreary convent, thankful that our lot was not cast in such a place!

The bread of Marsaba is held to be sacred. George offered me a piece of it, but it did not look tempting, so I declined it, and, with a look of deep reproach, he appropriated it to himself, muttering, "It is holy!" He said he should take it to Beyrout, where the members of the Greek Church would pay him "large money" for it.

About two and a half hours' ride from Marsaba took us to Bethlehem. The path was a mere slightly-marked bridle-track up the bare red mountain, and our improvised Sheikh showed that he had not over-rated his knowledge of the country, for, without hesitation or blunder, he led us over the wild monotonous route. The stony elevations and depressions succeeding one another were each like the preceding one, and not even a bush was there in this desert place to act as a landmark.

From one hill-top we had a glorious view eastward. The Dead Sea was lying two or three thousand feet below the desert range on which we stood, and looked like a beautiful blue lake. In the distance were the purple mountains of Moab, forming a brilliant contrast to the gloomy desert foreground. The only signs of life which we saw were some black tents of a Bedoueen encampment, and a group of French tourists camping out on their way from Jerusalem to Marsaba. With these exceptions silence and solitude reigned supreme in these regions, and it was with a sense of relief that, after a couple of hours' riding, we came to cultivated fields, and peasants busy with the harvest. The star of Bethlehem carpeted the road sides. Soon a party of armed Arabs met us, who stood across our path, and entered into a long harangue with Hani. Their voices were loud and threatening, but Hani, with some well-timed pleasantries, put them in good humour, their tone moderated, and finally, with smiles, they opened a way for us to pass through.

It was about two o'clock when we came in sight of Bethlehem, and halted for a short rest under the shade of a stone wall. The fields where the shepherds were abiding with their flocks by night, when the great news of the Saviour's birth was brought to them, lay before us. Once more we were surrounded by beautiful flowers, the bright-blue iris, scarlet and purple anemones, the star of Bethlehem, pink rock-roses, huge daisies, yellow pyrethrum, blue burrage, marigolds, ranunculuses, and mallows. This wealth of flowers was refreshing, but the heat was very great, and a little scorpion came out of the stone wall, only to meet its death at George's hands.

We were all tired, but we could not afford time for a long halt, and were soon on horseback again and starting for Bethlehem.

Bethlehem, situated on the side of a hill, looked beautiful as we approached it from the east. The houses rise one above another in tiers, and are very picturesque. The Convent and Church of the Nativity crown one side, with terraces of vines and olives below. For some miles round the country looks fertile, and is very carefully cultivated.

The population of Bethlehem is about 5,000, and almost entirely Christian.

We mounted the hill, and soon came to the Church of the Nativity, with Greek, Latin, and Armenian convents close by. The sacred building is the joint property of these three Churches.

We were received by a Franciscan monk who with the utmost courtesy showed us over the whole place.

The " Grotto of the Nativity " is a cave hewn out of the rock, about thirty-eight feet long and eleven wide. The basilica has been built over it, the grotto itself being under the chancel. There seems to be no doubt that rocky caverns of this description were in ancient times used as stables, and from the very earliest ages this grotto has been reverenced as the birth-place of Our Lord. At the east end, in the pavement, an inscription is found on a marble slab:

"*Hic de Virgine Maria Jesus Christus natus est.*"

Close to this is the site of the manger, which has been taken to Rome, and is to be seen in the basilica of Santa Maria Maggiore.

There were many native Christians on their knees before the altar, kissing the sacred stone and whispering prayers. As it was Easter Monday the crowds present were greater than usual.

We remained for some time in the grotto. When face to face with a holy site on which the mind has dwelt during a life-time, it is almost impossible to gather into one focus and concentrate into one great act of adoration all the various emotions which are felt at separate times, and it is somewhat disappointing not to have a stronger sense of enthusiasm at such moments. Human nature, after all, can only take in a certain amount of sensation, and no one, probably, is satisfied with his own depth of feeling in these sacred places, although it seemed intensely solemn and overwhelming to be kneeling in that rocky cavern where Our Lord Jesus Christ was born.

Immediately adjoining this, is another grotto, in which St. Jerome lived for many years, occupied in his Biblical labours. He died at the Armenian monastery close by.

Before we left the convent our attendant monk took us into the refectory, and regaled us with coffee, which was most refreshing.

As we rode back through Bethlehem the whole place seemed to be *en fête*. Men, women, and children were clothed in their best; the women in gay-coloured dresses, and wearing on their heads a sort of tall cone, over which a white veil is thrown, and on which strings of coins are loosely hung. The women of Bethlehem are noted for their beauty, and nowhere in Palestine did we see a more goodly array of the natives than we did at Bethlehem, crowding the streets, standing in the doorways, or watching us from the roofs of their houses.

Just outside the village is the traditional " well of Bethlehem that is at the gate," from which the three mighty men, after breaking through the host of the Philistines, brought water to David, but of which he would not drink, though he had longed for it, inasmuch as they had brought it "with the jeopardy of their lives."

A native woman was drawing water from it as we rode up, and we gratefully partook of some which she courteously offered us.

We cantered along the road from Bethlehem to Jerusalem, rough, stony, and full of ruts; but the sensation of being on a road at all was so novel that we felt as if we had returned to European civilization.

Since we came back to England we have been asked:

"How did you manage about travelling in Palestine? I suppose, being seven people, you just filled two carriages."

"Why, my good friend," was the answer, "there are only two roads in the Holy Land, one from Jaffa to Jerusalem, and the other from Jerusalem to Bethlehem, and they are worse than the worst parish road in the remotest district of England. As to vehicles, I never saw anything on wheels (not even a hand-barrow) except the carriage before described as jolting over the road from Jaffa."

Between Bethlehem and Jerusalem we came to the place where it is said that Elijah, flying from Jezebel, sat down under a juniper-tree, and requested for himself that he might die. Here he slept, and the angel fed him miraculously, and in the strength of that meat he went forty days and forty nights unto Horeb the mount of God.

We also passed Rachel's tomb, "in the way to Ephrath which is Bethlehem." "They journeyed from Bethel, and there was but a little way to come to Ephrath," and here "Rachel died and was buried, and Jacob set a pillar upon her grave."

It was about two hours after we left Bethlehem that we entered Jerusalem, and by that time it was almost dark. It was a marvel that we—the ladies of the party—were not over-tired, considering that we had been at least eight hours in the saddle.

Happily, we had no reason to regret entrusting ourselves to the care of Sheikh Hani. But even the road from Bethlehem to Jerusalem is not altogether safe. Not long before we came there, a rich Jew was robbed and murdered by one of the Arab peasants on the road; and the Bishop of Jerusalem told us that a few years ago his Arab muleteer, in charge of his baggage, was murdered on the road to Hebron. It is not often that the Arabs shed blood. They have a horror of it themselves; but when a murder occurs in a particular locality, and justice is demanded, the Pasha levies a heavy fine from the district, and thus enriches himself in the sacred name of justice!

We were sorry, on our return to the camp, to find that an owner had turned up who claimed our dog Beyrout as his private property. It was a great loss to us, for not only was he a general favourite, but, by dint of barking, growling, and fighting for the greater part of the night, he kept our encampment free from the inroad of jackals or the dogs of the city.

In the course of the evening we saw, by the expression of Hani's face, that something had gone wrong. He was evidently out of tune.

"What is the matter, Hani?"

"Lady, that Greek fellow, Giovanni, he is causing trouble."

"I am sorry to hear it. What has he done?"

"Ah! he is a villain. He is too much for me. He will not do what I tell him. He is not good to Tannous. Do you like him?"

"Yes. We have no fault to find. He is very civil, and waits upon us capitally."

And so there was an end of the conversation. But a day or two after we heard an uproar, and it turned out that Giovanni had threatened, in a paroxysm of jealousy, to kill Tannous, and poor Tannous, the steady-going and trustworthy Syrian, announced his intention of quitting our camp, if Giovanni remained.

Hani presented himself before us, and we had a cabinet council, the upshot of which was that Giovanni was to go. He was insupportable to his fellow-servants, and we infinitely preferred to keep the faithful Tannous.

That night, as my husband and I were reading in our tent, we were startled by the quiet and mysterious entrance of Giovanni, who crept through the curtain, and fell on his knees at my husband's feet, clasping his hands.

"Intercede for me, sir. I am persecuted. I am a worthy man. The rest are all against me because I am a Greek."

"I cannot interfere, Giovanni. Hani makes all his own arrangements, and we must abide by his decision."

"But if you knew how good I am, and how bad they are! It is because I am a Christian that they are all against me. Intercede for me, sir."

All this time he was on his knees in an attitude of abject entreaty, and I thought he would never go. At length, however, he left us, and went into the other tents, receiving much the same answer in each. After we had got rid of him, we had no more trouble or annoyance with our servants.

And now our time at Jerusalem was drawing to a close. Thoroughly had we enjoyed it. It had been a question with us whether we should remain in our tents or migrate into an hotel. There are two hotels in Jerusalem, the "Mediterranean" and the "Damascus," and one just outside the Jaffa Gate. They are all said to be fairly comfortable, but we formed such a pleasant party amongst ourselves that whenever the question was mooted it was always decided in the negative. At the same time, it must be allowed that the nights were very cold, and it required some acclimatization before we were reconciled to the gusts of wind which blew through the tents. Living, however, as we really were, in the open air both by day and by night, proved very healthy, which was a primary consideration. Tent-life is undoubtedly most invigorating.

The Damascus Gate, which was the nearest to our encampment, was interesting from a Scriptural point of view, for it is not difficult to trace in it the features which made the gate of the city in old times applicable to various purposes. The gate itself forms a covered archway of two sides, the one at right angles to the other. There are stone seats at the side. A staircase near the gate, outside the wall, leads to the battlemented top. It is easy, therefore, to imagine how in old times the King of Israel, and Jehoshaphat, King of Judah, sat in a void place in the entrance of the Gate of Samaria, and old Eli "fell from off the seat backward by the side of the gate," and how "David sat between the two gates, and the watchman went up to the roof over the gate unto the wall."

The Jerusalem shopkeepers seemed to have an idea that our time was drawing to a close, for, on the eve of our departure, our camp was turned into a native bazaar, and varied assortments of rosaries, olive-wood carvings, photographs, silver chains and bracelets, and a miscellaneous collection of antiquities and curiosities, were spread out on the ground for our inspection.

My husband and I thought it right, before leaving our camping-ground, to pay a visit to the Sheikh who had kindly allowed us to pitch our tents there, and a solemn and stately visit it was. The Sheikh was a tall man, with handsome features, unfortunately deformed by an obliquity of vision which made it a hopeless task to try to ascertain the direction of his gaze. He received us at the door of his house with much ceremony, and we followed him up a stone staircase to a little salon furnished all round with low divans. He placed us on these, and himself sat opposite to us cross-legged. Cigarettes and coffee were handed round, but as our knowledge of Arabic was confined to such few words as were necessary for giving orders, or dismissing importunate beggars, conversation with our host was a considerable difficulty, and the quarter of an hour spent in his drawing-room was decidedly awkward and perplexing. Smiles and shrugs of the shoulders were our only response to his volubility. We succeeded, however, in letting him know that we should like to see the view from the top of his tower. Thither, therefore, he led us, a black slave following us with seats. A little table was placed in front of us with well-sugared slices of orange. Then the son of the Sheikh, a lad of ten years old, came forward with a ewer of water, and poured it over our hands, after which the Sheikh showed us over the rest of the house.

The bed-room was merely a large bare room, with mattress beds on the floor, and a Persian carpet. There was not a single piece of furniture in it, not even a wash-hand stand. I went alone to the hareem, in which were three or four women of various ages, and several children, one a little infant only a few days old, of which they seemed very proud. They were much gratified at my admiration of the child. These rooms were equally bare of any furniture, save only mattresses and divans. One or two black slaves were in attendance, who continually came into the room grinning and showing their white teeth.

It was with some difficulty that we could persuade our host to let us go, and he accompanied us to the door of his house before finally parting from us, and just as we got out of the sight of the Sheikh's eye his little son ran after us with the cry of "backsheesh!"

We went alone to spend the evening hours of that day in the garden of Gethsemane, and on the Mount of Olives. There is a walled enclosure nearly opposite St. Stephen's Gate, which is held sacred as the scene of Our Lord's agony. It is well and reverently kept; ancient olive-trees, gnarled and rugged, cast a feeble shade over that solemn ground, and the only things that jarred upon us were the pictures of Our Lord's sufferings at the Latin Stations. In the garden of Gethsemane you do not need any adventitious helps to stir up devotion, and these poor representations seemed to us puerile and impertinent. Climbing higher up the hill, we sat down and read the prophecies concerning the wonderful future which is in store for Jerusalem, when the Lord Jesus shall return in power and great glory, and " His Feet shall stand upon the Mount of Olives." We felt that it was not likely that we should ever again see the holy places before us, and we lingered at every step on our homeward way, trying to stereotype in our minds the aspect of each sacred spot. How was it possible that we could leave Jerusalem and its surroundings without deep emotion and fond regret?

CHAPTER VII.

JERUSALEM TO NAZARETH.

DEPARTURE FROM JERUSALEM—RAMAH—BEEROTH—BETHEL—ENCAMPMENT AT SINJIL—THREATENING ASPECT OF A BEDOUEEN—JACOB'S WELL—NABLOUS—MOUNTS EBAL AND GERIZIM—MISSION WORK AT NABLOUS—THE SAMARITAN PENTATEUCH—SAMARIA—WONDERFUL RUINS—FULFILMENT OF PROPHECY—DOTHAN—JOSEPH'S WELL—CAMP AT JENIN—PLAIN OF ESDRAELON—GIDEON'S WELL—JEZREEL—SHUNEM—NAIN.

CHAPTER VII.

ON Wednesday, March 31st, we left Jerusalem. Our first stage was to Bethel, three hours and forty minutes.

It was a splendid morning, and the golden brilliancy of that early sunrise only made us the more sad to bid a long and last farewell to the Holy City. It was like parting from an old friend, and I could hardly have imagined that the place would have so entwined itself round our hearts, or become so dear to us in so short a space of time. But thus it was, and for evermore we shall carry the loving memory of that Holy City as an undying treasure, most precious and beautiful.

After riding through some olive-gardens up the rocky side of Mount Scopus, Hani suddenly drew up with the exclamation,

"After this, we see Jerusalem no more."

There was a general halt and silence, and then we went on our way over a dreary, treeless, stony track of table-land, meeting many strings of camels and donkeys laden with produce for the Jerusalem market. The camels were driven by poor-looking Arab fellaheens, armed with guns slung over the shoulder. Ramah, the home of Elkanah and Hannah, and the birth-place of Samuel, was soon passed, and Beeroth, now Birch, where tradition asserts that the absence of Our Lord from the company travelling from Jerusalem to Nazareth was first discovered by His Mother and Joseph. It seems, however, almost too near Jerusalem to allow of its being spoken of as "a day's journey."

Leaving Ramallah, a Christian village where Mr. Zeller has a successful mission, on our left, we soon reached Bethel, and here we halted in a little wheat-field, sown broadcast with stones, and were soon surrounded by the inhabitants of the few miserable hovels which now occupy the site of ancient Bethel.

Here Jacob had seen the heavenly vision; here the disobedient prophet sinned and met his punishment; here Jeroboam set up the golden calf corresponding to that at Dan in the north. But that which was foretold by Amos has come to pass, "Bethel shall come to nought" (Amos v. 5), and it now only furnishes one more example of fulfilled prophecy and of utter ruin in this land of buried greatness.

After a couple of hours' rest we resumed our way, bearing rather to the west. The cultivators of the soil have the habit of clearing their ground of stones, and depositing them in the bridle-path wherever it runs through their fields. The consequence is that, as it is nobody's business in particular to remove these stones, the riding is always difficult, and sometimes dangerous. Certainly the route from Bethel took us over the stoniest of stony ground, through a rich and extensive "wady" of fig-trees, to the gorge of the Robbers' Spring.

Happily for us, the defile was not true to its somewhat repelling name, but as we mounted the steep, rocky hill, nearly three thousand feet high, on which Sinjil—which was to be our camping-place for the night—is situated, we met a caravan of camels and armed Bedoueens. One of them deliberately placed his camel across the pathway, and stopped our advance. Hani peremptorily, according to Eastern fashion, insisted on our right of passage. The mounted Bedoueen obstinately refused, and placed his hand on his scimitar. High words passed between them, and the Bedoueen seemed to be furious, but Hani flourished his stick in the air, and the man sullenly gave way, muttering imprecations and curses against us.

I could not imagine what influenced those wild children of the desert, first to behave so churlishly, and then so completely to give way to our dragoman's orders; for he was perfectly defenceless, in accordance with his theory, that it was wiser never to carry fire-arms. I often wished it was otherwise, and that our Arabs, at any rate, had been armed, but he always persisted in saying that it was safer not; and once, pointing to my husband's pocket, in which he carried a small Bible, he added,

"Lady, that is our best protection."

Sinjil—so named from Raymond of Saint Gilles, who camped on the hill on his way to Jerusalem—turned out its whole population, men, women, children, babies and dogs, to stare at us, and a most ruffianly population they were. Our tents were pitched on a high green plateau just above the dirty mud village, overlooking an extensive tract of country. Not very far off, we could descry Shiloh, now little more than a heap of stones.

It was amusing to watch the rising generation of Sinjil in a thickly-packed semi-circle around us—dirty, bright-eyed boys and girls. We counted sixty at one time, all shouting, laughing, and keeping up a perpetual clatter of tongues. It was too much for Tannous. Generally he maintained a very quiet, measured, dignified bearing, but on this occasion his spirit was roused; he suddenly seized one of our riding-whips, and in a frenzy of indignation rushed at them, cracking it fiercely and ominously. There was a general stampede, but half an hour afterwards they had re-assembled, and sat huddled together on a great dust-heap out of the reach of Tannous' whip. From hence arose the cry of "Backsheesh!" till nightfall.

Sinjil has a bad reputation, and we heard afterwards that some travellers, who encamped there the very day after us, were robbed of a considerable sum of money. Hani specially warned us to be careful as to our bags, and always to place them under our beds before we went to sleep. The natives of the villages have a disagreeable habit at dead of night of either stealthily entering the tent, or introducing a hand under the side of the curtain, and appropriating whatever comes first. Sometimes, it is said, the camp-followers are in league with the thieves. But Hani was most cautious. Whenever a money transaction passed between him and my husband, it was always done in the evening, with the tent door closed, and with the utmost care that no sound of jingling coins should be heard. At Sinjil he immediately put us under the protection of the Sheikh of the place, but was not content with this, for by his orders some of our retainers kept watch by the camp-fire the whole night through. It is only fair to say that we never lost anything, even of the most trifling description, during the whole of our tour. So honest were our own men that a discarded shoe-lace was more than once brought to its owner at breakfast by the Arab who was packing up the sleeping-tents. My husband on one occasion said to him,

"Your men are very honest fellows, Hani."

"Ah, Governor," he replied, "I will tell you why. They are Syrians, from Beyrout. If I had Arabs, from Jaffa or Jerusalem, it would be a different story. I always take my own people, and then I am safe."

He was an enthusiast for Beyrout.

We left Sinjil betimes the next morning, April 1st. It was a relief to enter the richer country of Samaria, for Judæa maintains a distinct character for desolation, barrenness, and absence of trees, and, with the exception of the plain of Sharon, near Jaffa, the valley of Jericho, the neighbourhood of Bethlehem, and one or two other localities, it is desolate and dreary in the extreme. The descent from the heights of Sinjil is very precipitous, and until we came to the plain of Mukhnah the road was exceedingly rough and wearisome.

After nearly five hours' riding, we halted at Jacob's Well. This is one of the few places in Palestine over which no veil of uncertainty hangs. The verdict of all writers is unanimous in favour of its identity with the well which was dug by Jacob, " who drank thereof himself, and his children and his cattle." Here the weary Saviour rested after His toilsome journey over the stony hills and scorching plains of Judæa, and spoke those wondrous, life-giving words to the woman of Samaria.

Happily, the place is left in its natural condition. No stately ecclesiastical building is reared over it. No jealous custodian guards it from the common gaze. You simply see before you a cavernous aperture amid grassy mounds, and on descending into this hole a stone is seen covering the mouth of the actual well. This is now about seventy-five feet deep, and is dry in summer. In winter-time there is plenty of water in it. The view from the well is very interesting. Mounts Ebal and Gerizim towered a thousand feet above us. They stand facing one another at the entrance of the valley of Shechem like giant guardians. Close in front of us was the dome of Joseph's Tomb, and the huts of Sychar (now Askar) beyond. On the south the broad plain of Mukhnah, which looked like one vast corn-field, and must have suggested to Our Lord the words, "Lift up your eyes and look on the fields, for they are white already to harvest."

My husband read St. John iv. as we rested by the sacred well, and tried to gather up into our minds the beautiful memories which shine like a glory over this lonely place.

Nablous (the ancient Shechem) is about half an hour's ride from Jacob's Well. It is one of the most picturesque towns in Palestine, nestling in the gorge formed by Mounts Ebal and Gerizim, and embedded in groves and gardens of olives, oranges, citrons, figs, walnuts, mulberries, pomegranates, vines, and plums. Streams of water flow in abundance on all sides, and the sound of their constant ripple is very refreshing to the ear. Nablous is a sort of oasis in the grim, bare, rocky, mountainous scenery, as Damascus is in the arid plain.

It so happened that there was a Mohammedan *fête* on the day we were there, and the public olive-garden near the town was crowded with hundreds of little Moslem children, playing about, in rainbow-coloured chemises, girded round the waist with a sash or band, while the white-robed mothers were quietly watching them. It was like a garden of sprightly and moving flowers, or a swarm of butterflies.

Our ride through Nablous was very curious. The street is a mile long, lined on each side with bazaars. The paving was very uneven, and we rode in single file at great risk of falling, for our horses slipped at every step. The narrow street was crowded with the usual glorious confusion of natives, camels, mules, and dogs, and we had some difficulty in threading our way through the motley crowd. The people of Nablous, being chiefly Mohammedan fanatics, scowled at us as we passed along, but did not openly insult us, though we were told that a year or two ago it would not have been safe for us to have ridden through the town as we did. Our camp was pitched on high ground, quite at the south-west of the town, and so we had to run the gauntlet of the whole of the population of the place.

Mr. Karey, a native Christian who is zealous in good works among the inhabitants of Nablous, called on us soon after we had dismounted from our horses, and very kindly lionized us during our short stay.

We had intended to have gone up to the top of Gerizim, but unfortunately the day was very misty, and we reluctantly gave up the expedition, for we thought our time would be better occupied in the town. We spoke to Mr. Karey about the difficulty of hearing the blessings and the curses from the two sides of the valley, and he told us that only a fortnight before he had gone up Gerizim, while a friend of his ascended Ebal, and each had heard clearly what was said on the opposite mountain. The air here is peculiarly sound-conducting.

Mr. Karey is a member of the Supreme Council of Seventeen, under the Turkish Governor. Besides his wife, who is an Englishwoman, he has only one Christian companion of his own rank in the place, the Greek Bishop. He has a school for boys and girls, well attended. They are taught daily out of the Bible, and everything is done to steep them in the true faith. No open profession, however, is called for, nor are they baptised, or they would be murdered by their Moslem relatives for their apostasy. Mothers' Meetings are also held for Mohammedan women every week. The average attendance, according to Mr. Karey's statements, is as high as eighty. He reads "Line upon Line" to them, and questions them upon it, and they seem thankful to be instructed. But the work is essentially one of faith and hope, and it is impossible not to feel keen regret that they cannot openly acknowledge their faith by being brought to Holy Baptism, and thus enrolled into the fellowship of Christ's Church.

Better days will come, it is hoped, both religiously and politically, to this oppressed country. Religious liberty is abhorrent to the Mohammedans, but we must, as Christians, try more zealously to raise up the banner of the Cross in the midst of a land so dear to Our Lord, and carry out His last orders to the letter. Only thus will light break forth out of present darkness, and Palestine take its rightful place amongst Christian kingdoms. If the Holy Land were governed by Christian rulers, a great religious revival would in all probability soon begin.

It was quite refreshing, in walking round the town, to pass many fountains, rills, and reservoirs of water. The rippling and trickling sounded sweet and pleasant. Gardens and overhanging trees adorn the narrow pathways, in which the bulbul sweetly sings, without a rival amongst his unmusical compeers.

Through dim, arched, winding streets, Mr. Karey led us up a narrow flight of steps to a court-yard, deliciously fragrant with orange trees, in the corner of which was the Samaritan Synagogue, little more than a white-washed room with a small dome. There are not more than one hundred and seventy Samaritans remaining at Nablous, and none elsewhere. They believe in one God, the Pentateuch, Moses as lawgiver and prophet, and a coming Messiah. They celebrate the Passover on Mount Gerizim, a ceremony which Dean Stanley has graphically described, and also keep the feasts of Pentecost and the Atonement. Mr. Karey introduced us to the Samaritan High Priest, dressed in a purple robe and crimson turban, who sacredly guards the celebrated MS. copies of the Pentateuch. On the left-hand side as you enter the building is the Mizbah, a recess hidden by a sort of coloured curtain. Within this holy of holies the three sacred rolls are kept. The High Priest went behind the hanging and brought out for our inspection one of the manuscripts, written on parchment, and rolled on two rollers. It was enclosed in a brass and silver case, and the whole was carefully folded up in a silk wrapper, richly embroidered. The priest handled it very reverently and devoutly, and placed it on a stand. We asked to see another of the rolls, and he unlocked a cupboard, and brought out a second manuscript, still older, and enclosed in a more highly ornamented brass case. He read aloud some parts of it, and then we asked to see the oldest and most sacred scroll of all, the roll of Abishua, but he declined to bring it out. It is only shown to the Samaritans once a year, on the day of Atonement.

At night our camp was guarded by four Turkish soldiers, who kept up a series of dismal signal-whistles, the one answering the other, to prove that each was wakeful and watching. One of our horses broke loose, and rushed through some of the tent-ropes, which, coupled with a storm of rain, made our night rather disturbed. The tents, however, were perfectly waterproof. It was the first rain we had had since landing at Jaffa, so there was no cause to complain.

This downpour rather delayed our start the next morning, and we did not decamp till nearly half-past seven. It turned out ultimately a

RUINS AT SAMARIA. 189

regular April day, showers and sunshine alternately.

The route from Nablous to Samaria runs for a short distance through the rich valley of Shechem, abounding in streams, and producing crops that yield forty-fold. The barley was in full ear. Patches of great blue lupines were conspicuous amongst the wealth of wild flowers. Thistles took the place of ferns. There were a great variety of them, very graceful, with large, pointed leaves, deeply cut, and frosted like silver.

Crossing then over a succession of mountain tracks, after about a couple of hours' ride, we came to Sebaste, or Samaria, most commandingly placed on the top of a hill some four hundred feet high, in the centre of a plain.

A wonderful place indeed is Sebaste when viewed historico-prophetically. We are told that Omri "bought the hill of Samaria of Shemur for two talents of silver, and built it on the hill, and called the name of the city which he built after the name of the owner of the hill, Samaria" (1 Kings xvi. 23, 24). It then became the capital of the ten tribes. Ahab erected a splendid temple there for the worship of Baal, and after standing several sieges the city was well-nigh demolished, but rebuilt effectually by Herod the Great, who called it Sebaste (Augusta), after the name of his patron. Herod built a magnificent temple in honour of Augustus, on a terrace crowning the hill, which commands the whole valley. This temple appears to have been surrounded by a colonnade, many of the columns of which still remain standing. When the place was destroyed is not known, but certainly in its destruction the prophecies respecting it have been marvellously fulfilled.

It is said in Micah that for her sins:

"I will make Samaria as an heap of the field, and as plantings of a vineyard: and I will pour down the stones thereof into the valley, and I will discover the foundations thereof."

No eye-witness of the present state of the place could have more accurately described its appearance. The stones have been literally poured down into the valley. Columns rise up in every direction: some standing in the midst of corn-fields, some lying on their sides, almost overgrown with flowers, others broken into fragments, others cropping up in the valley beneath, even in their ruined state suggestive of past magnificence. The great colonnade, according to Lieutenant Conder, measured two thousand one hundred feet east and west, and six hundred and sixty feet north and south.

The present Samaria is the dirtiest Arab village imaginable. The inhabitants, numbering about four hundred, have a bad name, and Hani made us keep all together while we were in the place, for he said it would not be safe to ramble about alone.

We dismounted at the Pool of Samaria, where Ahab's chariot was washed, and where the dogs licked his blood. Close by are the ruins of the Crusaders' Church of St. John. Here John the Baptist is supposed to have been beheaded. Two side aisles remain, and some richly-carved capitals. The Moslems have possession of the church, and, curiously enough, they hold the tradition as to St. John's death here in sacred remembrance.

Unfortunately for us, the day was not clear, but the view from the summit of the hill, extending to the Mediterranean on the west and Hermon on the north, must indeed be grand.

After an hour or so spent at Samaria, we rode

down the side of the hill into the valley where Benhadad and his countless hosts once encamped, and where the forlorn, leprous men found that the enemy had fled in the twilight (2 Kings viii.).

The sun was very scorching after the morning hours, and it was refreshing to rest, as we did, on the terrace of a wooded hill, with a fine view of the plains below, and a clear spring of water close by, adorned with maiden-hair ferns. We made beautiful nosegays of wild flowers, which would have been received enthusiastically at Covent Garden.

After luncheon, we rode through the plain of Dothan (about seven miles long) to the well into which Joseph was cast by his unnatural brothers. There was water in it when we were there, but it is often dry. A young Arab galloped up to us, riding a high-spirited horse very cleverly without saddle or bridle. Others joined him, and we formed quite a large party round the old well. The village of Dothan, where Elisha was besieged by the King of Syria, and from whence his servant saw the mountain full of horses and chariots round about him, was on a low green mound just above us. There is something unspeakably impressive in being on the very spots where such miraculous wonders actually took place.

The Arabs of this district are singularly handsome, and so are the young girls, but they soon lose their good looks when they grow older. The men's dress is very simple, consisting of a white garment bound round the waist with a girdle, over which a rough woollen garment of broad white and brown stripes, with great sleeves, is thrown, called the abba. In this they wrap themselves up at night. The country women usually dress in dark blue flowing robes, which are very tasteful. Several of the men we saw "girding up their loins" for ploughing by simply tucking their garments under their girdle.

The rest of our journey from Dothan to Jenin, the ancient En-gannim, which was to be our resting-place for the night, lay for the most part through a beautiful valley, enamelled with flowers, and inhabited by a number of solemn-looking cranes. It was late before we reached Jenin, and just before we got there we passed a caravan with fifty-two camels, encamped for the night within a few hundred yards of the place where our own tents were pitched. They were on their way to Nablous. The bales of merchandise which these camels had carried were piled up in a huge mass on the grass.

We did not dismount from our horses till six o'clock, and were all very tired. Our baggage mules had only just arrived before us, and it was some time, therefore, before our coffee could be got ready; so we sat down on our camp-stools in the long dank grass under the grey olive-trees, and watched our men putting up the tents. The rapidity with which that wild, unkempt-looking olive orchard assumed the character of a civilized encampment was perfectly marvellous. Birds with grating notes, like those of a corn-crake, sang on all sides of us, frogs hopped about in the long grass, and we did not like the camping-ground at all, for it was sunless and damp. Hani, however, was not to blame in the matter, for the usual place was already occupied by two English travellers before we arrived. Three men from the town of Jenin guarded us during the night.

Notwithstanding the fatigue of the previous day, there was no loitering on the morrow, as our journals record—"Up at 5.30, off at 7.10." We looked forward to a day of intense interest, for in the course of it we should pass Gideon's Well, Jezreel, Shunem, Nain, Endor, and Mount Tabor, and finally reach Nazareth.

From Jenin we had a capital view of the plain of Esdraelon, the constant battle-field of the Israelites. We rode through miles of luxuriant wheat-fields, standing so thick with corn that it was not difficult to realise how such a sight would fill the inspired poets of old with enthusiasm. The wayside was beautifully furnished with acanthus plants, spreading out their huge, deeply-cut leaves on all sides in rich luxuriance. The natives eat some portions of it like an artichoke. The whole plain is excellent riding-ground, so that it was a perfect treat both for ourselves and our horses, and we could push on rapidly.

The Bedoueens from the other side of the Jordan used to make frequent raids into this rich corn-plain, and as recently as 1870 they levied black-mail on the settled peasantry. The Turks, however, sent some soldiers into the district, and the marauding parties disappeared. The plain of Esdraelon has the appearance of being one of the richest regions in the world. Even now, with but little care and labour, it produces abundant harvests of corn, millet, sesame, cotton, tobacco, and the castor-oil plant. Men with primitive ploughs —such as you see in old Scriptural pictures— were ploughing with yokes of small black oxen. Taanach lay on our left, Gilboa to the north-east, where Saul and Jonathan, "swifter than eagles," "stronger than lions," were slain, and Jezreel immediately in front of us, on a spur of the hill running out from Mount Gilboa.

Just as we reached the foot of the knoll on which Jezreel is built, we made a slight *détour* to the pool where Gideon selected his three hundred warriors because they lapped water with their hands. We observed constantly that the Arabs now-a-days invariably bow down upon their knees to drink at any spring or rivulet which would tally with the Scriptural account of there only being three hundred lappers with the hand out of a company of ten thousand men.

This well of Gideon is a beautiful, large, clear pool, with maiden-hair fern growing on the encircling rocks, and thousands of frogs croaking in the reeds beyond.

At Jezreel there are now no ancient remains at all, nor any trace of ruined buildings. The village is merely a collection of brown adobe hovels, with a watch-tower on one side which commands a fine view over the plain. From this very place the Israelitish watchman must have seen a chariot coming on rapidly across the plain, when he exclaimed,

"The driving is like the driving of Jehu, the son of Nimshi, for he driveth furiously."

Hence, too, Elijah might have been seen, with his loins girt, running before Ahab from Carmel to the entrance of Jezreel.

There is a plot of ground to the south-east of the village which is supposed to have been Naboth's vineyard, with traditionary ancient wine-presses close by, deserted and forsaken. The cultivation of the vine has now almost died out of Palestine, and Naboth's vineyard, as we saw it, seemed anything but a desirable inheritance.

We sat on a rocky height outside the dirty village, and looked over the great rich plain of Esdraelon to Mount Carmel and the blue sea on one side, to Nazareth afar off nestling like a tiny gleam of white in the dark mountains, and on the other side to the little hill of Hermon, dewless

Gilboa, and Mount Tabor. A group of young Jezreelites sat by and watched us. The girls had their eyes painted round the lashes with good effect, but they were disfigured by the universal blue tattoo-marks, in a trefoil pattern, on their foreheads, lips, and hands. Veils, which had once been white, were thrown over the head, and helped partially to conceal the rents and the dirt of the drapery with which they were clothed. But they were merry and good-natured, and we found them civil enough.

After crossing another stretch of the plain of Esdraelon we halted at Shunem for our midday repast. Shunem presents very much the same sort of general appearance as Jezreel, but it is redeemed from dreariness by being walled in by prickly pears, and in the middle of the village there was a lovely grove of orange and lemon trees, in full blossom, under the shade of which our carpets were spread. A stream of water from the little hill of Hermon flowed through the grove.

As usual, the principal personages of the village came to watch us during our meal. The men were exceedingly well-dressed in bright-coloured, flowing robes, and they moved about with a lofty dignity which, in such a mean place, was almost comical. One of them was much troubled by an incessant cough, so my husband gave him a mixture of tannin and ipecacuanha, which was the signal for all the other men to advance in a stately manner, and request that they might share in the distribution. They were accordingly dosed all round, and it is to be hoped that no ill effects followed.

On the roof of one of the Shunamite huts were two women "grinding at the mill." These constant Scriptural illustrations add a wonderful and vivid interest to the commonest objects in the Holy Land.

From Shunem we went round the spur of the hill to the village of Nain, which now consists of a few mud huts on the northern slopes of Little Hermon. There was a Bedoueen encampment just above the village. Mount Tabor was in full view in front of us—a circular mountain rearing itself up quite apart from any other, upwards of two thousand feet above the Mediterranean. There is nothing but the blessed memory of the Saviour's mighty power, and the mother's deep joy, to beautify Nain, for, like many another site in Palestine, it speaks not to the eye, but to the heart. Another two hours' ride across the plain and up the mountain side, and we found ourselves at Nazareth.

CHAPTER VIII.

NAZARETH TO SYRIA.

SITUATION OF NAZARETH—WHY LEFT SO INACCESSIBLE—THE VIRGIN'S FOUNTAIN—BEAUTY OF THE WOMEN—SUNDAY AT NAZARETH—VIEW FROM THE HILL ABOVE THE TOWN—CONCOURSE OF RUSSIAN PILGRIMS—THE HOLY SITES AT NAZARETH—CANA OF GALILEE—TIBERIAS—CAMP BY THE LAKE—CONTRAST OF THE PRESENT WITH THE PAST—DISPUTED SITES OF CAPERNAUM, BETHSAIDA, AND CHORAZIN—WE CAMP AT KAHN MINYEH—STORM ON THE LAKE—A QUIET MORNING—SAFED, "THE CITY SET ON AN HILL"—BEDOUEEN ENCAMPMENT—A METAWILEH SHEIKH—ALGERINE COLONY AT DESHUN—DISTRIBUTION OF MEAT—KADESH NAPHTALI—VANDALISM—DAN—SOURCE OF THE JORDAN—SCENE OF ROB ROY'S CAPTURE—BANIAS—WE LEAVE THE HOLY LAND.

CHAPTER VIII.

THE village of Nazareth lies embosomed in the hills at the north side of the plain of Esdraelon. It is surrounded on all sides by over-lapping mountains, "like the petals of a rose," and the ascent to it from the plain is up a steep and difficult bridle-path, rocky and precipitous. On expressing our surprise to Hani that so important a place should not even have a road leading up to it, he replied,

"The people of Nazareth are prosperous, and they fear the Bedoueens, who might be tempted to come across the Jordan and ravage the district, so they leave their pathway as rugged and inaccessible as possible, for the sake of safety."

The shadow of the Bedoueen darkens the land.

Nazareth, with its population of some four thousand souls, has a cheerful, well-to-do look.

The Franciscan convent, with the church of the Annunciation, the Greek church, the Protestant Mission church and orphanage, together with many well-built private houses, give quite a European air to the place. The population for the most part belong to the Roman Catholic or the Greek Churches, but there are a few native Protestants.

Towards evening we reached our camping ground on a grassy common outside the town, with a pleasant view of the whole village rising in terraces above us, gleaming white against the dark background of the hills.

We started off at once to the far-famed Virgin's Fountain, to see the women of Nazareth coming out to draw water from the well. The road thither was absolutely crowded with women and girls, wearing gay cotton-dresses with open bodices, and large, loose trousers of bright-coloured prints. They were gracefully balancing on their heads the heavy earthenware jars, which they filled at the well, and it was curious to watch them tuck up their trousers, wade into the pool of water in front of the well, fill these huge pitchers, and then help each other to balance them on little pads on their heads. It was a perfect "tour de force," and I never could make out how they were able to walk under the weight of those great jars, poised, as they always are, on one side.

The women of Nazareth, like their sisters at Bethlehem, have a great reputation for beauty, and as they are for the most part Christians, and therefore unveiled, we could judge of the truth of the report.

As we watched them coming and going we tried to recall the scene which, many hundred years before, must often have been witnessed at this spring, when, at the quiet evening hour, the pure and gentle Virgin-mother would draw near to fill her water-jar, accompanied, doubtless, by the Holy Child Jesus; and the sacred memories of His early life threw a halo of intense beauty and interest over that simple Eastern well.

It was just the same with a carpenter's shop into which we went, where a young Nazarene was busily employed in his trade, dressed, as all the youths are at Nazareth, in a long, striped cotton gaberdine, reaching down to the ankles, with a girdle round the waist, and tight sleeves. The interior of the shop was very primitive and simple, open to the street, and full of wood-shavings and old implements; and it was not difficult to imagine that Our Lord in His early manhood might, to the outward eye, have looked much the same as the carpenter in the workshop at Nazareth at the present day.

We had a complication of noises as usual to hush us to sleep in our camp-beds outside Nazareth; thousands of frogs in a neighbouring pool croaked loudly, jackals screamed close to the prickly-pear hedge behind our camp, and the dogs of the town answered them furiously. But towards morning the sounds were changed, and the bells of the Latin church welcomed the dawn of Sunday, heralding to us a most grateful day of rest.

There were Arabic services in the English mission-church both in the early morning and the afternoon, and it was interesting, at the former, to see a young layman of Nazareth come forth from the congregation to read the lessons, just as Our Lord might have done in the synagogue at Nazareth hundreds of years before. We had service in our own tent morning and evening, and read Dean Stanley's sermon on " Jesus of Nazareth,

The King of the Jews," which helped to deepen our impressions of the place.

In the afternoon we mounted a high hill behind the town, and saw from thence one of the finest views in Palestine. To the west lay Carmel, with the broad plateau on which the priests of Baal confronted the solitary prophet, and where the God of Elijah openly acknowledged His servant before the assembled multitudes. The silver shores of the blue Mediterranean stretched out beyond, with the bay of Acre, and the little town of Haifa. On the south were the mountains of Samaria, Gilboa, and little Hermon. The great plain of Esdraelon was spread out with its parti-coloured crops like a huge patchwork quilt just below us, while, beyond, the rounded mountain of Tabor and the distant range of the Galilean hills were seen. On the north the snow-capped Hermon reared its great, venerable white head into the deep blue sky, showing the extreme boundary of the Holy Land.

It was a magnificent view, glorified and ennobled by the wonderful thought that oftentimes Our Lord in childhood, youth, and manhood, must have escaped from the noise and wrangling of earthly voices in the town below to stand on this mountain top, amid the beauties of His own creative power, to hold communion with His Father in heaven.

We descended by a zig-zag path into the streets of Nazareth, and found them crowded with a long procession of Russian pilgrims, who had come hither from Jerusalem. A strange assemblage indeed they were, no fewer than fourteen hundred in number, headed by the Russian Consul and his two Cavasses, with gold-embroidered vestments, and wands of office in their hands. The poor things seemed very weary and footsore. They had left a thousand donkeys in the plains below, but a great number of them walk through their whole pilgrimage. Slowly they straggled along, with jaded faces and limping, halting steps. Many of them were very old. The men were clad in dark brown coats, full trousers tucked into high boots, and with fur caps on their heads; the women wore European short dresses of coarse brown material, dark homespun jackets, with pocket-handkerchiefs tied over their heads, and they carried ugly little bundles of necessaries, long staves, and, generally speaking, a tin can, tea-pot, or kettle dangling at their side. It is difficult to imagine a more hideous or repulsive-looking set of people, with their flat Kalmuck faces, small eyes, and broad noses.

The only redeeming features about the procession were the lovely nosegays of scarlet anemones and blue iris which most of the pilgrims held in their hands, and which contrasted strangely with their own uncouth and unattractive appearance. It was impossible not to make a comparison between the sombre character of their garments and the gay, bright appearance of the handsome Nazarenes in graceful Oriental dresses resplendent in kaleidoscopic colouring. The bells from the Greek church rang forth a welcoming peal as the pilgrims entered the town. Accommodation had been prepared for them at the Greek convent and in the church itself, but many of the Russians travelling through Palestine sleep out of doors.

There is something very pathetic in watching these poor wayworn travellers. Many of them die before the pilgrimage is over; they fall out from the ranks one by one, and suffer and pass away in this far-off land, lonely and forlorn. Occasionally they are drowned in the Jordan,

P

when bathing in its sacred waters, or lay in the seeds of a fatal fever from the chill of the stream. But the belief that the pilgrimage ensures their salvation, and that to die in the Holy Land is a certain passport to heaven, inspires them with an unconquerable endurance, and makes them bear patiently the many ills which they have to meet.

The question of the holy sites at Nazareth is a bone of contention between the Latin and the Greek Churches. In a crypt under the high altar in the Latin church the place is pointed out where the Virgin Mary received the angel's visit, and heard those gracious words,

"Hail! thou that are highly favoured. The Lord is with thee, and thou shalt bring forth a son, and shalt call His name Jesus."

Many of the native Christians were prostrating themselves, and kissing the marble slab which marks the place of the Annunciation. The church itself was crowded with men, women, and children, kneeling or sitting cross-legged on the stone floor of the church. The congregation follow the Mohammedan custom, and leave their shoes at the door, or carry them in their hands, and the women separated themselves from the men, and were congregated together at the west end of the church.

Vespers were going on when we were there, and the organ pealed forth most lovely secular music, which seemed greatly to delight the people. An Arabic litany was then sung, in which the congregation joined very heartily, every now and then spreading forth their hands towards heaven in an attitude of entreaty. We were not able to learn much about our own mission-work at Nazareth, for the Missionary happened to be away at Jerusalem for a conference; but one young Christian convert—Nasir-a-Saba—came to see us, and spent some time with us. He is apparently earnest in his wish to become a Missionary himself.

Our camp was quite lively as the afternoon closed in, for some native women with their babies paid us a visit, minutely examining into everything—our india-rubber baths, soap-tins, beds, sponges, looking-glasses, &c. They showed by signs and gesticulations that they greatly admired the appointments of our tents; but Hani was not fond of native visitors, and did not allow them to remain long within the sacred precincts of his encampment.

A terrific hurricane raged during the night, which threatened to blow down our tents, but they stood it out manfully, and no accident occurred, though the storm was so great that it kept me awake for hours. Early next morning we rode away up the steep mountain-side, north of Nazareth. The place had left a delightful impression upon our minds, in spite of the hurricane, and we parted from it regretfully.

Kefr Kenna, a small mud village, was the first place of interest which we passed. It disputes with another Kana, which we saw in the distance, the right of being "Cana of Galilee," but we were quite content to believe that we were in the very place where the first miracle was wrought. Some great water-pots are shown in the church, which are said to be fac-similes of the water-pots of stone used at the marriage-feast. The air in the neighbourhood of Cana was absolutely fragrant with the scent of the coronella. If it were not for the luxuriant growth of flowers, the country would be almost insupportably dreary, for, speaking generally, the absence of trees is a perpetual blank in Palestine.

We halted at midday on the summit of the

"Horns of Hattin." The view from hence over the Lake of Tiberias must be very fine, but the day was so cloudy that we could not see the distance at all clearly. Many have supposed the Horns of Hattin to be the Mount of Beatitudes, and the site of the feeding of the five thousand, and certainly a flat plateau near the top of the hill would be singularly well-suited for both. But the Mount of Beatitudes is now believed to be near the lake—whereas Hattin is two hours distant—and the feeding of the five thousand was probably at the other end of the Sea of Galilee.

Tiberias lies a thousand feet below Hattin. You do not see the town itself till some ten minutes or so before you come to it, and it seemed very strange to be approaching a place with a population of about 3,000 souls by a mere bridle-path across the rocky mountain-side. The air was thick and heavy, and a dark cloud hung over the water. We found that during the day hail-stones had fallen for the first time for half a century.

Tiberias, through which we rode in order to reach our camping-ground on the shore of the lake, is a walled-in, picturesque town, beautifully situated under the mountain slopes. The sea, as we drew near to it, looked dull and gloomy through the hazy atmosphere, and the heat was suffocating. We had changed the brisk, invigorating mountain air of Nazareth for the tropical heat of this lower region, 800 feet below the Mediterranean. Mosquitoes and a variety of annoying insects buzzed around us, and we felt a sudden collapse of energy, and an unaccountable longing for the *dolce far niente*. We congratulated ourselves that we had not begun our travels later in the year, for we felt it was better to bear the cold at night than to have run the risk of succumbing to the fierce heat by day of the later months.

Tiberias is one of the four cities of Palestine which are sacred in the eyes of the Jews, Jerusalem, Hebron, and Safed being the other three. The consequence is that the population to a great extent consists of Jews. A sallow, sickly lot they are, evidently enervated by the tropical climate. Their belief is that the Messiah will rise from the Sea of Galilee, and then reign in Safed.

We had an opportunity of seeing almost the whole of the population, for the next day, when we rode in single file through the town, the market-place (where there were broad beans in abundance, and plenty of fish from the lake) was thronged with buyers and sellers. It so happened that Hani had left us for a short time in order to replenish his commissariat department. Suddenly an old withered Jew, with hooked nose, long flowing beard, and flashing eyes, burst through the crowd just under our horses' heads, and, uttering fierce imprecations, rushed at a young man, whom he belaboured soundly. It was a furious assault, and, as the younger not unnaturally defended himself, the fight became hotter and hotter. We could not escape, and the crowd soon closed in around us. Suddenly Hani appeared on the scene, rode straight at the combatants with his stick held up aloft, and, with frantic menaces, abused them heartily. To our astonishment the men calmed down in a moment, looked at him with abject terror, and made him a humble obeisance. These Orientals are very like children, and Hani's bold, determined manner at once gave him unlimited power over them.

The bridle-path from Tiberias to Magdala follows the bend of the mountain slopes which border the lake, and affords a succession of most lovely views over the water, with the hills of Bashan in the distance. The day was rather cloudy, which made the effect of light and shadow all the more striking, and the hill-sides were carpeted with brilliant flowers in such lavish profusion that it was perfectly dazzling to look upon them. I never saw anything like the sheets of pink linum, giant pheasant's eye, and large rose-coloured mallows, interspersed with bands of buglos, blue daisies, alliums, anemones, ranunculuses, salvias, hyacinths, periwinkles, gold-coloured pyrethrum, and beautiful grasses of many sorts. They adorned the mountain slopes like a gorgeously embroidered kingly robe, and no words could fitly describe their splendour. The nebk, pomegranate, fig-trees, and oleanders grew down to the water's edge, and our syces amused themselves by decorating the horses' heads with their bright blossoms.

As we wound along this floral path overlooking the lake, we met a curious company of gypsies, who, with bag and baggage, were travelling southwards. Some were walking, some riding, all were clothed in rags and faded finery, and each had to help in conveying a share of their worldly goods. Most of the men carried barbarous-looking drums or "tom-toms," which seemed to be valuable family possessions.

It is hardly possible to imagine any part of Palestine where Our Lord's presence is more vividly realized than by the Sea of Galilee. Here on these beautiful hill-sides He had doubtless often walked alone, or in company with His disciples, or followed by the eager multitudes, passing and re-passing between villages and towns, ever about His Father's business, teaching, exhorting, healing, and manifesting forth His glory to the crowds that surged around Him.

But how changed is all now! Whereas Josephus asserts that the cities around the lake "lie very thick, and the very numerous villages are so full of people because of the fertility of the land that the very smallest of them contains above 15,000 inhabitants" (quoted in Farrar's "Life of Christ," vol. I., p. 178), Tiberias is now the only inhabited place of any importance on the lake. Certainly the wretched mud village of Mejdel, the ancient Magdala, has no attractions at the present day. It is just at the entrance of the plains of Gennesareth, a fertile tract of country about three miles long.

It took us some hours to ride from Tiberias to Ain-et-Tin, or Khan-Minyeh, where we had arranged to remain for the night. Many believe this to be the site of the old Capernaum. Our tents were pitched beneath the abrupt rocks which hang over Khan-Minyeh. A warm limpid spring bubbled up close by from under a wild fig-tree, and found its way through tall reeds and bulrushes to the lake. It was a damp and unhealthy camping-ground.

We rode on almost directly for another hour to Tel-Hum, passing El-Tabighah on our way thither. No point is more disputed than the identity of these three places with Capernaum, Bethsaida, and Chorazin, but we were content to identify them respectively with Khan-Minyeh, El-Tabighah, and Tel-Hum.

Tabighah is a picturesque but very poor fishing hamlet, consisting of two or three hovels of baked mud by the banks of a sparkling stream, full of crabs and fish.

Tel-Hum is nothing but a mass of ruins, and certainly no one remembering the once flourishing condition of these cities, and seeing now their absolutely ruined state, their very names being a matter of dispute, can doubt the utter fulfilment of those woes which Our Lord denounced against them. We stopped for several hours at Tel-Hum. The rank vegetation around is thickly strewn with broken walls, columns, and Corinthian capitals. There is one heap of ruins standing a little apart from the rest, with beautifully carved stones, which those who maintain that Tel-Hum was Capernaum identify with the synagogue built by the centurion whose servant Our Lord healed.

We were very glad that, whilst we were at Tel-Hum, a gale of wind arose, and in a few minutes the whole surface of the lake was changed. It no longer lay quiet, placid, and mirror-like beneath us, but was worked and lashed up into white-crested waves, and no boat would have ventured out upon such troubled waters. It was easy then to imagine the scene of old—the ship, in which the disciples were, tossed with waves, "for the wind was contrary;" the Lord Jesus walking to them on the sea, and calming their fears with those loving words, "It is I, be not afraid."

We had a charming ride back to Khan-Minyeh, on high ground overlooking the lake, and, as we were cantering along, a large snake was suddenly seen gliding amongst the rocks. It quickly, however, disappeared, but it gave Hani the opportunity of telling us thrilling stories of venomous snakes which are said to frequent the shores of the Sea of Galilee, and to be a source of great danger to the bare-legged natives.

A lovely night succeeded to the storm of wind, and we remained for long watching the darkness gradually gathering over the sacred waters, and picturing to ourselves our Saviour's God-like form passing noiselessly over those rippling waves. We felt more isolated and alone in that camping-ground at night than at any other place during our journey.

If this was really the site of Capernaum, what an amazing contrast between the past and the present!

Capernaum once exalted to heaven, teeming with human life, vessels crowding the harbour, multitudes following Our Lord along the shores of the blue sea: Capernaum, honoured with the title of His "Own City," where He healed the demoniac, cured Simon's wife's mother of a fever, restored the paralytic, called St. Matthew, healed the centurion's servant, and did many mighty works; and now the annihilation is complete and absolute—it is brought down so low that none can say for certain where it stood, and the great papyrus reeds and tangled maze of oleanders wave over the silent waters. The tide of life is extinct, and nothing but ruins remains to point the great moral of wasted opportunity and rejected blessing.

I could not sleep; the cry of jackals and the croaking of frogs made night hideous, and the Arab retainers began singing their wild, mournful songs, and shouting to a party of men who seemed as if they were coming down the rocky defile just above us. The noise increased, talking, hallooing, and quarrelling, till about three o'clock, when it subsided little by little, as the men dropped off to sleep, and in the morning we found that they had been enjoying an exceptional carouse—not with any alcoholic accompaniment, for they are all total abstainers, but with extra food and tobacco. I imagine they were afraid of sleeping long on this marshy ground, for it was so very damp and unwholesome, and that they kept themselves awake by these boisterous means.

April the seventh dawned at last over the lake in perfect repose and brilliancy; the wind had subsided into absolute calm, and the sea lay tranquilly rippling on the shore, and glittering like diamonds under a hot blazing sun.

Our baggage caravan was sent on to Safed immediately after breakfast, and we spent a quiet morning resting on the rocks over Ain-et-Tin, sketching, reading, gathering flowers, and dreaming. It was so delicious to linger about the sacred lake, and we found an exquisite place for our open-air *salon* on some great boulders of rock which stood near the tepid stream, just under the shade of a large wild fig-tree, full in leaf, which spread its branches over us, and shielded us from the great heat. We could watch the thousand silvery fish flitting about in the clear water, and coming in vast processions from the lake, to be fed with the *débris* of our meal.

What a "beautiful time" we had that day! It can never pass away from our memories, and words fail to describe the fascination of the Sea of Galilee. We parted from it sorrowfully when, at mid-day, we started for Safed, a town perched on the high mountain range which overlooks the whole country round.

An incident occurred as we were starting which may be worth mentioning as illustrative of native character. Alraschid, one of our syces, having been kicked by a horse, instantly flung himself on the ground and burst into tears, sobbing piteously. We were much alarmed, and asked to see the wound, which he displayed with renewed paroxysms of tears; it was only a scratch, which an English lad would have laughed at, but the great childlike Syrian be-pitied himself greatly, and his pathetic and dramatic gesticulations were quite touching.

Safed, for which we were bound, is nearly 3,000 feet above Khan-Minyeh. It is supposed to be "the city set on an hill," to which Our Lord pointed, and the position of the town is unique, built on a mountain range two hundred feet higher than Jerusalem, and overlooking the whole country round.

The ride from Khan-Minyeh to Safed took us four hours. As we passed through the rich plains bordering on the lake, the women at work in the fields there, for the first and only time, were scared at our approach, and ran away in alarm.

Mounting the hill in the midst of a wild open country, we passed a Bedoueen encampment; we descried their black tents in the distance, and were told that about two hundred Arabs from the other side of Jordan had come thither to pasture their flocks and herds for a time, and are under solemn promise to the Sheikh of Safed not to commit any depradations whilst they are there. A Bedoueen is always true to his word. They were, however, a wild looking lot, living as nomads in lonely isolation.

The last hour to Safed was up a steep climb, but it is well worth the effort, for the view from the ruined citadel, which is on a conical peak in the centre of the town, is quite magnificent— all Galilee seemed to be spread out like a map before us. The beautiful blue lake was embedded in a setting of range upon range of dark mountains; far away beyond the Sea of Galilee was the Land of Gilead, broken into ridges and broad ravines, and bounded by the hills of Bashan. Safed was beneath us, a town built in two parts, tier upon tier of houses on either side of the mountain.

We stood and gazed at the view till the sun went down in a golden glory behind Jebel Zebrid, flushing every mountain top with the purest rose colour. The night before we had been six hundred feet below sea level, in an almost tropical heat, and now we were two thousand feet above it, in a keen, cold air, which made us shiver. We found these sudden changes of temperature rather dangerous, and the woollen garments which we wore were quite the right sort for a tour in Palestine.

The citadel of Safed was destroyed by an earthquake in 1857, and has not since been rebuilt. The whole city suffered terribly at that time, for the houses being built on terraces, one above another, the upper tiers of buildings were thrown down upon the lower, and the consequent loss of life was very great. Nearly half the population perished. The town is divided into the Jewish and Mohammedan quarters, and, as we passed through the former, a fanatical young Jew pointed and snapped his gun at one of us. Luckily he was observed, and the gun was taken from him. He then began throwing stones and spitting at us, and we were glad to be out of the reach of this varied assortment of missiles.

We were more kindly treated by another citizen of Safed. A pretty little girl, who had followed us about for some time, suddenly rushed up to my cousin, seized his hand, kissed it, and pressed it to her forehead. He could not resist these graceful blandishments, and rewarded the child with some trifling present, but we had cause to repent of his good-nature, for the younger generation of Safed, in a variety of rags and tatters, assembled in such numbers that we could hardly move out of our camp without being surrounded by them, and, as we passed along, they stroked us and patted us, and raised a chorus of, "Backsheesh Setti." "Backsheesh Hawaji." It was a warning against future gifts; but these little Easterns have such pretty, coaxing ways, and they cajole you so patiently and perseveringly to notice them, that it is almost impossible to drive them away with a frown.

Our ride the next morning led us, as we descended the hill-side, through groves of fine old olive-trees of unusually large size; and from the heights which we mounted again directly afterwards we had a noble view of the long flat-ridged range of Lebanon, Mount Hermon covered with snow, and the Lake of Merom in the deep marshy valley lying at its foot. We thought this and the view from Safed quite the two finest in Palestine, and agreed that they might well stand a comparison with Swiss scenery.

During our day's journey we found some very fine specimens of the black Arum, which is, I believe, a specialité of the highlands in Palestine. The descent was so precipitous that we walked, and left the horses to file down along the narrow path, in the charge of Abdullah and Alraschid. Two of them broke away and careered over the mountain side, which caused Alraschid another flood of tears, and his dramatic gesticulations gave us a vivid idea of his agony of mind.

In crossing a stretch of table land we passed a grand-looking old Sheikh of the Metawileh sect, escorted by nine armed retainers. The Metawileh are the followers of Aly, the son-in-law of Mohammed, and are regarded as heretics by the orthodox. They are to be found northwards, in the neighbourhood of Baalbek, and in a few villages in the Lebanon, but they have a bad reputation as robbers. This chief, however, had very courteous manners, and he returned our salutations with much grace and dignity.

On the same cultivated upland a group of ploughers and sowers were busy at work; and the latter seemed to illustrate the parable of seeds sown on the roadside, on thorny, rocky, and good ground. They stopped and watched us attentively for some time, and then shouted to us. We took no notice. They shouted again, and one man ran towards us.

"Have you got a hakim (doctor) with you? For a woman here is ill, and wants you to cure her."

"No, my friend," said Hani, "we cannot help you. We have no doctor with us."

The poor man looked sadly disappointed, and I was excessively sorry for these people, out of reach of any remedies or relief for their sufferings, and having to depend on the precarious chance of a hakim passing by.

Our midday halt was at the bottom of a fine rocky gorge, by the side of a mountain torrent, and with no shade anywhere. The sun beat down in flames of fire; our rugs were spread by the rushing stream, and we hid ourselves under umbrellas. In half an hour the whole party was asleep, with the exception of my niece and myself, and we kept guard over our unconscious fellow-travellers for two hours, listening to the stream leaping and boiling on its way down into the valley, and admiring the grand, wild, lonely scenery. By-and-by sounds of music "crept in our ears," and a shepherd lad, with primitive Pan-pipes discoursed gruesomely to himself and his flock.

When everyone had awakened and remounted we ascended up to a great height, above a deep, narrow, and abrupt rocky defile. Far down below us, close to the torrent, on a platform of rock, we saw two Mohammedans at prayer, prostrating themselves, and bowing low before Allah. In the grand, natural temple of this mountain solitude there was something very solemn and suggestive in watching these men.

The place seemed one in which the presence of God could be felt without distraction, and I could imagine Elijah wrapping his face in his mantle, standing at the entrance of just such a rocky cave to listen for the " still small Voice," when the strong wind was hushed into silence, and the earthquake and the fire had passed away.

After a while we came to the village of Deshun, inhabited by an Algerine colony, who settled here when the French dispossessed them of their African homes. It was curious to see the houses with sloping roofs. The colonists are thriving and industrious, but they have to pay ten per cent on the produce of their land to the Turkish government. The village is well situated among the mountains, and we found the natives collected at the well, where a distribution of meat was taking place. Six goats had been killed, and the meat was piled up in little heaps, and apportioned to the various families. The Sheikh stood out prominently in the picturesque group, allotting the shares, and he came forward to receive our salutations with the never-failing courtesy of an Eastern. The Algerines seemed perfectly contented with his sub-division of the food, which, we were told, took place weekly. It seems as if —as far as butchers' meat, at any rate, is concerned—they had "all things in common." We lingered for some time watering our horses, and receiving great attention from the bystanders.

It always interested us to observe the calm, scrutinizing gaze of these grave people. We longed to know their thoughts, to interchange ideas with them, and dive below the outward surface of their lives, and we all found it very tantalising to travel in a country of the language of which we were wholly ignorant.

At Kedes (the ancient Kadesh-Naphtali) we were shown the ruins of the house of Barak. A spring of water gushes out just below it, and acres of olive-groves cover the slopes of the hills. Beyond stretches out a rich plain of two thousand acres, capable of yielding to the careful cultivator even a hundredfold, and answering to the description of the heritage of Naphtali, "Satisfied with favour, and full with the blessing of the Lord." Deut. xxxiii. 23.

Hedges and walls are unknown, the allotments being divided the one from the other by large stones, reminding us of the curse incurred by those who should venture to remove their "neighbour's landmark." The old ruins of Kedes are being fast demolished by some speculator, who has bought the ground on which they stand, and is about to use the ancient stones for his own new house. We heard that he had been made to pay somewhat exorbitantly by successive Governors of Damascus, who each in his turn managed to find some flaw in the original agreement, and by threats of eviction extorted a considerable sum of money. The original purchase-money of £2,000 had thus been gradually increased by these extortions to five times that sum.

We were very glad when we reached our resting-place for the night, Meis-el-Jebel, for one of our party was unwell. He went to bed at once, and slept without moving for thirteen hours, which completely cured him. His indisposition showed off our dragoman in a new character. No hospital nurse could have offered a patient clearer beef tea, or more smoothly-prepared arrowroot, than he furnished at a moment's notice.

About a couple of hours' ride the next day brought us to the fortress of Hunin, supposed by some to be the Beth-re-hob of Judges xviii. 28. The view from this ruined castle is very fine. Hermon, just in front of us, reared up his great snowy head above a corona of white clouds, which looked like an encircling glory resting on the summit, and between the castle on which we stood and Hermon lay the plains of Huleh and the Lake of Merom. The flat country was dotted about with Arab tents, but it looked marshy and unhealthy, and we were glad that we had chosen the longer route over the mountains, rather than a shorter one which leads through the plain. Into this flat country we now descended by a steep, precipitous path, and, after crossing the blue rushing torrent of the Hasbany, found ourselves at midday at Tel-el-Kadi, the ancient Dan, now consisting only of a mound some forty feet above the plain.

On the southern side of this height was the Temple of the Golden Calf, and its ruined foundations can still be traced. On the eastern side, bending over the clear stream which springs from a volcanic shaft in the ground, and is one of the sources of the Jordan, are two noble trees, a holm-oak and a terebinth. The latter is the largest in Syria. They cover the graves of Arab saints, and are the favourite resting-place for passing travellers. Oaks, poplars, reeds, and oleanders form a thicket on the western side, and the lovely white scented blossoms of the storax tree filled the air with fragrance.

In this romantic place we found two English travellers and their dragoman, who, unlike Hani, was well armed. It was pleasant to have a little intercourse with our fellow-countrymen again.

Not far from here Mr. Macgregor (Rob Roy) was captured by the natives, and Hani, who was his dragoman, entertained us with an account of some of his many adventures. He had been canoeing alone down this arm of the Jordan, and the natives near the Lake of Merom, seeing a strange object on the water, imagined that he was a supernatural being of the worst sort. They shot at him several times without wounding him, and finally took him prisoner. He managed to send a messenger to Hani, telling him of his danger, and asking him to come at once to his assistance. Hani, though a little suspicious of the man's tale, at once started off with him through the night, and, much to Rob Roy's relief, appeared suddenly, after some six hours' ride, on the scene of action. Great was Hani's indignation at the insults to which Mr. Macgregor had been subjected, and, by treating him with the deference due to royalty, he so impressed the Arabs with his exalted character that they at once released him. Hani threatened them that, if in any way they injured Rob Roy, the whole strength of the British nation would be put forth to annihilate them from the face of the earth. Under such awful threats they were thankful to let both him and his dragoman go away in peace.

As we rested under the old terebinth-tree a party of Druses, very well dressed, and wearing red tarbouches and white turbans, passed across the stream, and meeting some other Druses coming from Banias they embraced, and so passed on their way.

Another hour's ride ended this day, and we reached Banias, the ancient Cæsarea Philippi, early in the afternoon. Banias lies under Mount Hermon. On a precipitous hill immediately above it stands a castle, with a glorious view of the surrounding country. The lime-stone cliffs rise abruptly behind the town, and from a great, natural cavern the upper source of the Jordan bursts forth, a ready-made river, rushing, and boiling, and eddying, falling in cascades, and dashing over great boulders of rock amid thickets of fig-trees and mulberry-trees, maiden-hair ferns, reeds, and festoons of vines, all interspersed with ruins. There are carved inscriptions on the cliff which show that Pan and Baal were worshipped here.

The rock which overshadows this source of the Jordan is supposed to be the one to which Our Lord pointed when He said,

"Upon this rock I will build My Church, and the gates of hell shall not prevail against it." St. Matt. xvi. 18.

The appearance of the town of Banias is somewhat peculiar, for on the top of each flat roof the inhabitants erect wicker-work cages of oleander boughs, and stand them on four upright poles. These can only be reached by a ladder, and are used as sleeping places at night; the villagers hoping by this device to escape the scorpions and other insects which abound here during the summer heat. The people are said to suffer much from ague. A poisonous miasma rises from the marshes of Huleh in the autumn, and makes the place, fascinating though it was to our eyes, very unhealthy.

It is now generally supposed that it was on a spur of Hermon, not far from Banias, that the transfiguration of Our Lord took place. The mountain is beautiful, and seemed very appropriate for the glorious vision.

In the course of the evening some Druses came to our encampment, and finding my daughter reading at her tent-door, took the book into their hands, and made signs to show that they were aware that the Bible was to be treated reverently. They were interested in examining a writing-case, and other English articles, and as a token of friendship offered her a handful of raw beans, which they produced from under their flowing robes.

On leaving Banias we were parting from the Holy Land. We could no more tread in Our Lord's footsteps, or picture His Sacred Form in the towns and villages as we passed along, for, as far as we know, He never went beyond the "Coasts of Cæsarea Philippi." The change and void were felt by each of us with keen regret.

CHAPTER IX.

DAMASCUS.

FAREWELL TO PALESTINE—BITUMEN WORKS—MARONITE AND DRUSE WOMEN—THE RIVAL SECTS—THE MASSACRE OF 1860—SUNDAY AT HASBEYA—SOURCE OF THE JORDAN—RASHEYA—WELCOME BY SCHOOL-CHILDREN—RUINS OF RUKLEH AND DEIR-EL-ASHAYIR—HURRICANE AT DIMAS—NIGHT IN THE KHAN—BEAUTY OF THE ABANA—FIRST VIEW OF DAMASCUS—DIMITRI'S HOTEL—THE GREAT MOSQUE—BAZAARS—VISIT TO ABD-EL-KADIR AND THE GRAND MUFTI—HOUSES OF DAMASCUS—ALI BEY'S HAREEM—SUMMARY JUSTICE—BURIAL-GROUNDS—THE "STREET CALLED STRAIGHT"—MISSION WORK IN DAMASCUS—DANCING DERVISHES.

CHAPTER IX.

IT was remarkable that, immediately upon leaving Palestine and entering Syria, the land seemed to be more carefully cultivated, and the people were much better dressed.

Banias looked very lovely as we rode away on the 10th of April, and bade a sorrowful and loving farewell to the last place we should visit which had been honoured by Our Lord's Presence.

In passing through some corn-fields a strange, croaking noise was heard near, like a watchman's rattle. The natives at work in the fields were intently looking up into a tree with signs of alarm. It turned out that there was, coiled up in the branches, a large snake uttering those discordant sounds, and the people were preparing to kill it.

We had good cantering ground under Mount

Hermon, but at one place the whole surface of the ground was completely covered with bees which swarmed in myriads, and enveloped us on all sides. Groups of natives passed us as usual, and we had continual views of the snowy heights of Hermon and Lebanon.

It was intended that we should make a *détour* from Wady Kureibeh, and see the ruined temple of Hibbariyeh, which, according to Robinson, is "one of the most beautiful specimens of the many ancient temples with which Lebanon, Anti-Lebanon, and the valleys between are thronged," but after our week's continuous riding we were all tired, and elected to go straight on to Hasbeya. Shortly before coming to Hasbeya we visited some bitumen works. The manager was a friend of Hani's, and, happening to be at the door of the works as we passed, he recognized our dragoman, threw his arms round his neck, and insisted on our stopping to see all that was to be seen.

This superintendent was a most intelligent Syrian, clothed in a fine black cloth garment, with a crimson sash round his waist, and a fez cap. He told us that there are only three bitumen mines in existence, one in America, one near the

Dead Sea, which is not worked, and this one. The bitumen, after being well washed and picked over, is sent on mules and camels to Sidon for export to Europe. The Company which works the mine has to pay £800 a year to the Turkish Government. Down by the side of the Hasbany was the washing place, where, under a shed, we saw a wonderfully picturesque sight. A hundred and forty women and girls, Maronites and Druses, in gay cotton dresses and white veils, were sitting cross-legged, with round tins in front of them, washing the bitumen from earthy particles. Their arms and necks were adorned with silver bracelets and necklaces, some of them of considerable value. An Eastern woman wears her dower upon her person, for women are safe from robbery; whatever, therefore, they carry about with them is secure, and they consequently convert their money into ornaments as a safe investment.

The wage of these women is only half a franc a day. We observed that the Maronites wore their veils thrown back, while the Druse women covered their faces till the gentlemen had passed out. They are very strict with regard to this, not even unveiling themselves in the presence of their own brothers. When, however, the gentlemen had gone away, they at once threw back their veils, and, by way of salutation to us, gracefully placed their right hand, successively on the lips, forehead, and heart, in token that head and heart were at our service.

This was our first introduction to the rival sects of the Druses and Maronites, and it may be well to say a few words respecting them. The Maronites are Roman Catholics, followers of Maron, a hermit who lived in the fifth century. They live chiefly in the northern district of Lebanon, numbering about 200,000. They are warlike in their habits, bigoted, and intense in their hatred of their fellow Christians. They were expelled from the towns of Syria when condemned for heresy by the Council of Constantinople, and have ever since lived in the higher ranges of Lebanon.

The Druses are for the most part found in Southern Lebanon, and are of mixed Syrian and Arabian origin. Their creed is rather mysterious. They believe to a certain extent in the Koran, but explain it mystically, and the hidden meaning of it is supposed only to be known by the Okkals, or initiated, as opposed to the Djahels, or uninitiated. They are said by some in their secret rites to worship a calf, though it is generally supposed now that this is not the case. No stranger is ever allowed to be present at their services. They are themselves bound to secresy by awful oaths, and their temples are always built on the summit of mountains, far away from the habitations of men. They are brave and warlike. It is said that in the Lebanon there are no fewer than thirty-seven large towns and villages inhabited solely by Druses, and two hundred and eleven villages of Druses mingled with Christians. In Anti-Lebanon there are sixty-nine Druse villages or towns. Hasbeya and Rasheya are two of their capitals.

The Maronites and Druses are very bitter in their enmity the one against the other, and it will be long before the cruel memories of the massacres of 1860 fade away. We heard much about them in the regions of Hasbeya and Rasheya, for these two towns suffered dreadfully at that time. It was in that year that the smouldering ill-will between the two sects burst into a flame, fanned secretly, as we were constantly told, by the Government at Constantinople. At Beyrout, Deir-el-

Kamar, Tezeen, Hasbeya, Rasheya, Zachleh, and Damascus, the most frightful atrocities were perpetrated. Christians were massacred by hundreds, neither women nor children being spared; villages were in flames; at Sidon three hundred were slain by the sea-shore. Convents were attacked, monks slaughtered, and the Mohammedans vied with the Druses in the attempt to exterminate Christianity from the land. But Christian nations came to the rescue. English and French squadrons anchored off Beyrout. A body of French troops landed there in August, 1860, and the Maronites gradually regained confidence. It has been estimated that no fewer than eleven thousand of them were slain at that time, leaving twenty thousand widows and orphans. Many, too, died from destitution and misery.

A European Commission, in which England was well represented by Lord Dufferin, laboured for five months to restore the poor scattered Maronites to their homes, to appraise their losses, and to re-organise the government of Lebanon with a view to the safety of Christians. The Pasha of the Lebanon district is now required to be a Christian.

Our tents were pitched at Hasbeya, above the ravine of the river Hasbany, and in the course of the evening numbers of white-veiled girls, whom we had previously seen at the bitumen works, came to pay us a visit, and were made happy by presents of needles.

We were all tired, and I was thankful that we should not have to travel on the following day. I never realised so fully before what must be the weariness of a hard-working woman on Saturday night, or her joy in the prospect of Sunday, viewed merely as a day of rest.

Sunday, April 11th, was spent on the beautiful green plateau of Hasbeya, just under Hermon, in the most perfect repose. A wreath of white-robed women sat a little way off from our camp, and sundry groups of natives came to talk and smoke with our Arabs, but we felt little inclined to do more than have our own tent-services, and walk down, in the evening, through a beautiful olive-grove to the Hasbany, another source of the Jordan.

My husband had a great wish to climb up to the top of Hermon (9,300 feet) the next day, but a great deal of snow had recently fallen, and, to his regret, it was pronounced impossible. Our marching orders, therefore, were for Rasheya, a six or seven hours' ride through the wildest and dreariest of mountainous districts.

The town of Hasbeya was about a couple of miles above our encampment, splendidly situated on a spur of Hermon, overlooking a deep mountain gorge. Rich gardens, and terraces of vines, figs, and mulberries, covered the steep slopes, and owing to the beauty of its situation and its many arcades and picturesque buildings, interspersed with tall dark cypress-trees, the town had quite an Italian look. Hasbeya seemed to us to be one of the loveliest places in Syria.

We went up to the Seraglio, or Palace of the Ameer, which stands out above all the other buildings, adorned with a tower and arcades, and with a large piazza, or court, in front of it. Our cavalcade paused before the palace steps, and we looked around with mournful interest, for here, in 1860, one of the most terrible massacres had taken place. Into the court of the palace many Christians had fled, both from Hasbeya and from the villages around, and placed themselves under the protection of the Turkish governor. They were offered a written guarantee of safety on condition that they gave up their arms. Unfortunately, they believed in the Turkish Commandant's good faith, and consented to do so. Shortly afterwards, the Druses were admitted into the palace, and the poor Christians were cruelly slaughtered. Many were horribly mutilated. Wives and mothers in an agony of terror tried to screen their sons and save their husbands, but in vain. The men died like martyrs, hardly uttering a groan; and it is said that each in his turn, as he fell by the sword, fervently muttered the words,

"In Thy Name, O Lord Jesus.'

From a village near, which Hani subsequently pointed out to us, two hundred young Christian men were treacherously brought by their Mohammedan Sheikh, and then murdered. Numbers of women, we were told, shared the fate of the men by clinging to them in a grasp which only death could separate.

One of the princes came out of this palace, and, after a courteous greeting, urged us to partake of his hospitality, and go over the interior of the building. We reluctantly declined his kind offer, for we had a very long day before us, and there was no time to spare; so we bowed our thanks, made a complimentary speech through our dragoman, and went on our way.

The road from Hasbeya to Rasheya is rugged and rocky, "up and down, and a little roughy," as Hani expressed it. We went in single file along endless stony paths, without a yard of cantering ground, and exposed to the full blaze of the sun. Hermon, upwards of nine thousand feet, was on our right, and the Lebanon range, more than ten thousand feet high, on our left. Large, dark lizards and chameleons peered at us from behind rocks, but the flora of Syria is very different from that of Palestine, and we had little of beauty wherewith to refresh our eyes except the grand mountain scenery. We stopped for a few minutes, on a mountain ridge, at the little village of Elkfin, where the Christian school-master brought out all his scholars to greet us as we passed along, and in his simple hospitality presented to us a bowl of water.

It seemed to be the fashion of the country for the school-children thus to welcome travellers, for at Rasheya, which we reached at five o'clock, after six and a half hours' hard ride over cruel rocks and stones, not only did we find large crowds of people gathered round our tents, but also a whole school of children drawn up in line to receive us. They belonged to one of Mrs. Mott's Syrian schools, and the master could speak a little English. As we rode up they exclaimed, " Good evening." It was the only English phrase they knew, but smiles and salaams supplied all further expression of their good feeling towards us, and we quite understood that these cordial demonstrations were owing to Mrs. Mott's zealous educational work among them, which they thoroughly and gratefully appreciate.

We questioned the children through an interpreter, and they sang to us "in the English way," said their school-master, but it did not sound like anything we had ever heard before.

At the conclusion of their entertainment we drew our horses together in a semicircle, and sang some glees, which they clapped loudly, and after a final little speech, which was rendered into Arabic by Hani, we sought the grateful repose of our tents, and imagined they would go back to the town: but not so: they lingered for long about our camp, loth to depart, and did not finally disappear till it was dark.

As at Hasbeya, so too at Rasheya numbers of Christians were massacred in 1860. The village, of about three thousand inhabitants, looks extremely cheerful and thriving, but it does not bear a very good reputation.

Next morning, as usual, we were in our saddles by eight o'clock, and, after traversing a long valley, mounted high up on Hermon. Patches of snow were lying about, and it blew a hurricane all day. In one of the most secluded spots, nearly five thousand feet high, we came upon the ruins of Rukleh, at one time a temple of Baal. Massive stones, pillars, and capitals are huddled one upon the other in wild confusion, and seem to indicate the effects of an earthquake. Near the south-east corner of the ruined temple is a medallion with a finely-carved face upon it, supposed to be a representation of Astarte.

The wind continued to rise, and when we reached our halting place, under a great rock which sheltered us from the violence of the gale, it was curious to hear it thundering and raging over our heads while we were in comparative calm, and to see its effects on the trees and brushwood on the opposite side of the ravine. We had a grandly coloured view of the Zebedany valley and Anti-Lebanon. Every inch of available ground in the valleys was well cultivated.

Hani looked gravely at the stormy sky, and prophesied that no tents could be pitched if the gale reached Dimas, which was to be our resting-place for the night.

About an hour's ride from Rukleh brought us to another ruined temple of Baal at Deir-el-Ashayir. It is finer and more perfect than that at Rukleh, and stands nobly facing the Anti-Lebanon range. After seeing these temples, we seemed better able to realize the "high places" of Scripture.

Shortly before reaching Dimas we struck upon the new road from Beyrout to Damascus. This road was made by the French when their troops came to Damascus in 1860, and is now in the hands of a French Company. It is well engineered and kept in capital order.

Just as we came in sight of it, the diligence from Beyrout appeared in the distance. It was an exciting moment. We had not seen a carriage or a road for weeks. Our party set up a shout of exultation and delight, and, as Hani wanted to send some message by the driver to Damascus, we immediately started off at full speed after the coach. But all in vain. Whether the driver thought that our intentions towards him were evil or not will probably be always a mystery, but certain it is that he at once lashed his horses into a gallop, and we could not succeed in catching up the diligence.

On reaching Dimas we found that our men had been quite unable to pitch the tents. What was to be done? Should we push on for another four or five hours to Damascus? But we were all tired; the ride through a tremendous hurricane had been laborious and *pénible*, and we longed to get out of the sound and reach of this howling wind; anything would be better than another long spell of such distressful travelling. So we decided to take up our quarters for the night in the little Khan or caravansarai of this poor, miserable village. We rode up the narrow street between low, mud-baked houses, with the inhabitants all out and about, on their roofs and at their doors, staring at the benighted travellers, and were led through a low doorway into a courtyard, walled in, with a small covered gallery at one end, from which two rooms opened out. These were to be our quarters for the night. Both the walls and mud floor had been newly whitewashed. There were no windows, and the doors would not shut. They were entirely devoid of furniture, with the exception of some Damascus cabinets, inlaid with mother-of-pearl, and a shelf round the wall, on which were placed willow-pattern plates and a few ornaments. Each room had a large open chimneyed fireplace.

Our luggage was soon unloaded in the little courtyard, and our cook quickly set up his cooking apparatus in one corner of it. The owner of the two rooms (with a baby in her arms), in loose jacket and large trousers, and closely veiled, did all she could to assist, and in an incredibly short space of time the appearance of the rooms was transformed into comfort and homeliness by the introduction of beds, tables, camp-stools, &c. The ladies appropriated one room, the gentlemen the other, and our Arabs rolled themselves up, when night came on, in their abbas, and slept in the verandah or courtyard, just outside our rooms, making a chorus of snoring and heavy breathing which lulled us to sleep. The place was well sheltered from the violence of the gale which raged outside. We had nothing to complain of in this Eastern Khan, and it was no small comfort to be out of the grip of that frightful tornado, and in the quiet repose of those little rooms at Dimas.

When we started for Damascus the next morning the storm had rather abated, but the wind was still very high, and we were exposed to it without any shelter whilst crossing the dreary plain of Sahra, until we came to a sudden burst of luxuriant vegetation in a ravine fringing the beautiful river Barada (the Abana of Scripture), "the golden flowing." This impetuous mountain torrent rushes towards Damascus between bare arid rocks, carrying fertility wherever it can make its influence felt. The banks are clothed with poplars and walnuts, and the fertilising stream changes the whole aspect of the country. The water is so clear and blue that it is a joy to look at it, and we could sympathise with Naaman when he exclaimed, "Are not Abana and Pharpar, rivers of Damascus, better than all the waters of Israel?"

As we drew near to Damascus we turned off the main road, and raced our little Arabs up the mountain side to the Domed Wely, from which we were to get the celebrated view of far-famed Damascus. Each one was eager to be the first to catch sight of the beautiful city; and indeed the view, when we reached the top, was one worth coming any distance to see. We found ourselves suddenly on a bare peak of those desolate, arid mountains, with the vast sandy plain of the Hauran spread out before us, and at our feet a green oasis thirty miles in circumference, a garden of Eden, rich with orchards of orange, pomegranate, lemon, apricot, peach, plum, pear, walnut, and olive trees, and watered abundantly by the streams of the life-giving Barada. In the midst of this luxuriant greenery the city of Damascus, "the pearl of the East," flashes and gleams with gilded minarets, domes, mosques, palaces, and cupolas, looking very beautiful, fairy-like, and gorgeous in its rich setting. Far away in the distance lay the brown desert, stretching out in waves of sand-hills to purple mountains beyond. Sand storms swept wildly across the horizon, like some desolating fire stalking through the land. Behind us rose snow-capped Hermon, and the long range of Anti-Lebanon. A cloudless sky and a blazing sunshine glorified the whole scene.

When Mohammed first saw Damascus from this point of view, he is said to have uttered these words, "Man can only enter one Paradise, I prefer to go to the one above;" and then he turned his horse's head, and rode away from the beautiful city.

Not wishing to follow the example of Mohammed in shunning this earthly Paradise, we descended from the height by a steep path, and rode through green orchards and filthy streets to Dimitri's Hotel.

Damascus is more beautiful when viewed from afar than it is on closer inspection. Distance certainly lends enchantment to it, and the Paradisaical glamour passes away when you discover that it is rather more unpleasing to the olfactory organs than most Eastern cities. The high mud walls that shut in every road and street are grim and ugly. Heaps of offal lie outside the town, on which the carcases of dogs are decaying, while their half-starved surviving brethren, of funereal aspect, prowl about in a state of utter leanness and dejection. Cairo dogs are aristocratic in comparison with these.

The streets are narrow, always crowded, and the smells unspeakable.

Out of one of these dirty streets we passed through a low clamped doorway (which told a tale of insecurity of life and property), and suddenly emerged into an open, marble court, with a fountain playing in the centre, and exotic plants, trees, and trailing creepers growing luxuriantly, making the air heavy with sweet scents. Round this court were the rooms of the hotel, and a large alcove at one side, with another fountain in the centre, served the purpose of a salon. The sound of trickling water was cooling and refreshing.

Madame Dimitri, by birth a Greek, the widow of Monsieur Dimitri, formerly the master of the hotel, sailed forth to greet us, clad in a cotton dress with a long train, and her hair fastened in two plaits down her back. There was nothing Oriental in her appearance. She waved her hand majestically to one of the Syrian attendants, who showed us our bed-rooms. He led us up an outer staircase, across a flat roof, opening out on to which were our apartments. It was the first time we had been lodged in an hotel since we landed in Palestine, and we rather bemoaned our fate in being thus "cribbed, cabined, and confined."

Close to our windows was a minaret, from which, in the night, the Muezzin droned forth, in a lugubrious minor chaunt, the call to prayer. This weird and mournful sound, mixed up with the howling of dogs, wove itself unpleasantly into my dreams, and somewhat disturbed my rest.

One great happiness awaiting us at Damascus was good news from home. We had been out of reach of letters ever since we left Jerusalem, and the long silence, added to the feeling that it was impossible to hear from England, had been very trying.

The next day we began to lionise Damascus. Our first object was the Great Mosque, once a beautiful Christian church, with marble columns, and walls decorated with mosaics. The Moslems have white-washed the columns, and destroyed most of the mosaic-work in their bitter anti-Christian zeal, so that it has a very dreary and forlorn appearance. This mosque has three minarets. One of them is called the Minaret of Jesus, and the Mohammedans have a tradition that when Our Lord comes to judge the world He will first descend on this minaret, and then enter the mosque and call all men before Him to judgment. It is supposed by some that the temple of Rimmon stood on this very site; if so it would have been here that Naaman deposited the "two mules' burden of earth" brought from the Holy Land.

From the top of one of the minarets we had an interesting view of the town and the neighbouring country. We looked right into the courtyards of numberless houses, paved with marble, and over mosques, bazaars, and public buildings to the orchards, and farther still to the desert and ranges of mountains beyond.

The citadel, through which we passed in going to the mosque, was the scene of some of the most bloody incidents connected with the massacre of 1860. Our Syrian *valet de place* was a Christian, and had, with his family, lived there for some months, suffering terrible privations, and expecting that each day would be their last. We were told that the feeling between the Mohammedans and

Christians is still very bitter, and no one would be surprised at a fresh outbreak of fanaticism.

The bazaars are very quaint, almost more so than at Cairo. They consist of open stalls on each side of narrow lanes, with mud flooring, and are covered with raftered ceilings, which make them deliciously cool. In a corner of the recess the shopman sits, grave and solemn-looking, dressed in a long robe, and with a turban on his head, twirling his beads, studying the koran, or smoking a narghileh, and apparently quite indifferent as to his business.

Through these bazaars we threaded our way with difficulty amongst loaded camels, scavenger dogs, innumerable donkeys, and people of all colours and nationalities. Greatly did we admire the variety of Eastern merchandise displayed: the soft silks, antique armour, Damascus swords and daggers, gold and silver brocades, embroidered robes and portières, old china, brass-work, Persian carpets, Cashmere shawls, silver, gold, precious stones, and iron-work of every description, saddle-cloths, holsters, bridles, and trappings of brilliant colours embroidered with gold, and all the paraphernalia of Eastern magnificence.

As at Cairo, so here, the bazaars are apportioned out to distinct trades and merchandise. Distant countries have taken the place of Tyre in supplying her markets, and it may be said now, with a wider application than in the times of Ezekiel,

"Syria was thy merchant by reason of the multitude of wares of thy making: they occupied in thy fairs with emeralds, purple, and broidered work, and fine linen, and coral, and agate.

"Damascus was thy merchant in the multitude of the wares of thy making, for the multitude of all riches." (Ezek. xxvii. 16, 18.)

We had brought a letter of introduction to Abd-el-Kadir, the grand old Algerian leader, now for so many years exiled from his country, who acted so nobly by the Christians during the massacres of 1860. It is said that on one occasion he protected some Christians under his roof at the risk of his own life, for he laid himself down at the door of the room in which they were secreted at night, and declared resolutely that they should not be touched except over his own dead body.

He admitted Mr Heywood and my husband to an audience, and welcomed them with much grace and courtesy, but he is now old and feeble, and France would certainly have nothing to fear if the interdict as to his return to his old country were removed, and he were allowed to end his days there in peace and liberty.

We brought another letter of introduction to Mohammed Effendi Manzel, Mufti of Damascus, who gave us permission to visit some of the finest houses in the town. My husband had an interview with him, and he sent a gentleman with us to act as interpreter. The next day we placed ourselves under his guidance, and followed him through a narrow, dirty street, into a still narrower and dirtier passage, out of which we suddenly emerged into a large courtyard, coloured in stripes of red, white, and blue, with a beautiful tesselated pavement. Marble fountains were splashing and trickling, and sending forth thousands of refreshing diamond drops into the dry, hot air. Lemon, citron, and orange trees, and other shrubs and flowers, were growing luxuriantly in parterres, while jessamine trailed in profusion over trellis-work, making the most grateful shade. A delicious fragrance pervaded the whole atmosphere. On one side of the court was the Lewân, a raised dais, with divans round three sides of it, and a little fountain tinkled in the midst.

All the rooms opened on to the great court, and the reception halls were constructed after one uniform pattern. You enter, on the same level as the courtyard, into a chamber which has on one side a raised platform, richly carpeted and set round with divans and cushions, covered with satin embroidery of the gayest and most gorgeous colours, such as Easterns love. It is customary to leave your shoes or slippers on the lower level before advancing on to the raised dais, but we dispensed with this ceremony, and only carefully wiped the dust from our feet. The walls of one of these stately rooms were wainscoted, richly carved in beautiful arabesques, and inlaid with mother-of-pearl and gold. The windows were filled with stained glass, and the ceiling and shutters carved, like the walls, in the loveliest patterns.

We left the gentlemen standing in the outer court, while we were led through a winding passage to the rooms of the harcem. Here six ladies entertained us with coffee and cigarettes. The children of the family were present, and black and white slaves flitted about, who seemed much amused and gratified with a sight of Europeans. It is impossible to conceive a more useless, vacant, or deteriorating life than that which these Eastern women lead. They behaved like children, laughing at the most trifling things, and seemed to have very little intelligence. It is sad to think of them thus kept in ignorance and practical imprisonment, employing their time in little else than idle gossip, and the jealousies and inanities of their miserable life. We never saw a book or a bit of needlework in any hareem we visited, and it is difficult to imagine how their days are spent. I felt more strongly than ever the inestimable value of Zenana work, wherever it can be efficiently carried on.

We were shown their bath-rooms, with marble walls and floors, very cool and delicious in this hot climate. They seemed sorry when we left, and I wish I could have talked to them. As it was, we could only interchange ideas by signs.

When we emerged through the carefully-guarded doorway into the street again we succeeded in making our guide understand that we wanted to go to the palace of Ali Bey. Thither he led us, and Ali Bey met us at the door of his house, apparently in no wise disconcerted by our being nearly two hours later than we had intended to be. With Orientals time is a commodity of no great value.

Our host talked French well, and so we were able to converse freely with him. He led us courteously into the Salâm-leik, or reception-room, where coffee was soon handed to us, after which he offered to conduct the ladies into the hareem, where he said that his wife and sister, with his daughters by a former marriage, were waiting to receive us. We accordingly accompanied him to the women's quarters. The first person I saw was a very fair, handsome, blue-eyed woman, with a lovely baby in her arms, coming towards Ali Bey.

"Madame, c'est ma femme," he said.

I was struck with her beauty, and, forgetting for the moment the Eastern custom of never praising a wife to her husband, I could not help exclaiming,

"Comme elle est belle!"

To which Ali Bey replied, as though accounting for her prepossessing appearance,

"Je l'ai achetée pour deux cent cinquante livres !"

He then told me that he had seen her some years ago as a Circassian slave, at Constantinople, and had at once brought her to Damascus.

He had no other wife. She looked quite happy, and his manner was very kind to her. She was evidently curious to know the subject of our conversation, and said to Ali Bey, in Arabic,

"How I wish I could understand what you are saying !"

We were brought into a room decorated sumptuously with red satin hangings and divans, and carpeted with soft Persian rugs. It was soon filled with the other members of the harcem, and a number of black slave-girls, who came to inspect us, and stare wonderingly at us. After a while Ali Bey said he would fetch the gentlemen, and I was curious to know what would happen; for Eastern women must never be seen. In a few moments we heard a loud clapping of hands; it was Ali Bey's signal, and before he arrived with the rest of our party every woman and child had disappeared; but as he led us round the court we saw them laughing and peeping at us from behind doorways.

Nothing could exceed the courtesy of Ali Bey throughout our visit, and he only parted with us at his outer door with many salaams and complimentary speeches.

These beautiful old palaces show what Damascus must have been in its halcyon days. Now it is only a wreck of its former self, but even at the present time, in spite of dirt, ruin, and decay, there are beautiful bits of architecture and carvings peering out from among the houses and bazaars: old Moorish archways and doorways, lovely courtyards, and fountains, and ancient mosques, giving some idea of Oriental taste and magnificence in bygone ages. There are several modern palaces erected by rich Jews, which contrast mournfully with the exquisite old buildings and decorations. We paid a visit to one of these —the house of Lisbony. It is built on the old lines of a Damascene palace. The same courtyard, fountains, alcoves, divans, and reception-rooms were there, but all tricked out and vulgarised with French gilding, gaudy mosaics, bad frescoes, and tawdry colouring. It is thought very grand and fine, and certainly no expense has been spared, but we turned with enthusiasm to the sober, graceful beauty of the ancient palaces.

Justice or redress are hard to obtain in Damascus, and the simplest way seems to be for each man to fight his own battle. It happened that one day my daughter, with her cousin and Miss Stanhope, went into the bazaars to shop, with Georgé as their cavass. He was a great tall fellow, six feet high, and looked very imposing and aristocratic in his handsome Syrian dress. The young ladies stood outside one of the stalls, bargaining, and a crowd, as usual, had gathered round them. Suddenly they heard, to their horror, a resounding box on the ear being administered to some one close to them, and, on turning round, they saw Georgé in the act of beating a Turkish soldier; his face was crimson, and he looked infuriated. It was a regular fiasco.

"Georgé, que faites-vous donc! Qu'-est ce qu'il y a?"

Georgé drew himself up with great dignity, and pointed to the retreating figure of the soldier, who was disappearing in the crowd.

"Mais il voulait me voler la bourse, mademoiselle." And he struck his pocket significantly.

In this summary way Georgé administered

justice, without the intervention of handcuffs or police. The bystanders knew that he had right on his side, and so the affair ended at once, instead of turning, as they feared it might do, into a regular street row.

Damascus will ever be held dear in the memory of Christians as the birthplace of St. Paul to his high apostolic missionary life, and we should like to have seen the very spot which the oldest local tradition fixes as the scene of his conversion. It is twelve miles from Damascus, on the direct road to Tiberias, between the villages of Jûneh and Kaukab. We were not able to go there, but we rode outside the walls to the closed gate "Bab Kisan," near which St. Paul escaped, when through a window he was let down in a basket. Until quite lately the window in the wall was shown! Further on we came to the Bab Shurki, or Eastern Gate. About a quarter of a mile beyond it are the Roman Catholic, Jewish, and English cemeteries. Of these our own is the best kept. It is walled in and locked up, and, although rather dreary, it presents a pleasing contrast to the other burying places.

The Roman Catholic cemetery is little more

than a few open caves by the side of the road, and horrible stories are told of the hungry dogs emerging from the city after nightfall, and mangling the dead bodies; and robbers from Damascus are said to rifle the caves even of the very grave-clothes of those interred in them.

The Moslem cemetery is in a different quarter altogether, outside the Bab-es-Saghir, or Southern Gate. The Mohammedan tombs are of oblong shape, many of them ornamented with green cupolas and crescents. At each headstone there is a niche, for a pot of water and a myrtle-branch. On Fridays the Moslems come to mourn over their dead, and to read the Koran. We saw parties of women thus occupied, dressed in white izars, with their faces covered with the mandil, or coloured handkerchief. Tents were erected near the tombs, and in these they sat for hours, weeping, praying, or, as we occasionally observed, laughing, chatting, and gossiping.

Riding from these burying-grounds through the Bab Shurki, we passed into "the street called Straight." The bases of several columns have lately been discovered flanking this thoroughfare, which seem to indicate that in old times a colonnade ran along each side of it. The house of Judas, where St. Paul lodged, and the house of Ananias, are still shown in narrow streets diverging from the one "called Straight."

Service on Sunday was held in St. Paul's School. This establishment, under the charge of the British Syrian School Society, was opened in 1868, through the indefatigable labours of Mrs. Bowen Thompson. The sphere is one of great difficulty and danger, and requires in the conduct of the work much tact as well as Christian courage. We went over the establishment, which is well appointed and carefully looked after. Mr. Macintosh, the missionary schoolmaster, is greatly helped in his work by his wife. The children, to the number of one hundred and fifty, seemed happy and contented, and from their national fondness for garments of many colours the school looked very gay and cheerful. On the morning that we were there a Greek priest from the Hauran had been received into our Church. For a long time we were told he had been contemplating the step, but had been exposed to terrible persecution in consequence. He was obliged to give up wife and family, and was in danger of his life. At one time the Druses

T

protected him from the anger of his brother Christians.

For months he had been watched and prevented by force from coming to the English mission-house. The Greek Patriarch compelled him to sign a paper to the effect that he would never again hold intercourse with the Protestants.

That night he crept into the mission-house like Nicodemus, having escaped his watchers, and conferred with Mr. Macintosh as to his future. He was very miserable, and said that his relatives threatened to murder him if he joined the English Church. Mr. Macintosh placed the whole matter before him in its true light, and the result of the interview was that on that very evening the Greek priest went to the Patriarch's house, asked for the paper which he had signed, tore it up and wrote another, stating that his decision was made, and that he should at once seek to be admitted as a member of our Church.

He proved his sincerity by openly professing the faith. Of course his former means of livelihood had been cut off from him, and Mr. Macintosh hoped to be able to set him up in a book-shop in the town.

It was arranged that we should see the Dancing Dervishes, and accordingly we went to the circular hall where this extraordinary act of devotion was to take place. There were galleries all round, and a place railed off below for spectators. About one hundred persons were present. They left their shoes at the door, and sat crosslegged on the ground, solemnly awaiting the entrance of the performers. In a recess on one side was a mortuary chapel of departed dervishes, with several large tombs in it.

A band was stationed in the gallery. The instruments were reed-pipes, tambourines, tomtoms, and cymbals. A dervish was stationed with the band, who intoned some prayers in a nasal drone to their wild accompaniment, and the discordant noise was dreadful.

After we had waited a considerable time twenty dervishes in high, white felt hats, like flower-pots, white garments and over-coats, entered in single file. The skirt was done into a frill like a fan round them, and evidently weighted so as to stand out when they danced. Each had a broad belt round the waist.

The chief of the dervishes, to whom great respect was shown, wore a green cloth coat. When he entered the enclosure he bowed solemnly to the tombs of the deceased dervishes, and then sat down on a rug of sheep-skin, which is considered very sacred.

The ceremony began by the recital of some prayers by one of the men; they then prostrated themselves, kissing the ground, after which some hideous music began, and they all walked solemnly round the enclosure three times, kissing the breast of their chief as they passed him; he in return kissed each on the neck. More prayers were recited, and then half the number of dervishes doffed their outer coats, let down their white robes, and started off one by one, gliding round with outstretched arms, and closed eyes, and their heads lying on one side. For ten minutes they followed one another round the circular space with the greatest solemnity and decorum. There was no excitement, and they never jostled one another, although from their arms being extended it seemed almost impossible that their hands should not clash. But they never did. They were apparently in an ecstasy of devotion, and there was no sign of anything but reverence from first to last. At the end of ten minutes the second division of dervishes went through exactly the same performance. One of them always remained in the centre, the others whirling round him. A commemoration of deceased dervishes followed upon the dancing, and, after the ceremony had lasted about an hour, they solemnly filed out of the enclosure one by one, each in turn passing in front, and kissing the hands of those who still remained in the hall.

I had always fancied this dervish dance to be a sort of religious farce, and that it would be difficult to witness it without feeling it to be absolutely ridiculous and grotesque. It was nothing of the kind. The poor men seemed so intensely earnest and devout in their performance that the predominant feeling in our minds was a deep longing that such evident religious fervour might be gathered up into our own holy faith, and that the yearnings of these fanatics should be satisfied by a real and intelligent knowledge of the unknown God whom they ignorantly worship. Dervishes are held in great reverence by the Moslems, and are supposed to possess supernatural powers. Mohammedan mothers bring their sick children of all ages and place them under their feet, earnestly praying them to tread out the evil, and cure the disease. A friend of ours at Constantinople had seen a dervish thus standing upon a poor child who had been brought to him to be cured. The little creature, though wailing before being placed under the dervish's feet, was said to be perfectly quiet afterwards. Probably it had no breath left wherewith to express its feelings!

CHAPTER X.

DAMASCUS TO BEYROUT.

DEPARTURE FROM DAMASCUS—HALT AT AIN-FIJEH—BEAUTY OF THE BARADA—CAMP AT SUK-WADY-BARADA AND YAHFUFEH—WONDERFUL COLOURING OF THE BUKA'A PLAIN—WE REACH BAALBEK—MAGNIFICENT RUINS—MASSIVE STONES—INTERIOR OF A NATIVE HOUSE AT BAALBEK—ZACHLEH—LOVELY CAMP—REGRET AT ITS BEING OUR LAST—BACKSHEESH DISTRIBUTED—THE LEBANON PASS—FIRST SIGHT OF BEYROUT—OUR DRAGOMAN'S FAMILY—MRS. MOTT'S SCHOOLS, MOTHERS' MEETINGS, ETC.—PERSECUTION OF CHRISTIANS—INTERESTING SERVICE ON SUNDAY—NATIVE HAREEM—BRIDAL CUSTOMS—GENERAL DISLIKE OF THE TURKISH GOVERNMENT—FAREWELL TO SYRIA.

CHAPTER X.

ON Monday, April 19th, we left Damascus, amid profuse hand-shaking on the part of Madame Dimitri's Arab servants—willing, good-natured fellows they were, but terribly dirty withal, and miserably dressed.

Passing by the Merj—a grassy mead on the banks of the Barada which serves as a Hyde Park for the inhabitants of Damascus—we soon entered a gorge three or four miles long, of extraordinary fertility and great beauty. Red, bare, arid rocks rose up abruptly on all sides a thousand feet high. Fruit trees, forest trees, as well as flowering shrubs, in lavish profusion filled the narrow defile, and wafted sweet scents into the clear blue sky. Beneath us the Barada rushed along, roaring and eddying in its rocky bed, clear and sparkling. Some portion of the precious waters were diverted, and flowed in channels above the road, and it was easy to mark the boundary line of its refreshing influence.

The sister river, the Pharpar, we did not see. Under the modern name of Nahr-el-Awaj it flows between Jebel-el-Aswad and Jebel-Maniá, to the south-east of Damascus. It was described to us as being much the same sort of foaming torrent as the Barada.

Emerging from this exquisite defile, we toiled for a couple of weary hours through the Sahra desert, and then were rejoiced again to strike the gorge at a higher elevation.

At midday we reached Ain-Fijeh, the main source of the Barada. Here the beautiful blue stream bursts forth from under the great red rocky mountain in full-blown perfection, thirty feet wide and three or four feet deep. It forms a noble torrent of unspeakable loveliness, boiling, rushing, raving, and eddying amid groves of poplars, pomegranates, walnuts, orange, lemon, apricot, and peach-trees, rejoicing all nature in this thirsty land with its bounteous flow.

Immediately above the source of this river were the ruins of a massive temple, erected in old times to Baal. Here we rested for a while, and feasted our eyes on the beautiful view, with many thoughts of the past and the present. What scenes had been enacted here in bygone ages, when the cries of victims offered to Baal were muffled by the roaring of the new-born river! Now the place is perfect in its wild sylvan beauty.

The simple, harmless natives from a village near crowded around us with solemn curiosity, the women offering us for sale some of their silver armlets. We asked one woman, with a strikingly fine face, large dark eyes, and bare feet, what she would expect for her bracelet, and her reply was, "two napoleons." These women had also handsome nose and finger rings, as well as necklaces and ear-rings. The patterns of some of this native jewellery were exceedingly artistic. A peasant heiress carries her dower well in sight, and any admirer can easily calculate her material worth.

We camped at night at Suk-Wady-Barada, or Abila, the Scriptural Abilene, of which Lysanias was tetrarch. On a mountain near this village Abel is said to have been killed by Cain, and his tomb is pointed out.

Our tents were pitched under the lee of a rocky mountain side, two thousand seven hundred feet high, and seven hundred feet above Damascus, with the village just below us, imbedded in fruit-trees.

The next day's ride led us through romantic glens, at the bottom of which a branch of the Barada flows : now tumbling over massive rocks, now fertilizing green pastures, but always refreshing both to the ear and the eye, till we emerged into the plain of Zebedany.

High up on our right was perched the village of Bludan. The highest summit of Anti-Lebanon, seven thousand feet above the sea, rises up immediately behind it; vineyards cling to the steep sides of the mountain slopes, and little rills of water leap and murmur on their course to the rich plain below.

Bludan is the fashionable summer resort of the wealthy inhabitants of Damascus. When the heat of the town becomes overpowering they escape to this cool mountain village. It is the summer home of the English mission, the British Consul, and other Europeans, as well as of the natives.

In passing through Surghaya, a pretty village in a green valley some miles further on, I narrowly escaped a bad accident. We were quietly riding in single file through the little street of baked mud houses, and just as we reached the open plain my horse trod on a large, dead crane lying on the road, which I had not observed. The horse reared, and through the stirrup breaking I lost my seat and fell to the ground, but happily escaped with a few bruises. It seems to be the habit of the natives to leave dead animals unburied. Dead birds, cats, dogs, donkeys, horses, and camels may constantly be seen by the wayside, or lying in the fields. Happily dogs, vultures, and jackals act as scavengers, and usually leave nothing but the blanched bones to tell the tale of death.

We were able to make way rather rapidly across these high plains, as the ground was perfect for riding, and we reached our camp at Yahfufeh in good time.

Seven hours on horseback made us glad to lie down on the grassy common shut in by hills, and by the side of a mountain stream; here we enjoyed in delicious repose our well earned coffee.

The next day, April 21st, we climbed over wild

rocky mountains, and had a magnificent view of the snowy range of Lebanon, sixty miles long, the highest point being upwards of ten thousand feet high. The Cedars are about a thousand feet below this point, on the northern side. Owing to the quantity of snow which had recently fallen we were not able, much to our regret, to make an expedition to see these noble trees, about four hundred of which still remain.

It is impossible to describe the colouring of the Buka'a plain, and the two ranges of Lebanon and Anti-Lebanon, between which it lies. Grey rocks melted into purple; the red ground was cultivated in long brilliant streaks of cornfields, and various crops of differing shades; the pink tint on the lower spurs of the mountain deepened into rich browns, and gleamed under the glorious sunshine in an atmosphere which made every single feature and inflection of colour in the landscape stand forth with a vivid clearness unknown in our hazy climate. Syria would not be one half so captivating as it is, under a northern sky. In that latitude the heavens, both by day and by night, are a perpetual source of delight, and it is impossible not to say, in one's heart, "When I consider Thy heavens, the work of Thy fingers," the sun, "the moon and the stars which Thou hast ordained, what is man that Thou art mindful of him, and the son of man that Thou visitest him?"

For three hours we rode between these two great ranges, and then, winding round a shoulder of the mountain, we had our first sight of Baalbek. In the plain beneath us, on a knoll about a mile from the foot of the Anti-Lebanon range, the six beautiful columns of the Temple of Baal stood up erect, towering above massive walls, broken battlements, and ruined towers. A modern village of some hundred houses clustered on one side, through which a clear stream flowed. Graceful poplars reared themselves up amongst the ancient ruins, and the whole general effect was perfect. Even now Baalbek looks grand and splendid, and seems as though proudly asserting its right to rank as one of the noblest piles of buildings ever built up by the hand of man.

We rode under the gigantic walls, clattered over the ancient roadway, and entered by a long vault-like tunnel into the court of the Great Temple. On one side of the large area our tents were pitched amid massive *débris*, sculptured friezes, and broken columns. The ruins of the Temple of the Sun and the Great Temple were all around us, stupendous and wonderful.

We spent the afternoon for the most part in wandering about and trying to picture in our minds what these glorious temples had once been, and we soon became quite learned as to the different parts, the cella, the peristyle, the exedra, the stylobate, etc. We were never tired of admiring the exquisite carving of the entablatures, the graceful proportions of the temples, the richly ornamented friezes, with garlands of fruit and flowers, and the six beautiful columns of the peristyle standing in lonely grandeur, the last of their race, tottering gradually to their fall. These columns have in many cases been undermined by the natives in search of the metal clamps, which they extract and sell for a few piastres. Little respect, indeed, is paid to the ruins, for in the spirit of ignorant vandalism masses of the stone have been carried away for the building of new houses, or even for the making of roads.

The size of some of the stones employed is indeed gigantic. Three on the north and west sides of the Great Temple measure in length respectively sixty-four feet, sixty-three feet eight inches, and sixty-three feet. They are thirteen feet broad, and probably equally thick. From these stones the temple derived its name *Trilithon*. Six such blocks reared up on end would very nearly reach to the top of St. Paul's. How these enormous stones could be quarried, and raised to their present height— some twenty feet above the ground—is to this day a marvel unsolved. The old architects of bygone ages, whose very names have been obliterated from the pages of history, had giant minds and indomitable energy, and it is almost humbling to contrast the pigmy architecture of modern times with the grand proportions of these Old World buildings, rich in beautiful shape and workmanship, and of such stupendous size.

Fortunately for us the moon shone in all its glory on the night when we encamped at Baalbek. It brought out almost with the vividness of daylight the great court, four hundred feet from east to west, and the rich portal of the Temple of the Sun, with its sculptured borders, representing fruit, flowers, and little Cupids bearing bunches of grapes, crowned on the summit by an eagle (emblem of the sun) holding in his beak long, twisted garlands, the ends being held by flying genii. The six tall columns were well defined in the cold moonlight, flinging their long shadows right across the court, over piled-up ruins of broken sculptures, gems of carving and huge blocks of stone lying strewn about in all directions. It is impossible to convey even a faint idea of the solemnity and beauty of the scene, the brilliancy of the Syrian moonlight, the wonderful glory of the ruins, the silvery heights of Anti-Lebanon, and the perfect silence of those evening hours. Like fair Melrose, Baalbek to be seen in all its mysterious glory must be visited by the pale moonlight.

After most of us had retired to our tents, one of our party, who felt deeply the spirit of the place and scene, was anxious that Tannous (whose *repertoire* of English words was exceedingly limited) should share in the emotions which animated him.

"What a glorious place it is, Tannous!" he said.

Tannous placed himself in a sympathetic attitude and said, solemnly shaking his head,

"Baalbek!"

"What a brilliant and glorious moon lights up every corner of these noble ruins!" said our friend, raising his hand to the sky, and then describing a semicircle towards the earth.

Tannous followed the movement.

"Baalbek! The moon! The moon! Baalbek!"

"And think of the wonderful people who built these temples so many centuries ago!"

"Ah, ah," said Tannous, still more solemnly, "Baalbek!"

"And now it lies in ruin and decay, and desolation. What a lesson! What a strange picture of the vanity of all human greatness, is it not, Tannous?"

Tannous could only follow the tone of voice, and responded with deep emotion,

"Baalbek, Baalbek!"

He shook his head once more, and our moralising friend, finding that he could not extract any spontaneous or original thoughts from the mind of Tannous, was forced to content himself with feeding quietly on his own enthusiasm.

A visit next day to the temple of Venus in the village of Baalbek gave us the opportunity of seeing the interior of one of the native houses. It was a flat-roofed, mud-baked building, in which the fair custodian of the temple lived.

We made her understand by signs that we wanted to come inside it, and by the same universal language she intimated her willingness that we should do so. The floor was covered with matting; there were no tables or chairs, but one or two handsome inlaid cabinets, and plenty of china arranged on a high shelf all round the walls. A comfortable fire burnt in an open fire-place, and round it a few young people were gathered. A hole in the wall with a wooden-shutter served for the window.

I signed to her that we should be glad to see their sleeping arrangements, whereupon the good woman opened several cupboards in the wall, and drew out from thence a set of mattresses covered with scarlet, beautifully clean, and some coverlets. These she placed on the floor, and then acted the process of going to bed. She showed us her fresh-baked bread (for the Arabs bake daily), which looked like strips of badly washed flannel. It was thrown about carelessly, but was excellent eating, not unlike leathery oat-cake.

Altogether the interior of the house was far more comfortable than I should have expected from its external appearance.

On April 22nd, after spending the morning among the ruins of Baalbek, we rode along the rich Buka'a plain, which is absolutely treeless, into the mountains, and reached Zachleh in the evening. We saw the mirage very clearly several times as we rode along the valley. Sometimes a stream seemed to cross the road about a mile in front of us, and we began to wonder whether we should have to ford it. Then turning round in another direction a whole field would suddenly be transformed into a calm, still lake, and we had to look attentively to distinguish between the real and the unreal.

Zachleh is a beautifully situated town on the side of the hills, with a population of about twenty-five thousand Christians. They are for the most part Maronites—Roman Catholics. There are, however, a few Protestants, as there is a flourishing British Syrian School under Mrs. Mott's management. A Christian girl from this school, when she saw the English flag flying over our tents, came up to welcome us.

"Are you English?" she said, with a good accent. "Then I am glad!"

She remained for some time with us, though her knowledge of the English language was so limited that we could say but little to her.

Our camp was a very lovely one, pitched on a green plateau over an abrupt ravine, a torrent dividing us from the town of Zachleh. The spot is beautiful for situation, on a spur of Lebanon, mountains piled up high above it, and fir trees and cypress trees filling up the gorge beneath.

We could here see for ourselves the good effect of having a Christian Governor in the Lebanon. The place looked most thriving and well-to-do, and presented a great contrast to Mohammedan towns. Mohammedanism seems invariably to go hand in hand with misgovernment, and to bring a moral blight in its train wherever its power is felt.

This was to be our last night of camping out, and I think we were all grieving over the sad fact. We sat at the door of our tents, some of the ladies repairing the rents of the day, some writing their journals on their knees, which served as a table, some watching sadly, for the last time, Hani and the Arab cook huxtering with the sellers of eggs and chickens, and other dainties, outside the kitchen-tent, George cleaning the knives, Abdullah and Alraschid curry-combing the horses, the muleteers tethering their mules, and Tannous hanging the long Chinese lamps about the camp, lest perchance we might unwarily stumble over the tent-ropes. Tannous, the faithful, simple-hearted Syrian, was always good-natured, and ready to anticipate our smallest want. How often in the evening did we hear a call—

"Tannous."

"Yes, saar."

"Hot water, please."

"Vurry wull."

"Tannous."

"Yes, lady."

"Will you take my boots?"

"Vurry wull."

"Tannous."

"Yes, lady."

"Just light me across to the dining-tent."

"Vurry wull."

And the good-humoured fellow would carefully

walk in front, with his lamp close to the ground, so that you might avoid being entangled in the tent-ropes. There was something sad in the thought that these familiar sights and sounds would now be seen and heard no more. Yes— we had grown quite attached to our Arab retainers, and I am afraid that a certain Bohemianism had unconsciously crept over us all, and that the freedom of our wandering life had become very sweet and attractive. We had tasted the pleasures of nomad life, with all its romantic fascination, and now it had come to an end.

My niece, Miss Stanhope, and my daughter had bought presents at Damascus, which they distributed that evening amongst our faithful servants. Hani appeared the next day adorned in a gold silk kufiyeh, and with a Damascus sash round his waist over his European shooting coat. The others likewise were decorated with scarves or kufiyehs, and it must be confessed that our poor syces, Abdullah and Alraschid, looked most extraordinary in their dirty, ragged cotton trousers and over-shirts, with bare legs and feet, and lovely variegated striped kufiyehs bound over their heads. It was an ill-assorted match.

On this last evening I said a few words to Hani. As soon as I called, his tall figure appeared at the tent door.

"Yes, lady."

"We thank you very much for all your care of us. You have brought us the whole way in safety, without a single accident or *contre-temps* of any kind, and we owe you a great debt of gratitude."

Hani made a sign as though deprecating any necessity for thanks, and then raising his hand he said, solemnly,

"Lady, do not say that. It is not me; it is all God! Great mercy, lady, great mercy. Your service has done it" (alluding to our daily evening prayer). "I never made so good a journey before. Great mercy."

We intended to reach Beyrout the next day, but as it would be many hours' journey along a high road, and therefore somewhat tedious, arrangements were made that two carriages should meet us from Beyrout at a khan about ten or twelve miles from the town, half-way up the Lebanon pass.

It was a ride of five hours to this point along

the Damascus and Beyrout road, mounting upwards of five thousand feet over a spur of the Lebanon. Snow was lying about in patches, and from the top of the pass we had an exquisite panoramic view of Beyrout, the rich plains, and the blue sea beyond. The slopes of Lebanon were covered with villas and vineyards, and all manner of rich vegetation and verdure. The view was quite Italian.

As soon as ever Hani caught sight of Beyrout he waved his cap aloft and shouted out, enthusiastically,

"I see my home! my wife! my children! Ah! you shall know them all. My sons will come and meet us. You shall see!"

He was in a state of great excitement.

"That," pointing to the wild mountain slopes, "is where I come to shoot partridges in the autumn. There is Beyrout! Down there to the left of the town. That is my house. Ah! you shall see my little Josef; he is a droll! a *petit méchant!* a little Turk! But then, his mother spoils him. Oh yes, they all spoil him!"

"Except you, Hani."

"Lady, I do my best for my children. They are very good: you shall see."

Half way down the pass three tall young Syrians came running up the road towards us.

"Selim, Maron, Ayoob!" shouted Hani, and they fell on his neck and literally hugged him.

They brought us four beautiful large nosegays of roses and sweet-scented flowers, one for each lady, and we shook hands cordially all round.

Selim is a dragoman, like his father. He is much to be pitied, for, two years ago, a terrible accident befell him. He was acting as dragoman to some travellers, and on reaching Jerusalem the wind was so boisterous that he rather demurred to pitching the tents. The head of the party insisted that it should be done, and while he was trying to obey his orders a violent gust blew the tent down, and the tent-pole knocked him over, and frightfully crushed the upper part of his face. For weeks and months his life was in danger, but he gradually recovered, though he is hopelessly disfigured. He came with us afterwards as far as Constantinople, acting as valet to Mr. Heywood, and seemed thoroughly capable and trustworthy.

We lunched while the carriages were being got ready, and our repast was more sumptuous than usual, for Madame Hani had sent up from Beyrout some extra dainties for us by the hands of her sons.

It seemed strange and pleasant to be in a carriage once more, and the whole drive down the Lebanon to Beyrout, amid fig-trees, vines, mulberry and palm trees, cypresses and stone-pines, with lovely views of the blue sea and mountain slopes, was simply perfection. The air was mild and soft, the repose of the carriage after our tiring rides very delicious, and we had a feeling of satisfaction that our long journey was thus far safely accomplished, and a deep sense of gratitude that God's sheltering Hand had been so lovingly held over us.

As we drew near Beyrout, through a beautiful avenue of acacias in full, white blossom, several carriages filled with gaily-dressed ladies passed us, and there were evident signs that we had once more entered upon civilized regions.

The drive was a great deal too short, and we were quite sorry to reach the Oriental Hotel. We had pretty rooms looking over the blue Mediterranean, and the air felt deliciously warm. Beyrout had quite a European appearance, and we seemed already to have left Asia, and to be very near home.

Once more we were amongst sophisticated people, habited in cloth coats and tight dresses, and with half the romance of Oriental life gone. There is almost as great a difference between Eastern and Western life as there is between poetry and prose, chiefly, no doubt, because the grandest, noblest, and highest Life that was ever lived on earth throws a halo over this land, and weaves itself into every sight and sound, like the golden thread in a rich brocade, or the flood of light on a dull landscape. It pervades and glorifies the whole texture and aspect of a journey in the Holy Land, making beautiful the meanest and dreariest things, and exalting and ennobling every sense and feeling. We could thank God from our hearts that He had permitted us to tread in the footsteps of our Blessed Lord, and we longed that it might be a parable of deeper meaning influencing our daily life.

Mrs. Mott, who, as I have said before, takes the general management of the British Syrian Schools, lives at Beyrout, and, after morning service on Sunday, we went to her pleasant house on the hill, overlooking the town and sea. She herself was away in England, but her sisters,

Mrs. Henry Smith and Miss Lloyd, entertained us most hospitably, and gave us many interesting details respecting their philanthropic work.

My husband and Mr. Heywood went with the missionary to the Boys' Mission School, and also to a training institution, where there were about sixty young women under instruction for school teachers, and they thought them most intelligent and well educated.

Meanwhile I went with Mrs. Smith and Miss Lloyd to the girls' school, a large building erected by Mr. and Mrs. Mott just at the bottom of their garden. There were four rooms full of Eastern women (many of them with their little black-eyed babies in their arms), and native Christians were teaching them. Druses, Moslems, blacks, and Christians were in separate rooms, eagerly listening to the Scriptural Arabic lesson, singing hymns, repeating verses, and apparently very happy.

I spoke to them through an interpreter, and they unitedly sent a kind message to the members of my Mothers' Meeting at home, about which I told them. It was interesting to watch their excited eager faces, and their pleasure in hearing of their English sisters. Mrs. Smith said that they value these instruction classes so much that they come to them regularly through pouring rain, and, in some instances, from a considerable distance. They often times have to bear blows and cruel treatment from their Moslem husbands, who are enraged at them for attending these meetings.

On looking round over the motley crowd assembled in one of the rooms, there was a young white-veiled woman, who attracted my attention, and Mrs. Henry Smith told me her history. She had been cruelly persecuted. Having attended the classes, she much wished to become a Christian, but her mother, on discovering this, forced her to marry a bigoted Moslem, who, as she hoped, would forbid her daughter's attendance at Mrs. Mott's school. The young wife, however, was so good and gentle that the husband said he thought she learned no harm there, and that she might as well continue her visits. At this the mother was furious, and, by the most iniquitous means, brought about a divorce between the young couple.

Her next step (for daughters are mere puppets in their parents' hands, and have no voice in their matrimonial engagements) was to arrange a marriage between this divorced wife and a well-known aged Mohammedan fanatic. The agony of the young woman at being separated from a husband whom she loved, and the prospect of being married to an old man whom she looked upon with abhorrence, may be easily imagined. Fortunately, however, the old Moslem, after inquiring about his promised wife and finding out her Christian proclivities, declined to marry her. She was thus cast adrift by all her relations, so Mrs. Mott took her into her establishment, and she became one of the regular school-staff.

There was evening-service in the Presbyterian church, the only Protestant church, I am sorry to say, in Beyrout, and my husband, after reading our church prayers, addressed the converts. They sat in a large group, veiled in white, in one of the aisles. All those trained in Mrs. Mott's schools could understand English well, and thoroughly entered into the service and sermon. This was proved next day by their very intelligent answers to me concerning all that my husband had said to them the night before.

One afternoon, whilst we were at Beyrout, Hani gave us an entertainment in his house. It was quite patriarchal to see the tall, grey-haired, vigorous old man, and the round-figured, kindly mother, with their seven sons and four daughters. A goodly company they were: the eldest twenty-nine, the youngest two and a half years old. They stood up in a long row, Selim, Maron, Ayoob, Alexandre, Foudoulalla, Bechara, Hanné, Rosa, Régina, Maria, and little Josef. George was there too, and his sisters, and other relations.

They regaled us with coffee and sweet cakes, Turkish delight and other bon-bons, and Hani did the honours by showing us all over his house.

In the sitting-room, seeing only carpets, and no chairs, I asked,

"How do you all sit for dinner, you and Madame, and the children?"

"We will soon show you," said Hani, and immediately spread an imaginary table-cloth upon the floor, and sat round it with his wife and all the others, cross-legged.

In the house of a relation, to which he afterwards took us, they gave us, besides the usual coffee, orange-blossoms steeped in crystallized sugar. These are considered a great delicacy, and must

x

be eaten when freshly made. They have a deliciously scented taste.

Whilst we were at Beyrout I went with Mrs. Henry Smith and Massaba, the native hareem visitor, to Achmed Bey's hareem. We were fortunate in paying our visit just at the time that a fête was going on in connection with some religious service.

Madame Achmed, with a little infant in her arms, received us in a prettily-furnished room, set round with divans. All the women were decked out in bright-coloured dresses, and had artificial flowers in their hair. She herself looked very gentle and ladylike, and her manner was singularly attractive. She greeted us kindly, and the attendants brought glasses of rose-water, flavoured with orange-blossom, which was delicious, and the inevitable coffee in tiny cups. Several ladies and their children were of the party, and I found that it is the custom for rich families to invite their poorer friends, and give the feast for them in connection with religious festivals, thus saving them expense.

Madame Achmed, fortunately for me, talked French, and I found her very pleasant. She introduced me to her mother, saying fondly,

"What should I do without her when I am ill?"

She told me that she had seven sons, and she wept over the death of her only daughter, which did not look as if the common Syrian saying was always true:

"When a girl is born, the house goes into mourning for a fortnight."

The baby's cradle was quite lovely, carved in sandal-wood, lined with blue satin, and covered over with a lace veil.

From Madame Achmed's house Mrs. Smith took me again to see Mrs. Mott's schools. They seem to be most admirably conducted, and the children sang, recited, and answered questions with great intelligence and vivacity. In one part of the school-buildings blind girls are taught.

Massaba, seeing that I was interested in native habits and customs, asked me if I should like to come with her to visit a Mohammedan bride. I gladly assented, and we went to the house of Herisé Effendi. His son, aged twenty, had just been married to a pretty young bride of fifteen years old.

The marriage had been brought about as follows. Herisé Effendi happened to be paying a visit at a friend's house " twenty hours away," and had seen amongst his host's daughters a little girl who found great favour in his eyes. He immediately selected her as a wife for his son, and she had been married the Thursday before, having never even seen her husband until she came to Beyrout. There were altogether fourteen ladies in this hareem, mothers, daughters, and daughters-in-law, besides slave girls.

The young husband, with his brother and several sisters, received us. Both the bridegroom and his brother could speak French. The latter gave me his opinion very openly with regard to the way in which women are treated in the East.

"I wish," he said, "that they could be properly educated, and mix freely with their fellow-creatures as you do. Ours is a horrid system, and I detest it."

"Then," I said, "why do you not try to revolutionise it, and reform your customs?"

"Ah! Madame, you do not know the strength of fanaticism, or how Mohammedans dread Christian habits. Ah, it is terrible! We can do nothing. My compatriots are stupid and blind, they will not change."

We were then introduced to the little bride of fifteen, who during this interval had put on her bridal dress. She came in and stood in the middle of the room, gorgeously arrayed in her husband's gifts. Her dress was of crimson satin, heavily embroidered with gold; diamonds covered her head, neck, and bodice, and she had lovely flowers in her hair. Her eyelids and eyebrows were painted black, and her face shone with otto of roses, which fell in little drops on her neck.

Massaba told me that on her wedding-day she saw her sitting for hours in this splendid costume, with her eyes shut, according to the custom of the country, while all her friends and relations came to gaze upon her, the bride not being allowed to speak during the whole time. They offered us coffee, and, after mutual salutations, we left the house.

I cannot help hoping that this desire on the part of the more enlightened Mohammedans to educate the women, and allow them greater freedom of intercourse with the world at large, is becoming very general. At present their lives are utterly dreary, useless, childish, and inane, and it is fervently to be desired that a brighter and happier era may before long dawn upon them. There seems, too, on all sides a general detestation of the Turkish government. My husband had an interesting conversation with a Syrian shopkeeper, who spoke to him very openly with reference to politics, and expressed his opinion that the Turkish Government was so grossly corrupt and unjust that it could not last much longer. Bribery, dishonesty, and misrule, according to his account, paralysed everything. He said that the Syrians were heartily glad that the English were in occupation of Cyprus, and wished they had come on a little further. They felt that the presence of English troops even at Cyprus was to a certain extent a protection to life and property in their country. He evidently studied English papers, and was the first to give my husband the news of Mr. Gladstone being Prime Minister.

April 27th—the day on which it was arranged that we should leave Beyrout by the Austrian Lloyd Steamer *Hunyaria,* arrived only too soon. Our Arab retainers came to bid us good-bye.

They had hovered about our hotel perpetually during our stay to catch a sight of us, and always, when they met us in the streets, recognised us with delighted smiles. We were quite sorry to part from them, and when we gave them a farewell present of "backsheesh" they kissed our hands and placed them on their foreheads, wishing us long life and happiness.

The faithful Tannous was very miserable.

"Ah! I vis ve vus now at Jaffa," he said, "in de campment. You vull come again, von't you?" and tears filled his eyes.

Hani and three of his sons came in our small boat to the steamer to see us off, lading us with nosegays of beautiful flowers. Our parting with Hani was quite affectionate. He had been most faithful and attentive, and we looked upon him as a real friend. But at length the anchor was weighed, we said our last, long farewell to Syrian shores, and steamed away on a lovely evening from this wonderful land, which had been to us a country of deep emotions, sacred memories, graciousness, sunshine, and flowers!

CHAPTER XI.

WESTWARD HO!

CYPRUS: IMPROVED BY ENGLISH OCCUPATION—THIRD-CLASS PASSENGERS ON "THE HUNGARIA"—BEAUTY OF RHODES—A DAY AT SMYRNA—SUNDAY AT SYRA—GREEK EASTER—ARRIVAL AT ATHENS—MARS' HILL—THE PARTHENON—RESTORATION OF THE ELGIN MARBLES—FUNERAL PROCESSION—THROUGH THE DARDANELLES TO CONSTANTINOPLE—LOVELY VIEW OF THE CITY—THE SULTAN AT HIS DEVOTIONS—ASSEMBLAGE OF FASHIONABLES AT "THE SWEET WATERS"—THE MOSQUE OF ST. SOPHIA—CEMETERY AT SCUTARI WELL KEPT—MAGNIFICENCE OF THE DOLMA-BATCHI PALACE—WE LEAVE CONSTANTINOPLE FOR VARNA—ASPECT OF THE BULGARIANS—FROM RUSTCHUK TO BUCHAREST—WE REACH VIENNA VIA BUDA-PESTH—ARRIVAL IN ENGLAND.

CHAPTER XI.

ON the 28th of April we anchored off Cyprus, at about ten o'clock in the morning, after a run of thirteen hours.

Larnaca looked very inviting in the gay sunshine, with the mountain of Olympus rising five thousand feet in the background; and we quickly chartered a little boat and landed on the island, which had once been the home of Barnabas, and which was consecrated by the footsteps of St. Paul.

The town is much improved by English occupation. The once dirty and uneven streets have been fairly paved, and a neat quay has been made. We met an English officer who was drilling Cypriote recruits in motley costumes. He spoke well of the climate, which, after two years' residence at Larnaca, he declared to be extremely healthy.

We learned that the inhabitants of Cyprus wish very much that the English would take lasting possession of the island; for the uncertainty which exists in their minds as to the nature of the English tenure of the place completely paralyses enterprise. The news of Mr. Gladstone's appointment as Prime Minister had reached the island, and anxious fears were expressed as to what his intentions might be respecting it. The Greek inhabitants hailed his appointment with enthusiasm, as far as their own country was concerned, though they were anxious with regard to their future in Cyprus if it should be again handed over to Turkish rule.

The island is very fertile, and, in good hands, seems to be capable of a great future. At the present moment there are no carriage roads, and all locomotion is carried on on foot, or on horseback.

We were all anxious to see Nicosia, but it is fifteen miles distant, and our stay at Cyprus was not long enough to admit of our going there; so we were obliged to content ourselves with a walk under a burning sun, round the town and along the seashore. It was very curious, in the town, to see the mixture of Greek and English: "Picrides" Street led into "Wolseley" Street, and the first shop in "The Strand" was a "Pantopoleion."

We had brought a letter of introduction to Mr. Watkins, the manager of the branch of the Ottoman bank at Larnaca. He and his charming wife received us most kindly, and we were much interested in seeing his excellent collection of antiquities excavated in the island. He was good enough to give us some ancient glass tear-bottles as souvenirs of the place. Our visit was necessarily very hurried, yet we were glad even to have had this glimpse of Cyprus.

Life on board the *Hungaria* was pleasant enough. The sea was calm, our fellow-passengers agreeable, and the weather perfect. At night we left a trail of gleaming starry lights on the sea, from myriads of phosphorescent animalculæ. Unfortunately for us, the cargo included about one hundred and twenty Eastern third-class passengers, who lay about the deck in every direction, smoking, eating, and sleeping, and looking very hot and dirty. They seemed to have brought all their worldly possessions with them, including mattresses, bundles of clothes, and cooking apparatus, for they provide their own food, and cook it in little braziers, much to the jeopardy of their lives and the risk of the vessel. Sometimes they set fire to their bedding and chattels, which are then instantly and remorselessly thrown overboard. A piteous scene follows of wild despair and furious indignation, but there the matter ends.

The passage from Cyprus to Rhodes, our next station, takes about thirty-eight hours, and it was half-past three o'clock in the early morning of the last day of April that we first saw Rhodes by moonlight, and then watched the rising sun as, with a glow of light, it flushed the ancient towers and walls of the fortifications built by the Knights of St. John. Rhodes, following as it does the curves of the bay, looks very well from the sea. The harbour (across which, according to the old fable, the Colossus stood), and the modern town, adorned with minarets, interspersed with palm-trees and orange-groves, and with luxuriant hillsides rising up in the background, made altogether a charming picture.

We stopped for about an hour and a half at

Rhodes, and then, steaming on through the Archipelago, rounded Cnidus, and passed Halicarnassus, Cos, Samos, Patmos, Trogyllium, and many other islands, some wild and rocky, bare and uninhabited, others with soft green shores, and villages embedded in groves down to the water's edge. In and out our course lay, round points, through narrow channels, and among an endless variety of bays and rocky promontories, with vistas of islands upon islands, all set in a calm, lake-like sea of the most wondrous blue, and bathed in floods of golden sunshine:

> "The Isles of Greece—the Isles of Greece,
> Where burning Sappho loved and sung,
> Where grew the arts of war and peace,
> Where Delos rose and Phœbus sprung,
> Eternal summer gilds them yet,
> But all except their sun is set."

Patmos, which we saw in the distance, looked like a long broken ridge of hills. Samos is an independent island, governed by a Prince of its own, and with a separate flag—a white Greek cross on a blue ground. For the luxury of self-government it has to pay a subsidy of £20,000 a year to the Turkish Government.

Darkness came on as we caught the first glimpse of Scio (Chios), and at about ten o'clock on Saturday morning, May 1st, we steamed into Smyrna. Smyrna, the second largest town in the Turkish dominions, one of the Seven Churches, and the home of Polycarp, is beautifully situated at the head of the bay.

We intended to have made an expedition to Ephesus, as the steamer usually remains long enough to enable passengers to charter a special train there and back. Unfortunately the *Hungaria* had been delayed before reaching Beyrout, and we were therefore much behind our time. We could only stop at Smyrna for about four hours, and were obliged to content ourselves with a ramble over the town, and through the bazaars. There is here, as at Cairo, a strange juxtaposition of Eastern and European life. At one moment you meet a string of enormously large camels, the next moment you come upon a tramway, and shortly afterwards pass railway trucks on the quay.

The environs of Smyrna are said to be unsafe for defenceless travellers. We passed in the streets innumerable white lambs, painted with gay colours, and ready to be sacrificed at nightfall, according to custom, on the eve of the Greek Easter Day. There are a great number of Greek Christians in Smyrna.

At two o'clock in the afternoon, on May 1st, we left Smyrna in the *Delphino*, a much smaller boat than the *Hungaria* (which was going on straight to Constantinople), and reached Syra about half-past ten o'clock on Sunday morning, May 2nd.

It is a wonderfully picturesque town, built on three sugar-loaf shaped hills. The houses are all white, with green and yellow jalousies, reaching down, in closely-packed terraces, to the water's edge. The whole place was *en fête*, for it was Easter Day, and the vessels in harbour were gaily decked out with flags. We were distracted with the incessant firing of pistols, pétards, guns, crackers, and squibs. It seemed to be the object of every man and boy in the place to let off something which would make a noise, and at midday the great guns from the fort were fired, and by their booming drowned the lesser artillery.

After our own service on board we went on shore to the cathedral, which was almost filled with children carrying long, lighted tapers, to the imminent danger of their own and their neighbours' clothes. All, as they came into the cathedral, crossed themselves and kissed a picture of the Resurrection. There was a sort of enclosure at the east end, within which three or four priests chanted a service, and, by-and-by, a procession went round the church, the priest incensing the people. The service was not, as it seemed to me, either devotional or one that appealed to the senses. No instrument of music was used, and the singing was very poor.

As we returned my husband thought he would try how far his knowledge of ancient Greek would enable him to hold communication with a modern-speaking native. Remembering the visit of the Archbishop of Syra to England a few years ago he accosted an intelligent-looking man with the words,

Ποῦ ἐστιν ὁ οἶκος τοῦ Ἀρχιεπίσκοπου;

A blank look of astonishment was all the answer vouchsafed. No doubt the English pronunciation was perplexing, but an Athenian told him in the evening that colloquial Greek is so different from the ancient language that his question would hardly be understood by anyone now-a-days who had not studied the classics.

In the evening the town was illuminated, and looked lovely. We left Syra about eight o'clock, p.m., and, steaming past "Sunium's marbled steep," at half-past five o'clock in the morning of May the 3rd disembarked at the Piræus. Half an hour's drive along a straight, dusty road brought us to Athens.

It would be an impertinence in me if I were to attempt to describe too minutely what, in these days of travel, is so familiarly known. Suffice it to say that it was with a deep thrill of excitement and delight that we looked for the first time on the Acropolis rising up, rugged and grand, above the city, crowned with ruined temples, standing out against the clear morning sky in the perfection of beauty.

Athens! What a rush of memories for the classical scholar and the Christian! What a galaxy of great and noble names are linked with the thought of this city of art, poetry, and philosophy! And yet the eye of St. Paul pierced through all this earthly glamour, and his spirit was stirred within him, not because he was approaching "the eye of Greece," the "Mother of arts and eloquence," the home of intellect, genius, and human greatness, and the centre of civilization, but because with a saddened heart he saw the city wholly given to idolatry: it was of the earth, earthy; and as his Master wept over Jerusalem, so he mourned over the moral degradation and civilized heathenism of Athens.

We stood on Mars' hill, upon the very spot on which St. Paul had stood. It is a rocky eminence, just below the Acropolis, which rises about one hundred feet above it. Steps are cut in the rock leading up to this point, and there is a space immediately below, upon which, upwards of eighteen hundred years ago, the men of Athens, who loved to hear some new thing, were gathered together listening spell-bound, and with rapt attention, to the burning words of a humble foreigner, as he opened out to their wondering minds a new revelation of the unknown God Whom they ignorantly worshipped, of the Resurrection, and the Great Judgment to come.

From Mars' Hill we climbed up to the Acropolis, five hundred feet above the town, past the little Temple of Victory, commemorating the Battle of Marathon, and so through the Propylæum to the Parthenon. The Parthenon seemed to me to be faultlessly beautiful—pure Doric in style, and absolutely lovely, but the frieze of

Phidias is so high up that it is very difficult to see it satisfactorily.

The view from the Parthenon is quite enchanting. You look down upon the Athenian plain, rich in grey-green olive-groves and gardens, stretching out to the Piræus and Phalerum, the deep blue gulf of Ægina, Salamis, and the ranges of Pentelicus and Hymettus, with the nearer rocky heights of Lycabettus. Athens lay just beneath the abrupt precipice, with streets of glaring white houses, interspersed with old ruins, which peeped out here and there as though to record a silent protest against modern architectural taste. There were the little streams of Ilissus and Cephissus, the Arch of Hadrian, the Temple of Jupiter, with its fifteen Corinthian columns, Mars' Hill, the Stadium, where fifty thousand Athenians, in ancient times, could sit round to witness the chariot-races, the Bema, or platform, from whence Demosthenes enthralled and ravished the ears of his countrymen by his brilliant eloquence, and the Agora, where St. Paul disputed daily,—it was a perfect feast to the eye and mind, and it was easy by day-dreaming to re-people the beautiful old ruins, and to imagine the worldly grandeur of the ancient

Athenians in those days, when the chariots drove up through the marble columns of the Propylæa, and worshippers crowded into the Erectheum and the Parthenon in their long robes, amidst all the brilliancy of a splendid though corrupt ritual; and then we turned in thought to another scene when St. Paul gathered together a little band of Christian followers from out of the uncongenial idolatrous crowd, "among the which was Dionysius the Areopagite, and a woman named Damaris, and others with them."

Having just seen Baalbek, we could not fail to make a comparison between these two great relics of antiquity. The Temple of the Sun is richer and more splendid, and the whole mass of ruined temples and walls at Baalbek are on a grander scale than those at Athens. They have more of mystery hanging over them, and out of the far distant past so little can be gathered with certainty of the Phœnician builders of those huge, majestic old ruins standing in such stately solitude in the great Buka'a plain, and guarded by the long ranges of Lebanon and Anti-Lebanon, that their history will always, to a certain extent, remain veiled and sealed.

The Parthenon and the adjoining temples

seemed dwarfed by comparison with the great Syrian ruins, but, if Baalbek has size and breadth, nobleness and magnificence, the Parthenon has purity of style, absolute perfection of symmetry, and an unrivalled beauty of situation. "The finest ruin on the finest site in the world," is a description which I have somewhere read of the Parthenon. It was impossible not to feel a pang of regret that so much which constituted, in old times, the glory and beauty of the Parthenon has been removed from its natural home. The Elgin marbles, which, since the beginning of the present century, have been preserved in England, may testify, in the British Museum, to the liberality of the Turkish Government in generously parting with treasures of a subject nation, and possibly their existence at the present day may be due to the safety of the asylum in which they found refuge. But their restoration to their lawful owners would not, in these days, imperil their safety, and would surely be a graceful act, and one which would be appreciated to the full extent by the Greek nation. I honestly confess that it was with a feeling akin to shame that I saw the plundered and despoiled state of those glorious monuments of antiquity. No wonder that Lord Byron's indignation was aroused.

> "What! Shall it e'er be said by British tongue
> Albion was happy in Athena's tears?
> Though in thy name the slaves her bosom wrung,
> Tell not the deed to blushing Europe's ears;
> The Ocean Queen, the free Britannia, bears
> The last poor plunder from a bleeding land:
> Yes, she, whose generous aid her name endears,
> Tore down those remnants with a harpy's hand,
> Which envious Eld forbore, and tyrants left to stand.
>
> . . . .
>
> Cold is the heart, fair Greece! that looks on thee,
> Nor feels as lovers o'er the dust they loved;
> Dull is the eye that will not weep to see
> Thy walls defaced, thy mouldering shrines removed
> By British hands, which it had best behoved
> To guard those relics ne'er to be restored.
> Curst be the hour when from their isle they roved,
> And once again thy hapless bosom gored,
> And snatch'd thy shrinking gods to northern climes abhorr'd!"*

As we returned to our hotel the funeral procession of an aged professor of the college passed us. The body was laid on a bier, clothed in Academic robes; the fine, oval, pale face was exposed to view, with grey hair streaming over the pillow, and the hands in grey kid-gloves. There were Greek priests with candles and crucifixes in front, black-robed women, a military band, and large numbers of friends following behind. It was a

---

* *Childe Harold*—Canto ii. xiii. xv.

painful sight, but we were told that funerals are always conducted thus in Athens.

We felt a strange blank in having lost all traces of Orientalism: the flowing drapery, the veiled women, the camels, the dogs, the latticed-windows, the mosques, minarets, and palm-trees. Athens looked very prosaic and matter-of-fact with its modern white houses. It rather reminded us of Brussels, except when we remarked the shopkeepers' name and business painted in Greek letters over the doors, and saw the men walking about in very full, short white petticoats, elaborately embroidered waistcoats, and Greek caps, and the women in their pretty and becoming national dress.

The pepper trees, which have been planted in avenues in all directions, have died from the frost of the winter of 1879, and look as if a scathing fire had passed over them.

We were all sorry that, owing to the inexorable time-table of the steamers, we were obliged, after a couple of days, to leave Athens. Once more we were most fortunate in our weather, and had a beautiful and enjoyable voyage over a calm sea, with moonlit nights and sunny days, viâ Syra, to Constantinople; leaving Athens Tuesday evening, May 5th, and reaching Constantinople early in the morning of Friday, May 8th. We anchored for some seventeen hours at Syra, which was again *en fête*, and brilliantly illuminated at nightfall in honour of King George's "name-day."

We then steamed past Tenos, Mitylene, and other islands to Besika bay, on the threshold of the Dardanelles, from whence we looked over the plains of Troy. Leaving Tenedos on our left, we soon reached the straits, and, having sent a boat on shore to obtain permission to go through, we entered their narrow waters. Towards evening we passed Gallipoli, and various places well known in connection with the late Russian campaign. In the sea of Marmora we were constantly amused with watching the shoals of porpoises rolling and tumbling about in every direction.

The Turkish governor of Janina was on board, returning to Constantinople, with his secretaries, his wife, his sons, and his daughters, and a rabble of rough retainers. He was a gentlemanly and dignified-looking man, and consorted with the rest of the passengers at meal times, but the ladies were hidden away in the cabins, and only ventured to appear, closely veiled, in a retired corner of the deck, whilst dinner was going on downstairs.

We were up at five o'clock on the 7th of May to watch the sun rise over Constantinople. It was very beautiful to see the lovely confusion of glittering minarets and domes, dark cypress trees, hills covered with palaces, long reaches of the sea blue as azure running up into the Bosphorus and Golden Horn, steamers and vessels of all nations, caïques skimming hither and thither, and thousands of silver-winged sea-gulls, successively lit up by the soft rays of the rising sun, and our first sight of Constantinople was quite enchanting.

We disembarked at Galata, and walked up the steep streets to Missiri's Hotel.

It happened to be Friday, the Moslem Sabbath, on which we arrived at Constantinople, and our *valet de place* told us that on Friday afternoons the Sultan Ahmed always comes to worship in a mosque just outside the palace gates. This is *de rigueur*, and it is the only time when he can be seen by the people, for he never otherwise leaves the precincts of his palace grounds.

We therefore ordered a carriage, and drove to the little mosque below the Yildis gardens to see the Sultan. Here we took up our post, with many others, near the great gates, in the midst of a closely-packed, surging crowd of Arabs, Turks, Albanians, Egyptians, Europeans, Nubians, and many other nationalities. We were tightly hemmed in. Water-sellers, with earthenware jars on their backs, cried out, "Bous! bous!"—"Water! water!" while sellers of refreshing sweet drinks, of rice and milk, sweetmeats, Turkish delight, and pistachio nuts, were struggling painfully through the densely-packed multitude. Occasionally a tram-carriage driving along added to the confusion, and the excitement culminated when a hawker of coffee, armed with an array of cups and saucers, was kicked by two loose horses, and his whole paraphernalia fell to the ground, was smashed to pieces, and trodden under foot. The poor fellow, giving a look of anguish at his broken property, walked off, saying, "It is Allah."

Soon a large body of soldiers marched up to form guard outside the gates. The soldiers in Constantinople are better dressed and look a great deal smarter than those in the provinces. Bands played, carriages of Ministers and Court grandees drove up, and at last the great gates of the palace were thrown open, and the Sultan appeared, dressed in uniform, riding a handsome white horse, surrounded by aides-de-camp and ministers on foot, and two men walking in front of him perfuming the air with pastilles in silver bowls. The troops presented arms and shouted "Long live the Sultan." He is a good-looking man, about five and thirty years old, but strangely and unnaturally pale, as we saw him that day. We heard many stories as to conspiracies and mock conspiracies. Sultan Ahmed is said to be fairly clever and able, but he lends too ready an ear to the opponents of reform, and he is surrounded by flatterers, who conceal the truth from him. He is very nervous, and does not live, as the late Sultan did, in the Dolma Batchi Palace, close to the Bosphorus, but in a palace called Yildis Kiosk, on a hill outside the town, the grounds of which are surrounded on all sides with high walls.

In the afternoon we drove to "the Sweet Waters," a sort of promenade about four miles off, by the side of the river which flows into the Golden Horn. It would have been better if we had taken a caïque and rowed thither instead, but this we did not discover till afterwards. All the *beau monde* of Constantinople were congregated at the Sweet Waters. Innumerable carriages were there, filled with the hareem ladies, some of whom, leaving their broughams, walked about, or sat by the river-side, enveloped in bright-coloured silk izars, pink, yellow, or blue, and white muslin yashmaks, only showing their large dark painted eyes. There they sat in groups for hours, smoking, gossiping, and watching the gay caïques darting hither and thither, listening to singers and musicians, and eating sweetmeats.

It is very tempting to speak of the various sights which we saw in Constantinople, the museum of the Janissaries, with life-sized lay figures clothed in all the ancient costumes of bygone days, the thousand and one pillars of the old cistern of Basilius, the bazaars, the Sublime Porte—a gateway leading to the Government offices, and hence giving the title to the Government—the magnificent panoramic views of Constantinople from the hills above Scutari, the ancient walls, the many fountains, mosques, and palaces, and the glorious views of the Golden Horn, but I forbear. I must, however, say a few words about the mosque of St. Sophia, the cemetery at Scutari, and the Dolma Batchi Palace.

The mosque of St. Sophia was once a Christian church, but has been cruelly treated by the Turks; it has four minarets, endless domes,—the central one being said to be a little higher than St. Paul's,—marble columns of red porphyry from Baalbek, and others from the temple of Diana at Ephesus, and beautiful mosaics. The proportions of the whole building are exquisite, but all signs of Christianity have been rudely torn down or painted over, and every Christian emblem obliterated; the bronze from the doors has even been sold by the Turkish authorities. The outlines of crosses can, however, still be discerned under the colour used to paint them out. The whole floor of the vast area is carpeted, the pattern forming a succession of oblong spaces, each fitted for one worshipper. But as the building is Oriented, and the Mohammedan when praying must kneel towards Mecca, all the pattern is necessarily awry, which greatly spoils the general effect of the whole building. We were fortunate enough to be in the mosque at twelve o'clock, when the

Mohammedans were summoned to prayer. We went up into a gallery above, and were allowed to remain during this service. Some two hundred men stood shoulder to shoulder in military precision, bowing, prostrating themselves, and extending their hands towards Mecca, whilst one of them read the Koran at intervals and chanted out " Allah is great."

In the cemetery at Scutari we spent a quiet and deeply interesting hour. There could hardly be found a more lovely resting-place for our noble dead. It is a beautiful garden, with myrtles and camellias, Judas-trees and magnolias, growing luxuriantly. There are beds of bright-coloured flowers, and the turf is kept as in an English garden. The custodian, an old English Crimean soldier, thoroughly does his duty by the whole place; it slopes down to a low cliff straight above the water, with a lovely view of Constantinople, the Bosphorus, and the sea of Marmora. A stone obelisk is erected in the grounds, and on its massive base four guardian angels stand with folded wings and palms in their hands, looking down solemnly upon the quiet dead. A slab on each side records respectively in English, French,

Turkish, and Italian as follows: "In memory of the officers and men of the British army and navy, who, in the war against Russia in 1854, 1855, and 1856, died for their country, this monument was raised by Queen Victoria and her people in 1857."

There are large mounds over graves containing twenty or thirty bodies, and, near the cliff, marble crosses and memorial stones, with touching and beautiful inscriptions, mark the spot where the officers were buried. It was unspeakably pathetic to wander over this sacred ground and read the names and histories, and in some cases the words of blessed hope which cheered the dying hours of those brave heroic men, and shed a stream of light over their early deaths. We longed to tell their dear ones at home how beautifully they rest in God's acre, reverently guarded from all profane or common intrusion, in sure and certain hope of the resurrection to eternal life through our Lord Jesus Christ.

The Memorial Church in Pera was also built in memory of those who fell in the Crimean War. It is a handsome building, and the services there on Sunday were a great pleasure to us in this Mohammedan land.

Through the kindness of a friend at Court we had a special permit from the Sultan to see the magnificent palace of Dolma Batchi, a modern building erected by the late Sultan Abdul Aziz, overlooking the Bosphorus. The throne-room, one hundred and fifty feet broad, by one hundred and eighty feet long, lofty in proportion, and gorgeously decorated, is a magnificent hall. The Sultan had most courteously sent one of his aides-de-camp to lionize us, and a royal caïque was in readiness to take us to the Beyler Bey Palace on the opposite side of the Bosphorus, but we could not avail ourselves of his offer, for we were obliged to leave Constantinople that same afternoon, and our plans were Medo-Persian.

It was very well that we did not cross the Bosphorus, for we could only just get back to our hotel in time to make all necessary settlements before starting on the *Argo* for Varna. Bidding farewell to Constantinople and all its beauty, we steamed up the Bosphorus, past Therapia, between sloping hill-sides covered with palaces, houses, and villages, embedded in groves of cypress and pine trees, and the loveliest soft green of early spring. Great brown swallows were skimming close to the water in countless numbers, never resting in their ceaseless gyrations. Superstitious sailors believe them to represent the unquiet souls of dragomans.

The wind blew keen and cold, and the Black Sea was shrouded in fog as we crossed its gloomy waters. We reached Varna early in the morning, and I am indeed thankful that my lot in life is not cast there, for it is the most dismal place imaginable, built on flat, marshy, aguish ground, close to a large inland lake. We thought of old Crimean days, when English ships rode at anchor in the bay, and so many of our brave soldiers died of wounds and cholera in this unwholesome and fever-producing camping-ground.

There was a primitive station and still more primitive buffet at Varna. We laid violent hands on the simple fare carelessly set out in a wooden shanty, and which seemed to have no special owner. Happily, however, as soon as we had packed up our luncheon, an ostensible proprietor appeared on the scene.

The railway route from Varna took us right through Bulgaria. The country is still in a very unsettled state, and brigandage is said to be rife.

We heard that, not long before we were there, the guard and driver of the mail-cart from Rustchuk to Sofia had been murdered, and valuables stolen from the mail-bags. The Bulgarians whom we chanced to see looked peaceable and quiet, and were roughly clad in sheepskin coats turned inside out and embroidered, and with sheepskin hats dyed black. The women wear white upper and red under garments, which is rather picturesque. We passed Rasgrad, near one of the battle-fields of the Russo-Turkish War. Many of the villages on the road looked as though they had been recently rebuilt, and some were still in ruins.

Near Rustchuk we crossed the broad waters of the Danube in a little steamer, and landed at Giorgevo, in Roumania, on a broad plateau of ground, which, owing to recent rains, was converted into a lake of deep mud, into which our luggage was recklessly thrown for examination by the Roumanian douane.

The one train of the day for Bucharest was due to leave shortly, and it required almost superhuman efforts on the part of the gentlemen to pass our luggage through the custom-house, and transport it to the station, which was a couple of miles off. The carriages which conveyed us and our luggage were of the most primitive description, and quite in keeping with the roads, and the drivers looked as if they were capable of committing any enormity. We were not sorry to find ourselves, after a couple of hours, at Bucharest, where we stayed the night.

Bucharest, since the Turks have given up the country, has made vast strides in civilisation. It has now the aspect of a little Paris, with clean, well-paved streets, well-built houses, and boulevards. Our hotel was very comfortable, but frightfully exorbitant in its charges.

May the 13th, old May day, seemed to be celebrated by the Roumanians with an outburst of floral decoration. The station-houses along the line of railway, and even the engines, were adorned with flowers; and men, women, and children wore bunches of lilies of the valley. The gala costumes were gay and pretty, but, truth to tell, the appearance of these people contrasted badly with that of the graceful and handsome Orientals amongst whom we had been living, and Europe seemed tame and unpicturesque after the East.

We made a rapid journey across Roumania and Hungary to Buda-Pesth, and thence to Vienna. My husband had duties which recalled him to England immediately, and, as we were anxious to be at home again after our long absence, we parted sorrowfully and regretfully from our fellow-travellers at Vienna, and finished our journey alone.

Exactly three months after leaving home we found ourselves once more in Old England, and our "Holiday in the East" was over. But those three months had been so full of deep and absorbing interest, heightened and cheered by the society of our delightful companions, and crowned with such continual mercies, that they will ever be registered as red letter days in the history of our lives.

Sursum Corda.

APPENDIX.

WE have so often been asked about our outfit that it may be well to say that we found the "Lady Baker" helmets of white felt with patent air-chambers, and thick linen curtains, absolutely essential. Ours were bought at Ludlow's, No. 1, Pall Mall, London. Our riding-habits and dresses were of light woollen material. Ulsters, rugs, water-proofs, and India-rubber baths folding up into small flat cases (to be got at Carter's, 295, Oxford Street) are indispensable. Mule-trunks and Gladstone bags, with two locks, which are very convenient, we purchased at Sellers', 64, Strand, and they were well and strongly made. It is not necessary to take tea, or biscuits, or anything edible, for if you engage the services of a clever dragoman, he provides everything you can possibly want. Quinine and a few ordinary medicines should be taken. It may be well to give the address of our dragoman:

MICHEL-EL-HANI,
Care of Her Britannic Majesty's Consul,
Beyrout,
Syria.

If anyone wishes to take such a tour as we did in comfort and luxury, they cannot do better than place themselves with confidence in his hands.

LONDON: PRINTED BY DUNCAN MACDONALD,
BLENHEIM HOUSE.

13, GREAT MARLBOROUGH STREET.

MESSRS. HURST AND BLACKETT'S
LIST OF NEW WORKS.

MONSIEUR GUIZOT IN PRIVATE LIFE (1787-
1874). By His Daughter, Madame DE WITT. Translated by Mrs. SIMPSON. 1 vol. demy 8vo. 15s.

"Madame de Witt has done justice to her father's memory in an admirable record of his life. Mrs. Simpson's translation of this singularly interesting book is in accuracy and grace worthy of the original and of the subject."—*Saturday Review*.

"This book was well worth translating. Mrs. Simpson has written excellent English, while preserving the spirit of the French."—*The Times*.

"M. Guizot stands out in the pages of his daughter's excellent biography a distinct and life-like figure. He is made to speak to us in his own person. The best part of the book consists of a number of his letters, in which he freely unfolds his feelings and opinions, and draws with unconscious boldness the outlines of his forcible and striking character."—*Pall Mall Gazette*.

"This work is replete with interesting reminiscences, and the reading public may be congratulated on having a literary treat provided for them. It shows M. Guizot in the light of a most agreeable companion and capital correspondent, with a mind as capable of feeling interested in the little pleasure of society as in the great affairs of State. His descriptions of the life he passed in England during his last visit to this country are as lively as graphic."—*Globe*.

"We congratulate Mrs. Simpson on an excellent translation of a pleasing book. We heartily recommend it. The manner of the work is as charming as the matter, and we can scarcely say more."—*Whitehall Review*.

"Madame de Witt has accomplished her task with tact and judgment."—*St. James's Gazette*.

"We cannot but feel grateful for the picture that Mme. de Witt has given us of her father in his home. It is a work for which no one can be better qualified than a daughter who thoroughly understood and sympathised with him."—*Guardian*.

"It is especially delightful to have M. Guizot set before us, not only as he showed himself in his letters to relations and intimate friends, but also as he was at home at Val Richer. Everybody will read this book, and everybody will rise from it with a higher and truer estimate of the French character."—*Graphic*.

MY JOURNEY ROUND THE WORLD, via
CEYLON, NEW ZEALAND, AUSTRALIA, TORRES STRAITS, CHINA, JAPAN, AND THE UNITED STATES. By CAPTAIN S. H. JONES-PARRY, late 102nd Royal Madras Fusileers. 2 vols. Crown 8vo. 21s.

OUR HOLIDAY IN THE EAST. By Mrs. GEORGE
SUMNER. Edited by the Rev. GEORGE HENRY SUMNER, Hon. Canon of Winchester, Rector of Old Alresford, Hants. 8vo, with Illustrations. 15s.

AN ACTOR ABROAD; or, GOSSIP, DRAMATIC,
NARRATIVE, AND DESCRIPTIVE: From the Recollections of an Actor in Australia, New Zealand, the Sandwich Islands, California, Nevada, Central America, and New York. By EDMUND LEATHES. Demy 8vo. 15s.

"'An Actor Abroad' is a bright and pleasant volume—an eminently readable book. Mr. Leathes has the great merit of being never dull. He has the power of telling a story clearly and pointedly."—*Saturday Review*.

"A readable, gossipping, agreeable record of the chances and changes of an actor's career in far distant lands. Many of the sketches of character display considerable literary skill."—*Era*.

"A very readable book. It is a combination of the experiences of the voyager with those of the artist."—*Academy*.

"A bright, lively, entertaining volume, full of graphic description and acute observation."—*Sunday Times*.

1

13, GREAT MARLBOROUGH STREET.

MESSRS. HURST AND BLACKETT'S NEW WORKS—*Continued.*

ROYAL WINDSOR. By W. HEPWORTH DIXON.
Second Edition. Volumes I. and II. Demy 8vo. 30s.

CONTENTS OF VOLS. I. AND II.—Castle Hill, Norman Keep, First King's House, Lion Heart, Kingless Windsor, Windsor Won, Geoffrey Plantagenet, Windsor Lost, The Fallen Deputy, The Queen Mother, Maud de Braose, The Barons' War, Second King's House, Edward of Carnarvon, Perot de Gaveston, Isabel de France, Edward of Windsor, Crecy, Patron Saints, St. George, Society of St. George, Lady Salisbury, David King of Scots, Third King's House, Ballad Windsor, The Fair Countess, Richard of Bordeaux, Court Parties, Royal Favourites, Rehearsing for Windsor, In the Great Hall, Simon de Burley, Radcote Bridge, A Feast of Death, Geoffrey Chaucer, At Winchester Tower, St. George's Chapel, The Little Queen, At Windsor, Duchess Philippote, The Windsor Plot, Bolingbroke, Court of Chivalry, Wager of Battle, Captive Little Queen, A New Year's Plot, Night of the Kings, Dona Juana, Constance of York, The Norman Tower, The Legal Heir, Prince Hal, The Devil's Tower, In Captivity Captive, Attempt at Rescue, Agincourt, Kaiser Sigismund, The Witch Queen, Sweet Kate, The Maid of Honour, Lady Jane, Henry of Windsor, Richard of York, Two Duchesses, York and Lancaster, Union of the Roses.

"'Royal Windsor' follows in the same lines as 'Her Majesty's Tower,' and aims at weaving a series of popular sketches of striking events which centre round Windsor Castle. Mr. Dixon makes everything vivid and picturesque. Those who liked 'Her Majesty's Tower' will find these volumes equally pleasant."—*Athenæum.*

"A truly fine and interesting book. It is a valuable contribution to English history; worthy of Mr. Dixon's fame, worthy of its grand subject."—*Morning Post.*

"Mr. Dixon has supplied us with a highly entertaining book. 'Royal Windsor' is eminently a popular work, bristling with anecdotes and amusing sketches of historical characters. It is carefully written, and is exceedingly pleasant reading. The story is brightly told; not a dull page can be found."—*Examiner.*

"These volumes will find favour with the widest circle of readers. From the first days of Norman Windsor to the Plantagenet period Mr. Dixon tells the story of this famous castle in his own picturesque, bright, and vigorous way."—*Daily Telegraph.*

"Mr. Hepworth Dixon has found a congenial subject in 'Royal Windsor.' Under the sanction of the Queen, he has enjoyed exceptional opportunities of most searching and complete investigation of the Royal House and every other part of Windsor Castle, in and out, above ground and below ground."—*Daily News.*

VOLS. III. AND IV. OF ROYAL WINDSOR. By
W. HEPWORTH DIXON. *Second Edition.* Demy 8vo. 30s. Completing the Work.

CONTENTS OF VOLS. III. AND IV.—St. George's Hall, The Tudor Tower, A Windsor Comedy, The Secret Room, Treaties of Windsor, The Private Stair, Disgrading a Knight, In a King's House, The Maiden's Tower, Black Days, The Virgin Bride, Elegy on Windsor, Fair Geraldine, Course of Song, A Windsor Gospeller, Windsor Martyrs, A Royal Reference, Hatchment Down, The People's Friend, St. George's Enemy, Lady Elizabeth's Grace, Queen Mary, Grand Master of St. George, Deanery and Dean, Sister Temperance, Elizabeth's Lovers, Dudley Constable, The Schoolmaster, Peace, Proclaimed, Shakespere's Windsor, The Two Shakesperes, The Merry Wives, Good Queen Bess, House of Stuart, The Little Park, The Queen's Court, The King's Knights, Spurious Peace, King Christian, A Catholic Dean, Apostasy, Expulsion, Forest Rights, Book of Sports, Windsor Cross, In the Forest, Windsor Seized, Under the Keep, At Bay, Feudal Church, Roundheads, Cavalier Prisoners, The New Model, Last Days of Royalty, Saints in Council, Changing Sides, Bagshot Lodge, Cutting Down, Windsor Uncrowned, A "Merry" Cæsar, Windsor Catholic, The Catastrophe, Domestic Life, Home.

"Readers of all classes will feel a genuine regret to think that these volumes contain the last of Mr. Dixon's vivid and lively sketches of English history. His hand retained its cunning to the last, and these volumes show an increase in force and dignity."—*Athenæum.*

"Mr. Dixon's is the picturesque way of writing history. Scene after scene is brought before us in the most effective way. His book is not only pleasant reading, but full of information."—*Graphic.*

13, GREAT MARLBOROUGH STREET

MESSRS. HURST AND BLACKETT'S NEW WORKS—*Continued.*

CONVERSATIONS WITH DISTINGUISHED PERSONS
during the Second Empire, from 1860 to 1863. By the Late NASSAU W. SENIOR. Edited by his Daughter, M. C. M. SIMPSON. 2 vols. 8vo. 30s.

Among other persons whose conversations are given in these volumes are:—Prince Napoleon; the Duc de Broglie; the Marquises Chambrun, Lasteyrie, Pallavicini, Vogué; Marshal Randon; Counts Arrivabene, Circourt, Corcelle, Kergorlay, Montalembert, Rémusat, Zamoyski; Generals Changarnier, Fénelon, Trochu; Lords Cowley and Clyde; Messieurs Ampère, Beaumont, Chambol, Chevalier, Cousin, Dayton, Drouyn de Lhuys, Duchâtel, Dufaure, Dumon, Duvergier de Hauranne, Guizot, Lamartine, Loménie, Lavergue, Lanjuinais, Maury, Marochetti, Masson, Mérimée, Odillon Barrot, Pelletan, Pietri, Rénan, St. Hilaire, Slidell, Thiers, De Witt; Mesdames Circourt, Cornu, Mohl, &c.

"Mr. Senior's 'Conversations with M. Thiers, M. Guizot,' &c., published about a year and a half ago, were the most interesting volumes of the series which had appeared up to that time, and these new 'Conversations' are hardly, if at all, less welcome and important. A large part of this delightful book is made up of studies by various critics, from divers points of view, of the character of Louis Napoleon, and of more or less vivid and accurate explanations of his tortuous policy. The work contains a few extremely interesting reports of conversations with M. Thiers. There are some valuable reminiscences of Lamartine, and among men of a somewhat later day, of Prince Napoleon, Drouyn de Lhuys, Montalembert, Victor Cousin, Rénan, and the Chevaliers."—*Athenæum.*

"It is impossible to do justice to these 'Conversations' in a brief notice, so we must be content to refer our readers to volumes which, wherever they are opened, will be found pregnant with interest."—*The Times.*

"Many readers may prefer the dramatic or literary merit of Mr. Senior's 'Conversations' to their historical interest, but it is impossible to insert extracts of such length as to represent the spirit, the finish, and the variety of a book which is throughout entertaining and instructive."—*Saturday Review.*

CONVERSATIONS WITH M. THIERS, M. GUIZOT,
and other Distinguished Persons, during the Second Empire. By the Late NASSAU W. SENIOR. Edited by his Daughter, M. C. M. SIMPSON. 2 vols. demy 8vo. 30s.

Among other persons whose conversations are recorded in these volumes are:—King Leopold; the Duc de Broglie; Lord Cowley; Counts Arrivabene, Corcelle, Daru, Flahault, Kergolay, Montalembert; Generals Lamoricière and Chrzanowski; Sir Henry Ellis; Messieurs Ampère, Beaumont, Blanchard, Bouffet, Auguste Chevalier, Victor Cousin, De Witt, Duchâtel, Ducpetiaux, Damon, Dussard, Duvergier de Hauranne, Léon Faucher, Frère-Orban, Grimblot, Guizot, Laffitte, Labaunne, Lamartine, Lanjuinais, Mallac, Manin, Mérimée, Mignet, Jules Mohl, Montanelli, Odillon-Barrot, Quêtelet, Rémusat, Rogier, Rivet, Rossini, Horace Say, Thiers, Trouvé-Chauvel, Villemain, Wolowski; Mesdames Circourt, Cornu, Ristori, &c.

"This new series of Mr. Senior's 'Conversations' has been for some years past known in manuscript to his more intimate friends, and it has always been felt that no former series would prove more valuable or important. Mr. Senior had a social position which gave him admission into the best literary and political circles of Paris. He was a cultivated and sensible man, who knew how to take full advantage of such an opening. And above all, he had by long practice so trained his memory as to enable it to recall all the substance, and often the words, of the long conversations which he was always holding. These conversations he wrote down with a surprising accuracy, and then handed the manuscript to his friends, that they might correct or modify his report of what they had said. This book thus contains the opinions of eminent men given in the freedom of conversation, and afterwards carefully revised. Of their value there cannot be a question. The book is one of permanent historical interest. There is scarcely a page without some memorable statement by some memorable man. Politics and society and literature —the three great interests that make up life—are all discussed in turn, and there is no discussion which is unproductive of weighty thought or striking fact."—*Athenæum.*

13, GREAT MARLBOROUGH STREET.

MESSRS. HURST AND BLACKETT'S NEW WORKS—*Continued.*

HISTORY OF TWO QUEENS: CATHARINE OF ARAGON and ANNE BOLEYN. By W. HEPWORTH DIXON. *Second Edition.* Vols. 1 & 2. Demy 8vo. 30s.

"In two handsome volumes Mr. Dixon here gives us the first instalment of a new historical work on a most attractive subject. The book is in many respects a favourable specimen of Mr. Dixon's powers. It is the most painstaking and elaborate that he has yet written..... On the whole, we may say that the book is one which will sustain the reputation of its author as a writer of great power and versatility, that it gives a new aspect to many an old subject, and presents in a very striking light some of the most recent discoveries in English history."—*Athenæum.*

"In these volumes the author exhibits in a signal manner his special powers and finest endowments. It is obvious that the historian has been at especial pains to justify his reputation, to strengthen his hold upon the learned, and also to extend his sway over the many who prize an attractive style and interesting narrative more highly than laborious research and philosophic insight."—*Morning Post.*

"The thanks of all students of English history are due to Mr. Hepworth Dixon for his clever and original work, 'History of two Queens.' The book is a valuable contribution to English history."—*Daily News.*

VOLS. III. & IV. OF THE HISTORY OF TWO QUEENS: CATHARINE OF ARAGON and ANNE BOLEYN. By W. HEPWORTH DIXON. *Second Edition.* Demy 8vo. Price 30s. Completing the Work.

"These concluding volumes of Mr. Dixon's 'History of two Queens' will be perused with keen interest by thousands of readers. Whilst no less valuable to the student, they will be far more enthralling to the general reader than the earlier half of the history. Every page of what may be termed Anne Boleyn's story affords a happy illustration of the author's vivid and picturesque style. The work should be found in every library."—*Post.*

HISTORY OF WILLIAM PENN, Founder of Pennsylvania. By W. HEPWORTH DIXON. A NEW LIBRARY EDITION 1 vol. demy 8vo, with Portrait. 12s.

"Mr. Dixon's 'William Penn' is, perhaps, the best of his books. He has now revised and issued it with the addition of much fresh matter. It is now offered in a sumptuous volume, matching with Mr. Dixon's recent books, to a new generation of readers, who will thank Mr. Dixon for his interesting and instructive memoir of one of the worthies of England."—*Examiner.*

VOLS. III. & IV. OF HER MAJESTY'S TOWER. By W. HEPWORTH DIXON. DEDICATED BY EXPRESS PERMISSION TO THE QUEEN. Completing the Work. *Third Edition.* Demy 8vo. 30s.

FREE RUSSIA. By W. HEPWORTH DIXON. *Third Edition* 2 vols. 8vo, with Coloured Illustrations. 30s.

"Mr. Dixon's book will be certain not only to interest but to please its readers and it deserves to do so. It contains a great deal that is worthy of attention, and is likely to produce a very useful effect."—*Saturday Review.*

THE SWITZERS. By W. HEPWORTH DIXON. *Third Edition.* 1 vol. demy 8vo. 15s.

"A lively, interesting, and altogether novel book on Switzerland. It is full of valuable information on social, political, and ecclesiastical questions, and, like all Mr. Dixon's books, is eminently readable."—*Daily News.*

13, GREAT MARLBOROUGH STREET.

MESSRS. HURST AND BLACKETT'S NEW WORKS—*Continued.*

TALES OF OUR GREAT FAMILIES. *Second Series.* By EDWARD WALFORD, M.A., Author of "The County Families," "Londoniana," &c. 2 vols. crown 8vo. 21s.

CONTENTS:—The Old Countess of Desmond, The Edgcumbes of Edgcumbe and Cothele, The Lynches of Galway, A Cadet of the Plantagenets, The Proud Duke of Somerset, Lady Kilsyth, The Dalzells of Carnwath, The Ladies of Llangollen, The Foxes, The Stuarts of Traquair, Belted Will Howard, An Episode in the House of Dundonald, The Ducal House of Hamilton, The Chief of Dundas, The Duke of Chandos and Princely Canons, The Spencers and Comptons, All the Howards, The Lockharts of Lee, A Ghost Story in the Noble House of Beresford, A Tragedy in Pall Mall, An Eccentric Russell, The Lady of Latham House, Two Royal Marriages in the Last Century, The Boyles, The Merry Duke of Montagu, The Romance of the Earldom of Huntingdon, Lady Hester Stanhope, The Countess of Nithsdale, The Romance of the Earldom of Mar, Margaret Duchess of Newcastle, Lord Northington, The Cutlers of Wentworth, The Earldom of Bridgewater, The Carews of Beddington, A Chapter on the Peerage, The Kirkpatricks of Closeburn, The Cliffords Earls of Cumberland, The Homes of Polwarth, The Ducal House of Bedford, Tragedies of the House of Innes, The Ducal House of Leinster, The Royal House of Stuart, The Great Douglas Case, The Radcliffes of Derwentwater, The Rise of the House of Hardwicke, Field-Marshal Keith.

"The social rank of the persons whose lives and characters are delineated in this work and the inherent romance of the stories it embodies will ensure it a widespread popularity. Many of the papers possess an engrossing and popular interest, while all of them may be read with pleasure and profit."—*Examiner.*

"A second series of Mr. Walford's 'Tales of our Great Families' has by no means exhausted the rich field of material existing in the genealogy of the United Kingdom, and which gives proof that truth is stranger than fiction. There are few readers who will not bear testimony to the fascination of these family legends."—*Daily Telegraph.*

DIARY OF A TOUR IN SWEDEN, NORWAY, AND RUSSIA, IN 1827. By THE MARCHIONESS OF WESTMINSTER. 1 vol. Demy 8vo. 15s.

"A bright and lively record. So pleasantly are the letters written which Lady Westminster sent home, that her book is most agreeable; and it has this special merit, that it brings clearly before us a number of the great people of former days, royal and imperial personages, whose intimate acquaintance the traveller's rank enabled her to make."—*Athenæum.*

"A very agreeable and instructive volume."—*Saturday Review.*

"We recommend Lady Westminster's diary to all readers as a highly instructive book of interesting travel, replete with graphic sketches of social life and scenery, and abounding in many entertaining anecdotes."—*Court Journal.*

HOLIDAYS IN EASTERN FRANCE; Sketches of Travel in CHAMPAGNE, FRANCHE-COMTE, the JURA, the VALLEY of the DOUBS, &c. By M. BETHAM-EDWARDS. 8vo. Illustrations. 15s.

"Miss Edwards' present volume, written in the same pleasant style as that which described her wanderings in Western France, is so much the more to be recommended that its contents are fresher and more novel."—*Saturday Review.*

"Readers of this work will find plenty of fresh information about some of the most delightful parts of France. The descriptions of scenery are as graphic as the sketches of character are lifelike."—*Globe.*

MEMOIRS OF GEORGIANA, LADY CHATTERTON; With some Passages from her Diary. By E. HENEAGE DERING. 1 vol. demy 8vo. 15s.

"Lady Chatterton's Diary gives a sketch of society during a well known but ever-interesting period. Mr. Dering may be congratulated on having furnished a graceful epilogue to the story of an interesting life."—*Athenæum.*

13, GREAT MARLBOROUGH STREET.

MESSRS. HURST AND BLACKETT'S NEW WORKS—*Continued.*

THE VILLAGE OF PALACES; or, Chronicles of Chelsea. By the Rev. A. G. L'ESTRANGE. 2 vols crown 8vo. 21s.

"Mr. L'Estrange has much to tell of the various public institutions associated with Chelsea. Altogether his volumes show some out-of-the-way research, and are written in a lively and gossipping style."—*The Times.*

"These volumes are pleasantly written and fairly interesting."—*Athenæum.*

"Mr. L'Estrange tells us much that is interesting about Chelsea. We take leave of this most charming book with a hearty recommendation of it to our readers."—*Spectator.*

"One of the best gossiping topographies since Leigh Hunt's 'Old Court Suburb.' So many persons of note have lived in Chelsea that a book far less carefully compiled than this has been could not fail to be amusing."—*Daily Telegraph.*

"This is a work of light antiquarian, biographical, and historical gossip. Mr. L'Estrange is inspired by interest in his subject. The names of Chelsea celebrities, dead and living, including poets, novelists, historians, statesmen, and painters will be found thickly clustering in these volumes."—*Daily News.*

"Every inhabitant of Chelsea will welcome this remarkably interesting work. It sheds a flood of light upon the past; and, while avoiding the heaviness of most antiquarian works, gives, in the form of a popular and amusing sketch, a complete history of this 'Village of Palaces.'"—*Chelsea News.*

THE YOUTH OF QUEEN ELIZABETH. Edited, from the French of L. WIESENER, by CHARLOTTE M. YONGE, Author of "The Heir of Redclyffe," &c. 2 vols. crown 8vo. 21s.

"M. Wiesener is to be complimented on the completeness, accuracy, and research shown in this work. He has drawn largely on the French Archives, the Public Record Office, and British Museum, for information contained in original documents, to some of which notice is directed for the first time. M. Wiesener's work is well worth translating, for it is most interesting as showing the education and circumstances which tended to form the character of that extraordinary queen. Miss Yonge appears to have successfully accomplished the task which she has undertaken."—*Athenæum.*

A YOUNG SQUIRE OF THE SEVENTEENTH CENTURY, from the Papers of CHRISTOPHER JEAFFRESON, of Dullingham House, Cambridgeshire. Edited by JOHN CORDY JEAFFRESON, Author of "A Book about Doctors," &c. 2 vols. crown 8vo. 21s.

"Two volumes of very attractive matter:—letters which illustrate agriculture, commerce, war, love, and social manners, accounts of passing public events, and details which are not to be found in the Gazettes, and which come with singular freshness from private letters."—*Athenæum.*

"Two agreeable and important volumes. They deserve to be placed on library shelves with Pepys, Evelyn, and Reresby."—*Notes and Queries.*

RORAIMA AND BRITISH GUIANA. with a Glance at Bermuda, the West Indies, and the Spanish Main. By J. W. BODDAM-WHETHAM. 8vo. With Map and Illustrations. 15s.

"The author has succeeded in producing an interesting and readable book of travels. His remarks on every-day life in the tropics, his notes on the geography and natural history of the countries he visited, and, above all, his vivid descriptions of scenery, combine to form a record of adventure which in attractiveness it will not be easy to surpass."—*Athenæum.*

"Mr. Whetham writes with vigour, and describes the life in the forests and on the rivers and prairies of South America with a picturesqueness and freshness of interest not inferior to that of the late Mr. Waterton's immortal wanderings. Mr. Whetham travelled in portions of Guiana little known, meeting with many adventures, seeing many strange sights, and taking notes which have furnished matter for a book of fascinating interest."—*Daily News.*

13, Great Marlborough Street.

MESSRS. HURST AND BLACKETT'S NEW WORKS—*Continued.*

ROUND THE WORLD IN SIX MONTHS. By Lieut.-Colonel E. S. Bridges, Grenadier Guards. 1 vol 8vo. 15s.

"The author may be congratulated on his success, for his pages are light and pleasant. The volume will be found both amusing and useful."—*Athenæum.*

"Colonel Bridges' book has the merit of being lively and readable. His advice to future travellers may be found serviceable."—*Pall Mall Gazette.*

A LEGACY: Being the Life and Remains of John Martin, Schoolmaster and Poet. Written and Edited by the Author of "John Halifax." 2 vols. crown 8vo. With Portrait. 21s.

"A remarkable book. It records the life, work, aspirations, and death of a schoolmaster and poet, of lowly birth but ambitious soul. His writings brim with vivid thought, touches of poetic sentiment, and trenchant criticism of men and books, expressed in scholarly language."—*Guardian.*

"Mrs. Craik has related a beautiful and pathetic story—a story of faith and courage on the part of a young and gifted man, who might under other circumstances have won a place in literature. The story is one worth reading."—*Pall Mall Gazette*

LIFE OF MOSCHELES; WITH SELECTIONS FROM HIS DIARIES AND CORRESPONDENCE. By His Wife. 2 vols. large post 8vo, with Portrait. 24s.

"This life of Moscheles will be a valuable book of reference for the musical historian, for the contents extend over a period of threescore years, commencing with 1794, and ending at 1870. We need scarcely state that all the portions of Moscheles' diary which refer to his intercourse with Beethoven, Hummel, Weber, Czerny, Spontini, Rossini, Auber, Halévy, Schumann, Cherubini, Spohr, Mendelssohn, F. David, Chopin, J. B. Cramer, Clementi, John Field, Habeneck, Hauptmann, Kalkbrenner, Kiesewetter, C. Klingemann, Lablache, Dragonetti, Sontag, Persiani, Malibran, Paganini, Rachel, Ronzi de Begnis, De Beriot, Ernst, Donzelli, Cinti-Damoreau, Chelard, Bochsa, Laporte, Charles Kemble, Paton (Mrs. Wood), Schröder-Devrient, Mrs. Siddons, Sir H. Bishop, Sir G. Smart, Staudigl, Thalberg, Berlioz, Velluti, C. Young, Balfe, Braham, and many other artists of note in their time, will recall a flood of recollections. It was a delicate task for Madame Moscheles to select from the diaries in reference to living persons, but her extracts have been judiciously made. Moscheles writes fairly of what is called the 'Music of the Future' and its disciples, and his judgments on Herr Wagner, Dr. Liszt, Rubenstein, Dr. von Bülow, Litolff, &c., whether as composers or executants, are in a liberal spirit. He expresses cheerfully the talents of our native artists; Sir S. Bennett, Mr. Macfarren, Madame Goddard, Mr. J. Barnett, Mr. Hullah, Mr. A. Sullivan, &c. The volumes are full of amusing anecdotes."—*Athenæum.*

HISTORIC CHATEAUX: Blois, Fontainebleau, Vincennes. By Lord Lamington. 1 vol. 8vo. 15s.

"A very interesting volume."—*Times.*

"A lively and agreeable book, full of action and colour."—*Athenæum.*

CELEBRITIES I HAVE KNOWN. By Lord William Pitt Lennox. *Second Series.* 2 volumes demy 8vo. 30s.

"This new series of Lord William Lennox's reminiscences is fully as entertaining as the preceding one. Lord William makes good use of an excellent memory, and he writes easily and pleasantly."—*Pall Mall Gazette.*

COACHING; With Anecdotes of the Road. By Lord William Pitt Lennox. Dedicated to His Grace the Duke of Beaufort, K.G., President, and the Members of the Coaching Club. 1 vol. demy 8vo. 15s.

"Lord William's book is genial, discursive, and gossipy. We are indebted to the author's personal recollections for some lively stories, and pleasant sketches of some of the more famous dragsmen. Altogether his volume, with the variety of its contents, will be found pleasant reading."—*Pall Mall Gazette.*

13, GREAT MARLBOROUGH STREET.

MESSRS. HURST AND BLACKETT'S NEW WORKS—*Continued.*

WORDS OF HOPE AND COMFORT TO THOSE IN SORROW. Dedicated by Permission to THE QUEEN. *Fourth Edition.* 1 vol. small 4to, 5s. bound.

"These letters, the work of a pure and devout spirit, deserve to find many readers. They are greatly superior to the average of what is called religious literature."—*Athenæum.*

"The writer of the tenderly-conceived letters in this volume was Mrs. Julius Hare, a sister of Mr. Maurice. They are instinct with the devout submissiveness and fine sympathy which we associate with the name of Maurice; but in her there is added a winningness of tact, and sometimes, too, a directness of language, which we hardly find even in the brother. The letters were privately printed and circulated, and were found to be the source of much comfort, which they cannot fail to afford now to a wide circle. A sweetly-conceived memorial poem, bearing the well-known initials, 'E. H. P.', gives a very faithful outline of the life."—*British Quarterly Review.*

"This touching and most comforting work is dedicated to THE QUEEN, who took a gracious interest in its first appearance, when printed for private circulation, and found comfort in its pages, and has now commanded its publication, that the world in general may profit by it. A more practical and heart-stirring appeal to the afflicted we have never examined."—*Standard.*

OUR BISHOPS AND DEANS. By the Rev. F. ARNOLD, B.A., late of Christ Church, Oxford. 2 vols. 8vo. 30s.

"This work is good in conception and cleverly executed, and as thoroughly honest and earnest as it is interesting and able."—*John Bull.*

LIFE OF THE RT. HON. SPENCER PERCEVAL; Including His Correspondence. By His Grandson, SPENCER WALPOLE. 2 vols. 8vo. With Portrait. 30s.

"This biography will take rank, as a faithful reflection of the statesman and his period, as also for its philosophical, logical, and dramatic completeness."—*Post.*

THE SEA OF MOUNTAINS: AN ACCOUNT OF LORD DUFFERIN'S TOUR THROUGH BRITISH COLUMBIA IN 1876. By MOLYNEUX ST. JOHN. 2 vols. With Portrait of Lord Dufferin. 21s.

"Mr. St. John has given us in these pages a record of all that was seen and done in a very successful visit. His book is instructive, and it should be interesting to the general reader."—*Times.*

"Mr. St. John is a shrewd and lively writer. The reader will find ample variety in his book, which is well worth perusal."—*Pall Mall Gazette.*

THE THEATRE FRANCAIS IN THE REIGN OF LOUIS XV. By LORD LAMINGTON. 1 vol. demy 8vo. 15s.

"A most valuable contribution to dramatic literature. All members of the profession should read it."—*Morning Post.*

"A work on a most attractive subject, which will be perused with keen interest by thousands of readers. It is written in a style singularly vivid, dramatic, and interesting."—*Court Journal.*

MY YOUTH, BY SEA AND LAND, FROM 1809 TO 1816. By CHARLES LOFTUS, formerly of the Royal Navy, late of the Coldstream Guards. 2 vols. crown 8vo. 21s.

"A more genial, pleasant, wholesome book we have not often read."—*Standard.*

ACROSS CENTRAL AMERICA. By J. W. BODDAM-WHETHAM. 8vo. With Illustrations. 15s.

"Mr. Boddam-Whetham writes easily and agreeably."—*Pall Mall Gazette.*

"A bright and lively account of interesting travel."—*Globe.*

13, GREAT MARLBOROUGH STREET.

MESSRS. HURST AND BLACKETT'S NEW WORKS—*Continued*.

LONDONIANA. By EDWARD WALFORD, M.A., Author of "The County Families," &c. 2 volumes crown 8vo. 21s.
"A highly interesting and entertaining book. It bristles with anecdotes and amusing sketches. The style is vivid, graphic, and dramatic, and the descriptions are given with a terseness and vigour that rivet the attention of the reader. The historian, the antiquarian, and the lover of romance will combine in pronouncing 'Londoniana' one of the most readable books of the day."—*Court Journal.*
"There is variety and amusement in Mr. Walford's volumes."—*Pall Mall Gazette.*

HISTORY OF ENGLISH HUMOUR. By the Rev. A. G. L'ESTRANGE, Author of "The Life of the Rev. W. Harness," &c. 2 vols. crown 8vo. 21s.
"This work contains a large and varied amount of information. It is impossible to give any idea of the wealth of anecdote and epigram in its pages."—*John Bull.*

A MAN OF OTHER DAYS: Recollections of the MARQUIS DE BEAUREGARD. Edited, from the French, by CHARLOTTE M. YONGE, Author of "The Heir of Redclyffe," &c. 2 vols. 21s.

MY YEAR IN AN INDIAN FORT. By Mrs. GUTHRIE. 2 vols. crown 8vo. With Illustrations. 21s.

RECOLLECTIONS OF COLONEL DE GONNE-
VILLE. Edited from the French by CHARLOTTE M. YONGE, Author of the "Heir of Redclyffe," &c. 2 vols. crown 8vo. 21s.

THROUGH FRANCE AND BELGIUM, BY RIVER AND CANAL, IN THE STEAM YACHT "YTENE." By W. J. C. MOENS, R.V.Y.C. 1 vol. 8vo. With Illustrations. 15s.

MY LIFE, FROM 1815 TO 1849. By CHARLES LOFTUS, formerly of the Royal Navy, late of the Coldstream Guards. Author of "My Youth by Sea and Land." 2 vols. crown 8vo. 21s.

A BOOK ABOUT THE TABLE. By J. C. JEAFFRESON. 2 vols. 8vo. 30s.

COSITAS ESPANOLAS; OR, EVERY-DAY LIFE IN SPAIN. By Mrs. HARVEY, of Ickwell-Bury. *2nd Edition.* 8vo. 15s.

PEARLS OF THE PACIFIC. By J. W. BODDAM-WHETHAM. 1 vol. Demy 8vo, with 8 Illustrations. 15s.
"The literary merits of this work are of a very high order."—*Athenæum.*

TURKISH HAREMS & CIRCASSIAN HOMES. By MRS. HARVEY, of Ickwell-Bury. 8vo. *Second Edition.* 15s.

MEMOIRS OF QUEEN HORTENSE, MOTHER OF NAPOLEON III. Cheaper Edition, in 1 vol. 6s.

RECOLLECTIONS OF SOCIETY IN FRANCE AND ENGLAND. By LADY CLEMENTINA DAVIES. *2nd Edition.* 2 v.

THE EXILES AT ST. GERMAINS. By the Author of "The Ladye Shakerley." 1 vol. 7s. 6d. bound.

THE NEW AND POPULAR NOVELS.
PUBLISHED BY HURST & BLACKETT.

FIXED AS FATE. By Mrs. HOUSTOUN, Author of "Recommended to Mercy," "Twenty Years in the Wild West," &c. 3 vols.

JEANNETTE. By MARY C. ROWSELL, Author of "Love Loyal," &c. 3 vols.

GERALDINE AND HER SUITORS. By Mrs. SIMPSON, Author of "Winnie's History," &c. 3 vols.

"Mrs. Simpson's novel displays considerable literary merit. The descriptions of scenery, men, and manners are lifelike and good. The interest is well sustained from first to last."—*Court Journal.*

STRICTLY TIED UP. 3 vols.

"This novel may be described as a comedy of life and character, and in the changing society to which we are introduced the author shows abundant knowledge of the world. There is humour as well as sufficient excitement in the volumes, and not a few of the descriptions, both of people and scenery, are exceedingly graphic and piquant."—*Saturday Review.*

"'Strictly Tied Up' is entertaining. It is in every sense a novel conceived in a light and happy vein."—*Athenæum.*

"'Strictly Tied Up' is a very cleverly constructed novel, as amusing as it is ingenious."—*St. James's Gazette.*

LITTLE PANSY. By Mrs. RANDOLPH, Author of "Gentianella," &c. 3 vols.

"This novel is sure to be popular. It is a most amusing story. Little Pansy is a charming creature."—*Sunday Times.*

"'Little Pansy' will assuredly take precedence of all Mrs. Randolph's works, brilliant as they were. Her characters are thoroughly true to nature."—*Court Journal.*

ROY AND VIOLA. By Mrs. FORRESTER, Author of "Viva," "Mignon," "Dolores," &c. *Third Edition.* 3 vols.

"'Roy and Viola' is an admirable tale; told by one who can vividly describe, and incisively comment, on the manners and personnel of modern society."—*The World.*

"Mrs. Forrester has a very bright, animated way of writing, and a knack for dialogue amounting to talent."—*Daily News.*

"An interesting story, containing very well-drawn sketches of character."—*John Bull.*

ST. MARTIN'S SUMMER. By SHIRLEY SMITH, Author of "His Last Stake," &c. 3 vols.

"There is freshness and variety in this story, and some of its characters are very prettily conceived. The book is well worth reading."—*Athenæum.*

"There is plenty of smart writing in 'St. Martin's Summer.' The author has a clever, graphic way of setting people forth, and a certain power of easy, lively talk."—*Daily News.*

"A novel of no common merit. It is brightly and vivaciously written; it abounds in sprightly cleverness and shrewdness; it contains a great deal of dialogue at once lively and natural, spontaneous and amusing."—*Pall Mall Gazette.*

FORESTALLED. By M. BETHAM-EDWARDS, Author of "Kitty," "Bridget," &c. 2 vols. 21s.

"The plot of this story is both ingenious and novel."—*Athenæum.*

"Those who appreciate a quiet, original, interesting, and carefully-written story will welcome 'Forestalled' with satisfaction."—*Spectator.*

A VERY OPAL. By C. L. PIRKIS. 3 vols.

"A novel of considerable merit. There is a minuteness of observation and at times a kind of quiet humour which reminds one of Jane Austen."—*Athenæum.*

"'A Very Opal' is likely to be read with considerable interest."—*Morning Post.*

"A clever and interesting novel, written in good English."—*Spectator.*

THE NEW AND POPULAR NOVELS.
PUBLISHED BY HURST & BLACKETT.

DIMPLETHORPE. By the Author of "St. Olave's,"
&c. 3 vols.
"'Dimplethorpe' is a well-written, ingenious, agreeable, and interesting story. The characters are naturally drawn."—*St. James's Gazette.*
"The study of character which the author proposed to herself is exhibited with considerable skill. She describes the better sort of village people with pleasant humour."—*Athenæum.*
"For quiet humour, careful observation, and cultivated style, 'Dimplethorpe' is equal to any of the author's previous works."—*John Bull.*

LORD BRACKENBURY. By AMELIA B. EDWARDS,
Author of "Barbara's History," &c. *Third Edition.* 3 vols.
"A very readable story. The author has well conceived the purpose of high-class novel-writing, and succeeded in no small measure in attaining it. There is plenty of variety, cheerful dialogue, and general 'verve' in the book."—*Athenæum.*
"A story that can be read with not a little interest. The plot is contrived with much skill, and in the double hero and heroine the reader is provided with a great deal of both exciting and tender reading."—*Saturday Review.*
"Miss Edwards is far too clever and experienced an author not to have produced a pleasant book, and 'Lord Brackenbury' is pleasant reading from beginning to end."—*Academy.*
"A very good story—plenty of reading, plenty of variety, and some amusing sketches of modern society."—*Daily News.*

THE TENTH EARL. By JOHN BERWICK HARWOOD,
Author of "Lady Flavia," "Young Lord Penrith," &c. 3 vols.
"'The Tenth Earl' has plot and substance, incident and vitality."—*Athenæum.*
"The reader will find 'The Tenth Earl' very amusing reading."—*John Bull.*
"A fascinating novel. The plot is deeply interesting, the characters are true to nature, while the language is remarkable for power."—*Court Journal.*

WOOERS AND WINNERS. By Mrs. G. LIN-
NÆUS BANKS, Author of "The Manchester Man," &c. 3 vols.
"A thoroughly readable, fresh, and wholesome novel."—*John Bull.*
"An excellent novel. It must be recommended to all readers."—*Graphic.*

MERVYN O'CONNOR. By the EARL OF DESART,
Author of "Kelverdale," &c. 3 vols.
"Lord Desart shows his accustomed liveliness in description which is always distinct and never prolonged so as to become wearisome."—*Athenæum.*
"A bright, lively story, full of interest and action."—*Sunday Times.*

MISS BOUVERIE. By Mrs. MOLESWORTH, Author
of "Hathercourt Rectory," "The Cuckoo Clock," &c. 3 vols.
"'Miss Bouverie' is a pure and pretty story."—*Athenæum.*
"One of the prettiest stories which has appeared for years."—*Post.*
"A very charming story. In these delightful volumes Mrs. Molesworth has produced a capital book."—*Graphic.*

POET AND PEER. By HAMILTON AÏDÉ, Author of
"Penruddocke," &c. DEDICATED to LORD LYTTON. 3 vols.
"'Poet and Peer' is a novel of unusual merit, the work of a cultivated man of the world, who describes what he has himself seen. It is the best of Mr. Aïdé's novels, and will interest and amuse every reader who takes it up."—*Athenæum.*
"A thoroughly readable and attractive novel."—*Morning Post.*

A MODERN GREEK HEROINE. 3 vols.
"A very attractive and clever story, which is unusually successful. It is the work of a refined mind, and is carried out with considerable skill."—*Athenæum.*
"As entertaining and original a composition as we have met with for a long time. The heroine is delightful. We advise the reader to send at once for 'A Modern Greek Heroine.'"—*Blackwood's Magazine.*

Under the Especial Patronage of Her Majesty.

Published annually, in One Vol., royal 8vo, with the Arms beautifully engraved, handsomely bound, with gilt edges, price 31s. 6d.

LODGE'S PEERAGE
AND BARONETAGE,
CORRECTED BY THE NOBILITY.

THE FIFTIETH EDITION FOR 1881 IS NOW READY.

LODGE'S PEERAGE AND BARONETAGE is acknowledged to be the most complete, as well as the most elegant, work of the kind. As an established and authentic authority on all questions respecting the family histories, honours, and connections of the titled aristocracy, no work has ever stood so high. It is published under the especial patronage of Her Majesty, and is annually corrected throughout, from the personal communications of the Nobility. It is the only work of its class in which, *the type being kept constantly standing*, every correction is made in its proper place to the date of publication, an advantage which gives it supremacy over all its competitors. Independently of its full and authentic information respecting the existing Peers and Baronets of the realm, the most sedulous attention is given in its pages to the collateral branches of the various noble families, and the names of many thousand individuals are introduced, which do not appear in other records of the titled classes. For its authority, correctness, and facility of arrangement, and the beauty of its typography and binding, the work is justly entitled to the place it occupies on the tables of Her Majesty and the Nobility.

LIST OF THE PRINCIPAL CONTENTS.

Historical View of the Peerage.
Parliamentary Roll of the House of Lords.
English, Scotch, and Irish Peers, in their orders of Precedence.
Alphabetical List of Peers of Great Britain and the United Kingdom, holding superior rank in the Scotch or Irish Peerage.
Alphabetical list of Scotch and Irish Peers, holding superior titles in the Peerage of Great Britain and the United Kingdom.
A Collective list of Peers, in their order of Precedence.
Table of Precedency among Men.
Table of Precedency among Women.
The Queen and the Royal Family.
Peers of the Blood Royal.
The Peerage, alphabetically arranged.
Families of such Extinct Peers as have left Widows or Issue.
Alphabetical List of the Surnames of all the Peers.
The Archbishops and Bishops of England and Ireland.
The Baronetage alphabetically arranged.
Alphabetical List of Surnames assumed by members of Noble Families.
Alphabetical List of the Second Titles of Peers, usually borne by their Eldest Sons.
Alphabetical Index to the Daughters of Dukes, Marquises, and Earls, who, having married Commoners, retain the title of Lady before their own Christian and their Husband's Surnames.
Alphabetical Index to the Daughters of Viscounts and Barons, who, having married Commoners, are styled Honourable Mrs.; and, in case of the husband being a Baronet or Knight, Hon. Lady.
A List of the Orders of Knighthood.
Mottoes alphabetically arranged and translated.

"This work is the most perfect and elaborate record of the living and recently deceased members of the Peerage of the Three Kingdoms as it stands at this day. It is a most useful publication. We are happy to bear testimony to the fact that scrupulous accuracy is a distinguishing feature of this book."—*Times.*

"Lodge's Peerage must supersede all other works of the kind, for two reasons: first, it is on a better plan; and secondly, it is better executed. We can safely pronounce it to be the readiest, the most useful, and exactest of modern works on the subject."—*Spectator.*

"A work of great value. It is the most faithful record we possess of the aristocracy of the day."—*Post.*

"The best existing, and, we believe, the best possible Peerage It is the standard authority on the subject."—*Standard.*

HURST & BLACKETT'S STANDARD LIBRARY
OF CHEAP EDITIONS OF
POPULAR MODERN WORKS,
ILLUSTRATED BY SIR J. GILBERT, MILLAIS, HUNT, LEECH, FOSTER, POYNTER, TENNIEL, SANDYS, HUGHES, SAMBOURNE, &c.

Each in a Single Volume, elegantly printed, bound, and illustrated, price 5s.

1. SAM SLICK'S NATURE AND HUMAN NATURE.
"The first volume of Messrs. Hurst and Blackett's Standard Library of Cheap Editions forms a very good beginning to what will doubtless be a very successful undertaking. 'Nature and Human Nature' is one of the best of Sam Slick's witty and humorous productions, and is well entitled to the large circulation which it cannot fail to obtain in its present convenient and cheap shape. The volume combines with the great recommendations of a clear, bold type, and good paper, the lesser but attractive merits of being well illustrated and elegantly bound."—*Post.*

2. JOHN HALIFAX, GENTLEMAN.
"This is a very good and a very interesting work. It is designed to trace the career from boyhood to age of a perfect man—a Christian gentleman; and it abounds in incident both well and highly wrought. Throughout it is conceived in a high spirit, and written with great ability. This cheap and handsome new edition is worthy to pass freely from hand to hand as a gift book in many households."—*Examiner.*

3. THE CRESCENT AND THE CROSS.
BY ELIOT WARBURTON.
"Independent of its value as an original narrative, and its useful and interesting information, this work is remarkable for the colouring power and play of fancy with which its descriptions are enlivened. Among its greatest and most lasting charms is its reverent and serious spirit."—*Quarterly Review.*

4. NATHALIE. By JULIA KAVANAGH.
"'Nathalie' is Miss Kavanagh's best imaginative effort. Its manner is gracious and attractive. Its matter is good. A sentiment, a tenderness, are commanded by her which are as individual as they are elegant."—*Athenæum.*

5. A WOMAN'S THOUGHTS ABOUT WOMEN.
BY THE AUTHOR OF "JOHN HALIFAX, GENTLEMAN."
"A book of sound counsel. It is one of the most sensible works of its kind, well-written, true-hearted, and altogether practical. Whoever wishes to give advice to a young lady may thank the author for means of doing so."—*Examiner.*

6. ADAM GRAEME. By MRS. OLIPHANT.
"A story awakening genuine emotions of interest and delight by its admirable pictures of Scottish life and scenery. The author sets before us the essential attributes of Christian virtue, with a delicacy, power, and truth which can hardly be surpassed."—*Post.*

7. SAM SLICK'S WISE SAWS AND MODERN INSTANCES.
"The reputation of this book will stand as long as that of Scott's or Bulwer's Novels. Its remarkable originality and happy descriptions of American life still continue the subject of universal admiration."—*Messenger.*

8. CARDINAL WISEMAN'S RECOLLECTIONS OF THE LAST FOUR POPES.
"A picturesque book on Rome and its ecclesiastical sovereigns, by an eloquent Roman Catholic. Cardinal Wiseman has treated a special subject with so much geniality, that his recollections will excite no ill-feeling in those who are most conscientiously opposed to every idea of human infallibility represented in Papal domination."—*Athenæum.*

9. A LIFE FOR A LIFE.
BY THE AUTHOR OF "JOHN HALIFAX, GENTLEMAN."
"In 'A Life for a Life' the author is fortunate in a good subject, and has produced a work of strong effect."—*Athenæum.*

HURST & BLACKETT'S STANDARD LIBRARY

10. THE OLD COURT SUBURB. By LEIGH HUNT.
"A delightful book, that will be welcome to all readers, and most welcome to those who have a love for the best kinds of reading."—*Examiner.*

11. MARGARET AND HER BRIDESMAIDS.
"We recommend all who are in search of a fascinating novel to read this work for themselves. They will find it well worth their while. There are a freshness and originality about it quite charming."—*Athenæum.*

12. THE OLD JUDGE. By SAM SLICK.
"The publications included in this Library have all been of good quality; many give information while they entertain, and of that class the book before us is a specimen. The manner in which the Cheap Editions forming the series is produced, deserves especial mention. The paper and print are unexceptionable; there is a steel engraving in each volume, and the outsides of them will satisfy the purchaser who likes to see books in handsome uniform."—*Examiner.*

13. DARIEN. By ELIOT WARBURTON.
"This last production of the author of 'The Crescent and the Cross' has the same elements of a very wide popularity. It will please its thousands."—*Globe.*

14. FAMILY ROMANCE.
BY SIR BERNARD BURKE, ULSTER KING OF ARMS.
"It were impossible to praise too highly this most interesting book."—*Standard.*

15. THE LAIRD OF NORLAW. By MRS. OLIPHANT.
"The 'Laird of Norlaw' fully sustains the author's high reputation."—*Sunday Times.*

16. THE ENGLISHWOMAN IN ITALY.
"Mrs. Gretton's book is interesting, and full of opportune instruction."—*Times.*

17. NOTHING NEW.
BY THE AUTHOR OF "JOHN HALIFAX, GENTLEMAN."
"'Nothing New' displays all those superior merits which have made 'John Halifax' one of the most popular works of the day."—*Post.*

18. FREER'S LIFE OF JEANNE D'ALBRET.
"Nothing can be more interesting than Miss Freer's story of the life of Jeanne D'Albret, and the narrative is as trustworthy as it is attractive."—*Post.*

19. THE VALLEY OF A HUNDRED FIRES.
BY THE AUTHOR OF "MARGARET AND HER BRIDESMAIDS."
"If asked to classify this work, we should give it a place between 'John Halifax' and 'The Caxtons.'"—*Standard.*

20. THE ROMANCE OF THE FORUM.
BY PETER BURKE, SERGEANT AT LAW.
"A work of singular interest, which can never fail to charm."—*Illustrated News.*

21. ADELE. By JULIA KAVANAGH.
"'Adele' is the best work we have read by Miss Kavanagh; it is a charming story, full of delicate character-painting."—*Athenæum.*

22. STUDIES FROM LIFE.
BY THE AUTHOR OF "JOHN HALIFAX, GENTLEMAN."
"These 'Studies from Life' are remarkable for graphic power and observation. The book will not diminish the reputation of the accomplished author."—*Saturday Review.*

23. GRANDMOTHER'S MONEY.
"We commend 'Grandmother's Money' to readers in search of a good novel. The characters are true to human nature, and the story is interesting."—*Athenæum.*

HURST & BLACKETT'S STANDARD LIBRARY

24. A BOOK ABOUT DOCTORS. By J. C. JEAFFRESON.
"A delightful book."—*Athenæum*. "A book to be read and re-read; fit for the study as well as the drawing-room table and the circulating library."—*Lancet*.

25. NO CHURCH.
"We advise all who have the opportunity to read this book."—*Athenæum*.

26. MISTRESS AND MAID.
BY THE AUTHOR OF "JOHN HALIFAX, GENTLEMAN."
"A good wholesome book, gracefully written, and as pleasant to read as it is instructive."—*Athenæum*. "A charming tale charmingly told."—*Standard*.

27. LOST AND SAVED. By HON. MRS. NORTON.
"'Lost and Saved' will be read with eager interest. It is a vigorous novel."—*Times*. "A novel of rare excellence. It is Mrs. Norton's best prose work."—*Examiner*.

28. LES MISERABLES. By VICTOR HUGO.
AUTHORISED COPYRIGHT ENGLISH TRANSLATION.
"The merits of 'Les Miserables' do not merely consist in the conception of it as a whole; it abounds with details of unequalled beauty. M. Victor Hugo has stamped upon every page the hall-mark of genius."—*Quarterly Review*.

29. BARBARA'S HISTORY. By AMELIA B. EDWARDS.
"It is not often that we light upon a novel of so much merit and interest as 'Barbara's History.' It is a work conspicuous for taste and literary culture. It is a very graceful and charming book, with a well-managed story, clearly-cut characters, and sentiments expressed with an exquisite elocution. It is a book which the world will like."—*Times*.

30. LIFE OF THE REV. EDWARD IRVING.
BY MRS. OLIPHANT.
"A good book on a most interesting theme."—*Times*.
"A truly interesting and most affecting memoir. Irving's Life ought to have a niche in every gallery of religious biography."—*Saturday Review*.

31. ST. OLAVE'S.
"This charming novel is the work of one who possesses a great talent for writing, as well as experience and knowledge of the world.'—*Athenæum*.

32. SAM SLICK'S AMERICAN HUMOUR.
"Dip where you will into this lottery of fun, you are sure to draw out a prize."—*Post*.

33. CHRISTIAN'S MISTAKE.
BY THE AUTHOR OF "JOHN HALIFAX, GENTLEMAN."
"A more charming story has rarely been written. Even if tried by the standard of the Archbishop of York, we should expect that even he would pronounce 'Christian's Mistake' a novel without a fault."—*Times*.

34. ALEC FORBES. By GEORGE MAC DONALD, LL.D.
"No account of this story would give any idea of the profound interest that pervades the work from the first page to the last."—*Athenæum*.

35. AGNES. By MRS. OLIPHANT.
"'Agnes' is a novel superior to any of Mrs. Oliphant's former works."—*Athenæum*.
"A story whose pathetic beauty will appeal irresistibly to all readers."—*Post*.

36. A NOBLE LIFE.
BY THE AUTHOR OF "JOHN HALIFAX, GENTLEMAN."
"This is one of those pleasant tales in which the author of 'John Halifax' speaks out of a generous heart the purest truths of life."—*Examiner*.

37. NEW AMERICA. By HEPWORTH DIXON.
"A very interesting book. Mr. Dixon has written thoughtfully and well."—*Times*.
"We recommend every one who feels any interest in human nature to read Mr. Dixon's very interesting book."—*Saturday Review*.

HURST & BLACKETT'S STANDARD LIBRARY

38. ROBERT FALCONER. By GEORGE MAC DONALD.
"'Robert Falconer' is a work brimful of life and humour and of the deepest human interest. It is a book to be returned to again and again and for the deep and searching knowledge it evinces of human thoughts and feelings."—*Athenæum.*

39. THE WOMAN'S KINGDOM.
BY THE AUTHOR OF "JOHN HALIFAX, GENTLEMAN."
"'The Woman's Kingdom' sustains the author's reputation as a writer of the purest and noblest kind of domestic stories.—*Athenæum.*

40. ANNALS OF AN EVENTFUL LIFE.
BY GEORGE WEBBE DASENT, D.C.L.
"A racy, well-written, and original novel. The interest never flags. The whole work sparkles with wit and humour."—*Quarterly Review.*

41. DAVID ELGINBROD. By GEORGE MAC DONALD.
"The work of a man of genius. It will attract the highest class of readers."—*Times.*

42. A BRAVE LADY. By the Author of "John Halifax."
"A very good novel; a thoughtful, well-written book, showing a tender sympathy with human nature, and permeated by a pure and noble spirit."—*Examiner.*

43. HANNAH. By the Author of "John Halifax."
"A very pleasant, healthy story, well and artistically told. The book is sure of a wide circle of readers. The character of Hannah is one of rare beauty."—*Standard.*

44. SAM SLICK'S AMERICANS AT HOME.
"This is one of the most amusing books that we ever read."—*Standard.*

45. THE UNKIND WORD.
BY THE AUTHOR OF "JOHN HALIFAX, GENTLEMAN."
"The author of 'John Halifax' has written many fascinating stories, but we can call to mind nothing from her pen that has a more enduring charm than the graceful sketches in this work."—*United Service Magazine.*

46. A ROSE IN JUNE. By MRS. OLIPHANT.
"'A Rose in June' is as pretty as its title. The story is one of the best and most touching which we owe to the industry and talent of Mrs. Oliphant, and may hold its own with even 'The Chronicles of Carlingford.'"—*Times.*

47. MY LITTLE LADY. By E. F. POYNTER.
"There is a great deal of fascination about this book. The author writes in a clear, unaffected style; she has a decided gift for depicting character, while the descriptions of scenery convey a distinct pictorial impression to the reader."—*Times.*

48. PHŒBE, JUNIOR. By MRS. OLIPHANT.
"This novel shows great knowledge of human nature. The interest goes on growing to the end. Phœbe is excellently drawn."—*Times.*

49. LIFE OF MARIE ANTOINETTE.
BY PROFESSOR CHARLES DUKE YONGE.
"A work of remarkable merit and interest, which will, we doubt not, become the most popular English history of Marie Antoinette."—*Spectator.*
"This book is well written, and of thrilling interest."—*Academy.*

50. SIR GIBBIE. By GEORGE MAC DONALD, LL.D.
"'Sir Gibbie' is a book of genius."—*Pall Mall Gazette.*
"This book has power, pathos, and humour. There is not a character which is not lifelike."—*Athenæum.*

51. YOUNG MRS. JARDINE.
BY THE AUTHOR OF "JOHN HALIFAX, GENTLEMAN."
"'Young Mrs. Jardine' is a pretty story, written in pure English."—*The Times.*
"There is much good feeling in this book. It is pleasant and wholesome."—*Athenæum.*

www.ingramcontent.com/pod-product-compliance
Lightning Source LLC
Chambersburg PA
CBHW031423230426
43668CB00007B/407